Faculty Misconduct
in Collegiate Teaching

Faculty Misconduct
in Collegiate Teaching

John M. Braxton and Alan E. Bayer

The Johns Hopkins University Press ▪ Baltimore and London

To
E.M.B & A.J.S.
and our graduate students who choose
academic professional careers

© 1999 The Johns Hopkins University Press
All rights reserved. Published 1999
Printed in the United States of America on acid-free paper
9 8 7 6 5 4 3 2 1

The Johns Hopkins University Press
2715 North Charles Street
Baltimore, Maryland 21218-4363
www.press.jhu.edu

Library of Congress Cataloging-in-Publication Data

Braxton, John M.
  Faculty misconduct in collegiate teaching / John M. Braxton and Alan
E. Bayer
     p.   cm.
  Includes bibliographical references and index.
  ISBN 0-8018-6125-X (alk. paper)
    1. College teachers—Professional ethics—United States.   2. College
teaching—Corrupt practices—United States.   I. Bayer, Alan E., 1939– .
II. Title.
LB1779.B73   1999
378.1'25—dc21   99-11238 CIP

A catalog record for this book is available from the British Library.

CONTENTS

TABLES

ACKNOWLEDGMENTS

Good fortune and good friendship are key ingredients to a fulfilling collaboration. It was our good fortune to have the friendship of John Smart, who recognized our mutual interest in the study of the American professoriate and our shared perspectives for analysis. He was instrumental in making sure we became personally acquainted rather than knowing each other only through our writings, and he introduced us to each other at an annual meeting of the American Educational Research Association more than fifteen years ago.

We are indebted as well to a large number of other colleagues at our home institutions for their help and comments when we first embarked on designing the College Teaching Behaviors Inventory (CTBI). In addition to these colleagues, we wish to acknowledge in particular the thoughtful comments and suggestions of Martin Finkelstein and James Michaels. We are also indebted to members of the American Sociological Association's Project on Teaching, especially Carla Howery, for many helpful suggestions in developing the CTBI.

Michael Gavlick and Jean Hendrix provided conscientious assistance in drawing our representative samples of colleges and universities and randomly selecting the faculty members who taught at them. We would also like to thank the members of the graduate-level course titled the American Academic Profession offered in spring 1997 at Peabody College of Vanderbilt University. The students in this course, Francis Alexander, Mia Alexander-Snow, Susanna Baxter, Robert Buckla, Juanita Buford, James Coaxum, Rodney Cohen, Marietta Del Favero, Karen Elsey, Darlene Franklin, Scott Gilmer, Patricia Helland, Barbara Johnson, Anthony Jones, Laurel Raimondo, Monique Robinson-Wright, Ross Scott, and Evans Whitaker, were helpful in generating the recommendations for policy and practice described in Chapter 10.

In addition, Michael Clark and Eric Crutchfield were instrumental in setting up procedures for tracking survey responses, data entry, and preliminary data processing for initial frequency distributions on survey questions.

We wish to thank Cynthia Crawford and Kimberly MacInnis for their patience and persistence in typing numerous versions and revisions of the CTBI. We also acknowledge the thorough and careful keyboarding assistance of Monica Bryant, Susan Mead, and Kate Murnane in preparing tables, the fictional vignettes, and major portions of the manuscript text.

Many individuals provided us gracious assistance in collecting the documents discussed in Chapter 9. Many of our friends and colleagues scattered at academic institutions across the country generously responded to our call for help in collecting a variety of student instructional rating forms. Patricia Hyer and Gary Rhoades offered fruitful leads in acquiring other materials. Stephanie Bird generously provided us with a copy of her extensive collection of professional association codes of conduct and ethics. We are grateful to the National Education Association, particularly Christine Maitland, for releasing to us the CD-ROM version of their vast collection of higher education collective bargaining contracts.

Our gratitude is also expressed to the Johns Hopkins University Press. They engaged two preliminary reviewers and other reviewers who offered numerous constructive recommendations in response to our initial proposal to undertake this book. While we retain responsibility for any shortcomings in the published version, we are especially indebted to an anonymous reviewer who read the full draft manuscript and made a number of constructive suggestions for improvement before we went into production, to Jean Eckenfels for extraordinary care in copyediting, to Mark McKnight for his care in producing the index, and to Kimberly Johnson, Senior Production Editor, for overseeing the final stages. We are also indebted to Editor-in-Chief Jacqueline Wehmueller, at the Johns Hopkins University Press, who shepherded our work from initial concept through final contract. Jackie's wise counsel, support, and enthusiasm helped make this collaborative endeavor an especially enjoyable one.

We are grateful also to the several individuals at our affiliated universities who believed in our endeavor in sufficient degree that they were instrumental in awarding us small grants to continue our enterprise and data collection. Funding for this project was received, in part, from Syracuse University, Vanderbilt University–Peabody College, and the College of Arts and Sciences at Virginia Polytechnic Institute and State University.

Finally, we would be remiss if we did not acknowledge the significant support of our partners, Ellen Brier and Arlene Stevenson. Their patience, moral support, and active encouragement of our work together over the years has been our source of strong inspiration and heightened enthusiasm for our collaboration and colleagueship.

ONE

Introduction: The Centrality of Norms to Academic Work

The standards of behavior that the American professoriate expects of students are frequently no longer being met. College and university faculty members are reporting a dramatic rise in incivility in the classroom (Amada, 1994; Schneider, 1998) where the behavioral expectations for college students regarding their decorum and civility toward teachers and fellow students seem to be fracturing and dissolving.

While many explanations have been offered—changing demographic backgrounds of college students, exposure to media and video violence, poor secondary schools, inadequate or permissive parenting, to name a few—rarely has the professoriate looked inward toward itself as a possible source of deviance in academe. Might not faculty misconduct in teaching provoke this growing problem of student misbehavior in the classroom? Consider the following:

- Professor Willburn is always too busy to prepare for her first day of class. She never has her syllabus ready, and her students find it hard to catch up.
- Mr. McLaughlin is habitually late for class, he often cuts classes short, and sometimes, without any explanation, he doesn't show up at all. This is extremely annoying to students and, for some, his frequent profanity in the classroom merely exacerbates their aggravation.
- Professor Hasselman appears impervious to signals of disdain from some of his students, especially the women students. Seldom will he let a class hour pass without a digression to an off-color joke. He appears to hear only the uproarious laughter of a few of his men students but to be unaware of the deafening silence from most in his classroom.
- Mr. Barkley regularly demeans his students. They quickly become reticent to participate in class, but when they do take the risk, Barkley frequently embarrasses them. He is quick to humiliate his students publicly for what he characterizes as simple, uninformed, or "stupid" questions or comments.

- Dr. Pierce doesn't think her office hours or student appointments are of particularly high priority. If something else comes up, she doesn't feel it necessary to arrange other things around her scheduled times to meet students.
- Professor Walcott seems to have found only coercive solutions to maintaining class attendance and keeping his students up-to-date with their reading assignments: threats, scolding, and intimidation. He goes on a tirade in class and gives a pop quiz when only a few students show up for class or no one appears prepared to answer questions on their assigned reading.

Could these hypothetical anecdotes provide models for corresponding student disregard for expected behavior? Perhaps students come to class late and unprepared, use profanity, show disrespect, voice hostile public criticism of others, including their teachers, make sexist remarks, and engage in a wide variety of other unapproved behaviors in part as a result of their experiences with some of their instructors.

If so, it may be that the growing concern over student incivility is simply another classic case of "blaming the victim" (Ryan, 1971, 1976). Indeed, Gerald Amada (in Schneider, 1998) suggests that misconduct by college and university faculty members encourages students to behave as badly. Robert Boice (1996) extends this observation, suggesting that *most* student incivility in the classroom may be prompted by professorial incivility.

In this volume, we will address the issue of impropriety or misconduct in the teaching role at the postsecondary level. Do members of the professoriate view certain actions as faculty misconduct in teaching? Do faculty members across various collegiate settings share views about appropriate and inappropriate behaviors by their colleagues in the teaching role similar to the expectations they share for colleagues in regard to endeavors in research and scholarship? By *expectations*, we mean normative systems or normative domains. Hence, we begin with a discussion of the role of norms for the professions generally, and for the professoriate in particular.

The Role of Norms in the Professions

Behavioral norms are shared beliefs within a particular social or professional group about behavior expected or desired in a given situation or circumstance (Gibbs, 1981; Rossi and Berk, 1985). More specifically, Merton (1968, 1973) defines norms as *prescribed and proscribed patterns of behavior.* The various degrees of moral outrage or indignation that result when norms are violated indicate the social significance of a normative orientation (Durkheim, 1995 [1912]). Hence, norms represent "the collective conscience" of a social group (Durkheim, 1982 [1894]).

For professions, norms provide a guide to appropriate and inappropriate behavior with respect to colleagues and clients (Goode, 1957). In the case of college and university faculty, norms specify prescribed and proscribed patterns of behavior in the performance of research, service, and teaching roles.

Norms, the informal variants of professional ethics, are central in three theoretical perspectives on the nature of professions: functionalism, monopoly or power theory, and professionalization. The functionalist perspective on professions holds that norms serve to control the work of individual professionals so that the welfare of clients is safeguarded (Abbott, 1983). In contrast, power theory holds that norms, or codes of conduct, play a role in helping an occupational group maintain a monopoly on its services by governing the behavior and obligations of colleagues (Abbott, 1983). Berlant (1975) asserts that such behaviors and obligations assure solidarity among the profession's members, which, in turn, assists a profession in maintaining a monopoly over the services members provide to clients. Formal statements of norms are also important in the formulations of professionalization theory. Wilensky (1964) states that the last stage occupational groups pass through on their way toward professionalization is the establishment of a code of ethics.

Norms: A Notion Central to Academic Work

Norms constitute a central phenomenon in the study of academic life as well as in the day-to-day life of college and university faculty members. The centrality of norms arises from several important issues concerning academic work.

First, most college and university faculty members possess a great deal of autonomy in their roles as teachers and researchers. Norms serve as guides to their performance of these roles. Without norms, faculty members would be free to follow their own unconstrained and idiosyncratic preferences in teaching and research. This formulation stems from Durkheim's (1951 [1897]) supposition that nonconformity is the natural human condition, whereas conformity is abnormal.

Second, norms specify permissible actions for realizing group goals (Merton, 1968). Because norms represent the "collective conscience" of a social group (Durkheim, 1982 [1894]), they provide an indication of the most important goals, deep-seated values, and moral precepts of the professoriate. Hackman (1976) asserts that norms develop for behaviors viewed as important by most group members. The conditions under which groups are likely to enforce norms offer additional evidence on the value of norms as an indicator of important professorial goals. Feldman (1984) posits that group norms are enforced if they promote the survival of the group, if they assist a group in avoiding embarrassing interpersonal problems, and if they symbolize the central values of the group and clarify the group's identity.

Third, norms provide one marker of the professionalization of college and university teaching. Sociologists of the professions offer perspectives on traits that accord status as a profession to an occupational group. Occupational groups vary in the traits or characteristics they possess (Vollmer and Mills, 1966), and the degree of professionalization depends on how many of these characteristics they exhibit (Carr-Saunders and Wilson, 1933; Barber, 1963; Millerson, 1964; Greenwood, 1957; Harries-Jenkins, 1970; Moore, 1970). These defining characteristics include an extensive period of training and socialization, the existence of a systematic body of theory, the creation of professional associations, and the existence of a code of conduct.

A code of conduct may be formal or informal (Goode, 1957; Greenwood, 1957; Strauss and Bucher, 1961). Because norms prescribe and proscribe professorial behavior, they function as an informal code of conduct. Thus, the existence of a normative structure for faculty performance provides an indicator of the extent of professionalization achieved by college and university faculty as an occupational group.

Fourth, the centrality of norms also stems from their role in assuring the ideal of service to clients. Goode (1969) contends that the core generating traits of professionalism are: the mastery and control of a basic body of abstract knowledge and the ideal of service to clients. The ideal of service, or "the collectivity orientation" (Parsons, 1939), is the obligation of professionals to base their professional choices on the needs and welfare of their clients (Goode, 1969). As an informal code of conduct, norms assure that the professional choices adhere to the ideal of service. Clients of the academic profession include the academic discipline (Schein, 1972), the cause of learning (Goode, 1969), the knowledge base of an academic discipline (Braxton, 1990), students in groups (Schein, 1972), and students as individuals (Blau, 1973).

Fifth, norms play an important role in professional self-regulation. The lay public grants autonomy to professions that assure that the professional performance of individuals adheres to the ideal of service to clients

(Goode, 1969). Norms serve to encourage faculty behavior consistent with the ideal of service to the various clients of teaching and research.

Sixth, norms are central to college and university faculty because they facilitate or hinder changes in the way professorial roles are carried out. Because of the autonomy most faculty have, they are free to enact new policies and procedures according to their own preferences. If norms supportive of such policies and procedures are present, then faculty are more likely to implement such policies and procedures in a reliable manner (Braxton, Eimers, and Bayer, 1996).

Normative Structure for Research Role Performance

Because norms are central to academic work, a fundamental question emerges: What are the normative structures for faculty role performance? An extensive body of theory and research concentrates on the existence of a normative structure for the performance of research (Braxton, 1986; Zuckerman, 1988). Merton (1942, 1973) describes this normative structure as composed of four core patterns: communality, disinterestedness, organized skepticism, and universalism. Communality means that the research findings are the intellectual property of the research community. Scholars should, however, receive appropriate recognition for their contributions. Disinterestedness bars individuals from conducting research for personal or financial gain, merely to receive recognition, or simply to gain prestige. The desire to advance knowledge should be the primary motive for conducting research. Organized skepticism stipulates that research findings not be accepted without peer assessment based on empirical and logical criteria. Universalism prescribes that research be judged on the basis of merit and not particularistic criteria such as race, nationality, or social origin.

Conformity to these norms is instrumental to the advancement of knowledge because they are derived from the goals and methods of science (Merton, 1942, 1973). Thus, the client of the research role is the knowledge base of an academic discipline (Braxton, 1990).

From their reviews of research on compliance with the Mertonian norms of science, Braxton (1986) and Zuckerman (1988) both conclude that conformity to these norms is variable. They are neither consistently binding nor routinely violated (Zuckerman, 1988). Conformity varies from one facet of communality or universalism to another in the studies of these two well-researched normative patterns (Braxton, 1986).[1]

1. The Mertonian norms of science have, however, been the object of much criticism (Mulkay, 1969, 1976; Barnes and Dolby, 1970; Rothman, 1972; Mitroff, 1974). Mulkay's (1969, 1976) criticisms are particularly noteworthy. He argues that the norms of science should be

Undergraduate Teaching Performance Norms: A Neglected Topic

Although teaching and research make up an integrated core of activities for the academic profession (Parsons and Platt, 1973; Braxton and Toombs, 1982), teaching is the primary interest and activity of most college and university faculty (Boyer, 1990). Yet the body of scholarship focusing on normative preferences for undergraduate teaching is considerably less extensive than that for research.

This scant scholarly attention to teaching improprieties is troubling given the public perception that academic misconduct is widespread (Braxton and Bayer, 1994, 1996). Evolving higher education institutional policy and new governmental rules and agencies are evidence of the formal response to malfeasance, improprieties, and misconduct by the professoriate (Hackett, 1994). These formal responses follow growing public perceptions of high levels of misconduct based primarily upon well-publicized cases of individual misconduct (Braxton and Bayer, 1994, 1996), particularly fabrications of scientific results and sexual misconduct, and upon novels, exposés, and anecdotal accounts. But the perception is also based on reality: recent research suggests that incidents of misconduct are not at all as rare as may once have been assumed (Swazey, Anderson, and Louis, 1993: Office of Inspector General, 1990).

Professorial impropriety generally falls within one of four domains: (1) scholarly or scientific misconduct (e.g., plagiarism, fabrication of laboratory data); (2) academic or teaching misconduct (e.g., habitual failure to meet classes, public ridicule of students); (3) professional service misconduct (e.g., failure to meet commitments at professional meetings, failure to fulfill responsibilities of committee assignments); and (4) employee misconduct (e.g., embezzlement of institutional funds, theft of property).

Most institutions have formal rules governing scholarly and research misconduct (Steneck, 1994). Moreover, definitions of such misconduct

---

viewed as an ideology rather than as a binding code of conduct for research. Moreover, Mulkay (1976) asserts that the norms of science are vocabularies used by elite scientists to gain political favor and preserve autonomy for research. However, Zuckerman (1988) cogently argues that it is theoretically unsound to put aside the norms of science, as she argues that these norms are instrumental to the advancement of knowledge and are binding on scientists. She also points out that the social significance of these norms is reflected in the moral indignation scientists express when they are violated. Zuckerman concludes that norms are "at a great distance from merely ideological statements designed to defend the autonomy of science and from mere rationalization of action offered after the fact" (1988, p. 517).

The centrality of a normative structure to faculty research role performance is strongly reflected in the criticisms of Mulkay and others as well as Zuckerman's response to such criticisms.

have taken shape (Price, 1994; Commission on Research Integrity, 1995) in the past two decades. Given that the primary activity of most college and university faculty members is teaching, it is all the more remarkable that this domain of possible impropriety has been relatively neglected.

What little empirical research on the teaching norms held by the professoriate that has been conducted has been based largely on faculty at unspecified types of four-year colleges and universities (Tabachnick, Keith-Spiegel, and Pope, 1991) or at only selected types of research universities and comprehensive colleges and universities (Braxton, Bayer, and Finkelstein, 1992; Boice, 1996; Braxton, Eimers, and Bayer, 1996). Braxton, Bayer, and Finkelstein (1992) delineated four violations of normative behavior patterns espoused by faculty in the academic disciplines of biology, mathematics, history, and psychology holding academic appointments. These patterns represent inviolable norms that require strong sanctions when ignored: interpersonal disregard, inattentive planning, moral turpitude, and particularistic grading. These normative behavior patterns represent inviolable norms likely requiring administrative action when ignored. Braxton, Bayer, and Finkelstein also focused on faculty espousal of these four normative behavior clusters and identified institutional and disciplinary differences for breaches of them.

Research Questions

The research described in this volume extends that of Braxton, Bayer, and Finkelstein (1992) by addressing a set of questions not posed by them. The five questions posed in the current research are:

1. *What inviolable patterns of behavior comprise the normative structure of undergraduate college teaching?* Norms differ in the degree of moral outrage or indignation their violation elicits (Durkheim, 1995 [1912]). Norms are considered inviolable when academics believe severe sanctions are warranted by the transgression of such norms.

2. *What admonitory patterns of behavior comprise the normative structure of undergraduate college teaching?* Transgressions of admonitory norms evoke less condemnation than transgressions of inviolable norms do. Moreover, the reaction of colleagues to transgressions of such norms is unpredictable, although individual academics are advised not to ignore such normative behavioral configurations.

3. *Are any of the inviolable norms or admonitory patterns similar across all types of educational institutions? Are there core inviolable or admonitory patterns for all types of colleges and universities? Are there inviolable or admonitory normative arrays that vary in their level of disapproval among fac-*

ulty by institutional type? Institutional structures are greatly influenced by the mission of a college or university (Ruscio, 1987). Institutional structures, in turn, influence academic work (Ruscio, 1987; Blackburn and Lawrence, 1995). Consequently, faculty espousal of inviolable and admonitory norms may differ across different types of colleges and universities.

4. *Are there core inviolable or admonitory norms across academic disciplines? Are there inviolable or admonitory normative arrays that vary according to academic discipline in their level of faculty disapproval?* Braxton and Hargens (1996) concluded from a comprehensive review of research that the differences among academic disciplines are "profound and extensive." These differences are organized around the paradigmatic development of an academic discipline, that is, the degree of consensus a discipline has reached on such matters as theoretical orientation, research methods, and the importance of research questions (Kuhn, 1962, 1970; Lodahl and Gordon, 1973; Biglan, 1973a, 1973b). Braxton and Hargens (1996) note that the paradigmatic development of a discipline influences the importance faculty members attach to the roles of teaching and research. The academic disciplines of biology, mathematics, history, and psychology illustrate the variation in the level of paradigmatic development (Biglan, 1973a). As a consequence, faculty espousal of inviolable and admonitory proscriptions may vary across these four academic disciplines.

5. *Do individual faculty characteristics—for example, administrative experience, gender, professional status, research activity, and tenure status—affect espousal of inviolable or admonitory normative patterns above and beyond the effects of institutional type and academic discipline?* Faculty characteristics constitute sources of personal control. Reiss (1951) describes personal controls as the individual's ability to avoid norm violations that may occur as a result of personal needs. By extension, personal controls or individual faculty characteristics may also influence faculty espousal of inviolable or admonitory normative orientations. More extensive formulations for the possible influence of each of these five faculty characteristics on norm espousal are described in Chapter 7.

For a normative structure to be institutionalized and binding (Mulkay, 1976), faculty members must avoid transgressions of all inviolable and admonitory proscriptions in undergraduate teaching. Such transgressions constitute teaching misconduct. This book advances practical formulations to account for such misconduct and posits theoretical formulations about the mechanisms of deterrence and detection of misconduct. It also explores sanctions and advances the necessity of greater formal codification of the normative system of teaching in both associational and institutional policy documents, given evidence assembled here that suggests a relative deficiency of such formalized teaching proscriptions.

Theoretical Perspective

Because the specific inviolable and admonitory normative clusters are not known a priori, theoretical formulations predicting faculty variation by institutional type, academic discipline, or individual characteristics cannot be advanced. Nevertheless, this research is theoretically informed. Two orienting theoretical notions undergird this research. First, norms are proscribed (as operationalized in this book) patterns of behavior that carry social significance to college and university faculty and their clients. The index of their social significance lies in the degree of moral outrage or indignation such proscribed behaviors evoke (Durkheim, 1995 [1912]). Such moral outrage or indignation can be assessed by ascertaining the severity of sanctions faculty perceive as befitting such prohibited behaviors. Second, the severity of sanctions faculty perceive as befitting a particular proscribed normative pattern varies according to the value patterns and role identities academics have with respect to performance of their teaching role. This orientation stems from Rokeach's supposition that values influence behaviors (1973). Thus, faculty espousal of the inviolable and admonitory norms identified in this volume may vary across different types of colleges and universities and academic disciplines. Moreover, individual faculty characteristics may also influence the espousal of inviolable and admonitory normative arrays.

Overview of the Book

Chapter 2 recounts the methodology used in conducting the research reported in this book. Instrumentation, sampling designs, and characteristics of obtained samples are described in this chapter. Chapters 3 and 4 describe the normative structure of undergraduate college teaching identified by this piece of research. Chapter 3 delineates the set of inviolable normative proscriptions identified. Chapter 4 delineates the set of admonitory normative patterns derived. In both chapters, fictional vignettes are presented for each of the inviolable and admonitory normative configurations identified. These vignettes offer a crisper perspective on the meaning of each inviolable and admonitory normative cluster than mere statistical descriptions do.

Chapter 5 identifies those inviolable and admonitory normative patterns found to be core norms across various types of colleges and universities. Those inviolable and admonitory normative clusters that differ by institutional type are also described in Chapter 5.

Chapter 6 delineates those inviolable and admonitory normative arrays established as core norms across academic disciplines. Building on the findings of Chapter 5, core inviolable and admonitory norms across institutional type and academic discipline are also recognized. Moreover, those inviolable and admonitory normative clusters that vary across academic disciplines are discussed in Chapter 6.

Chapter 7 reports the influence of the five individual faculty characteristics on the espousal of inviolable and admonitory normative proscriptions.

Theoretical formulations for teaching misconduct are advanced in Chapter 8. This chapter also postulates some formulations concerning the deterrence, detection, and sanctioning of teaching misconduct.

In Chapter 9, we analyze and review a variety of materials and documents that have appeared over the past decade in order to ascertain the degree to which recent materials contain components of the norm clusters identified in Chapters 3 and 4 as well as the degree of formal codification of teaching proscriptions current in academe. Included are selected volumes addressing ethical standards and appropriate behaviors of college teaching and handbooks on college teaching; professional association policy documents and codes of conduct; collective bargaining agreements; and selected institutional documents, including student instructional rating forms and criteria employed for post-tenure review of the professoriate.

Chapter 10 offers conclusions, recommendations for further research, and implications for professional- and institutional-level policies and practice. Misconduct by the professoriate in all work role domains, including teaching behavior, is shown *not* to be as rare as is often popularly assumed. We propose that the research results reported in this volume offer evidence of the need for increased formalization and articulation of behavioral standards for teaching faculty in academe.

TWO

Design for the Studies

By the end of the 1980s, the notion of self-regulation by the academic profession had been thoroughly challenged as regards the research and scholarly roles of the professoriate. Media coverage of research improprieties and outright fraud had raised public consciousness and public skepticism of the ethical dimensions of the profession. By 1990, the National Science Foundation concluded that one-fifth of scientists have directly encountered fraud and an equal proportion of graduate deans have dealt with verified cases of scientific misconduct over the previous ten years (Office of the Inspector General, 1990).

This has resulted in a comprehensive literature identifying the classification and dimensions of scientific misconduct, a proliferation of policies, statements of standards and responsibilities in professional codes of conduct, and establishment of formal mechanisms from the federal level to individual institutions to address scientific misconduct (Braxton and Bayer, 1994, 1996). While anecdotal accounts of misconduct in the teaching role suggest that academic administrators and faculty panels spend far more time addressing this type of misconduct than that of improprieties in the scholarly and research roles, relatively little parallel formal response has been made. Indeed, in 1987, the American Association of University Professors endorsed its Statement on Professional Ethics, which was less than two pages long and contained merely a paragraph outlining the ethical standards on teaching expected of college and university faculty members (American Association of University Professors, 1990, pp. 75–76). Similarly, perhaps the most widely used primer for preparing college teachers, Wilbert J. McKeachie's *Teaching Tips: A Guidebook for the Beginning College Teacher*, contained nothing addressing teaching ethics in its many editions and updates through its seventh edition. Not until the eighth edition (1986) was there a chapter titled "Ethical Standards in Teaching," and it was only a two-page excerpt from the code of ethics of the American Psychological Association. Finally, in its most recent edition

(1994), there is a chapter, titled "Ethics in College Teaching" (9 pages), that attempts to set out some explicit standards for teaching behavior.

It is against this backdrop of the late 1980s that we began to formulate plans for undertaking an assessment of the prevailing ethics and normative standards on teaching held by the American professoriate. Our earlier collaborative research on misconduct in science provided a template for what needed to be done to understand misconduct in the teaching role. Like the earlier literature on scientific fraud and misconduct, the initial phase needed to be an assessment of consensus on what improprieties deserve sanctions and thus were "core" norms of behavior in the teaching role. Toward this end, we needed to design a survey instrument comprised of various teaching behaviors that might be subject to normative criteria. This chapter reports the design of the instrumentation and studies we conducted to attain this objective. Three separate surveys were conducted using the instrument we developed: one of faculty in research universities and comprehensive colleges and universities, one of faculty in both highly selective and less selective liberal arts colleges, and one of faculty in community colleges. Subsequent chapters report the analytical results from these studies and provide the groundwork for the next steps, including ascertaining prevalence of various forms of misconduct, developing statements of standards, and establishing social control mechanisms to replace professional self-regulation, which has now broken down; these steps parallel those found in the history of actions and in the literature on scientific misconduct.

Survey Instrument

While public school teachers were subject to massive bureaucratic procedures by the late 1980s, including written prescriptive and proscriptive behaviors, an online literature search and perusal of literature indexes yielded no codifications of teaching norms or delineations of expected teaching behaviors for college and university faculty members. Moreover, perusal of codes of ethics of selected professional associations with a large proportion of the membership coming from academe yielded few statements of an explicit nature regarding specific ethical behaviors (other than as regards sexual harassment) in the teaching role (for more detailed content analysis, addressing more recent professional association codes, see Chapter 9).

Consequently, we used several methods in gathering statements to integrate into a survey instrument addressing specific teaching norms of the professoriate. One approach was simply to ask a convenience sample of faculty colleagues to provide a list of the normative expectations they had in terms of their associates' teaching behavior. A second approach was to compile a list of specific behaviors expected of college teachers that could be derived from the literature on ethics in college teaching: included for this assessment was the work by Baumgarten (1982), Robertson and Grant (1982), Schurr (1982), Scriven (1982), and Wilson (1982). Third, we developed parallel behaviors for teaching that we derived as analogous to the norms emerging in the process of our doing research on scientific misconduct, including derivations from the four norms of science identified by Robert Merton (1942, 1973). Fourth, we added to this list those incidents we had encountered over our years in higher education teaching and in academic administration from college students registering complaints about some of their instructors' actions or from faculty who conveyed criticisms of teaching practices of some of their colleagues.

Finally, we submitted a compilation of teaching behaviors that might meet normative criteria derived from these procedures to a panel of 23 experts on college teaching from the membership of the Project on Teaching of the American Sociological Association. Each worked independently and was invited to critique the list they were provided and to add to that list other proscribed behaviors they believed were part of the general normative structure regarding college teaching practice. A substantial number of additional improprieties were derived from these participants.

Remarkably, our first approach to generating a list of norms was the least fruitful. We asked more than 20 of our faculty colleagues (all social scientists, and most sociologists) to compile a list of the "specific normative expectations you hold for college teachers." Approximately half chose to translate this request to listing their expectations regarding *student* behavior. With the exception of one person who provided specific behavioral statements regarding normative expectations of college faculty members, all the remaining responses were simply vague generalities, for example, "respect students," "teach well," "grade fairly."

A compilation of identified behaviors from all sources resulted in 126 specific statements. Because there were so many, we grouped them into categories so respondents would find it easier to deal with the survey list. Eight categories were formed: preplanning for the course (14 behaviors), first day of class (14 behaviors), in-class behaviors (21 behaviors), treating course content (9 behaviors), examination and grading practices (25 behaviors), faculty-student in-class interactions (9 behaviors), relationships with colleagues (16 behaviors), and out-of-class practices (18 behaviors).

In an initial pretest, some behaviors were listed in positive terms and others in negative terms. Respondents were asked to evaluate the importance of each in terms of their perception of the general standards applied to college teachers of the average undergraduate class in their field. This response category setup proved both confusing and difficult for the respondents. It was abandoned. In its place, we turned to bedrock sociological insight: the general principle advanced by Durkheim in 1912 that norms are best recognized when they have been violated (Durkheim, 1995 [1912]).

Consequently, the 126 specific behaviors subsumed under the eight categories of behavioral context were all worded *negatively* so as to cast each behavior in the form of a violation of possible preferred conduct. Individuals were asked to indicate their opinion on each specific behavior as might ideally apply to a faculty member teaching a lower-division college course (intended primarily for first- and second-year students) in their field of about 40 enrolled students regardless of whether they ever taught such a course.

While one often thinks of proscriptive norms as being either existing or not existing as regards a particular behavior, the sanctions that can be applied to such a behavior lie along a continuum of severity. We later build on this fact by distinguishing between the strongest, "inviolable" norms (see Chapter 3), and somewhat lesser norms, which we call "admonitory" norms (see Chapter 4). Survey respondents used the following rating system to indicate the degree of their reaction to each behavior: (1) appropriate behavior, should be encouraged; (2) discretionary behavior, neither particularly appropriate nor inappropriate; (3) mildly inappropriate behavior, generally to be ignored; (4) inappropriate behavior, to be handled informally by colleagues or administrators suggesting change or improvement; and (5) very inappropriate behavior, requiring formal administrative intervention. This item format composed the core of what is called the College Teaching Behaviors Inventory (CTBI). This section of the instrument remained precisely the same for all three subsequent studies of faculty in various types of institutional settings. The liberal arts college version of the CTBI is shown in Appendix A.

While it may be obvious, one more point about these 126 behavioral items needs to be emphasized: they are not exhaustive. Nor is it possible to compile a complete finite array of all behaviors that might meet normative standards applicable to college and university teaching faculty. Indeed, since we have compiled our list of behaviors, a similar independent endeavor, but one targeted only to college teachers in psychology, has been developed (Tabachnick, Keith-Spiegel, and Pope, 1991). In this case, 63 behaviors were identified. Many of these items paralleled those on our list, but some reflect other transgressions that we had not identified (e.g., accepting a publisher's rebate for adopting a textbook, accepting an expensive gift from a student, using films without educational value to fill class time and reduce preparation work for teaching). Nevertheless, while many other specific individual improprieties in teaching may be identified, the range of incidents represented by the 126 items in the CTBI likely represent the full spectrum of general categories of improprieties that might be uncovered by factor analysis, cluster analysis, or similar statistical techniques.

In addition to assessing faculty opinion about the severity of transgressions represented by the 126 items, the survey instrument included a short section on personal demographics and educational background, career characteristics, current teaching activity, and information about the employing institution and department. When warranted by the employing institutional type for a particular study survey, these questions were modified slightly. For example, in our survey of community college faculty, an additional response category was added to the tenure status question ("on contract, institution does not offer a tenure system") and to the academic rank question ("institution does not have academic rank designation").[1]

Survey Samples

Three separate surveys using the CTBI were conducted over a span of six years. Each survey targeted faculty members in a different segment from the approximately 3,000 higher education institutions classified by the Carnegie Foundation for the Advancement of Teaching (1987). The three surveys selected faculty at institutions from the following Carnegie categories:

Survey I: Research universities I (RUI), that is, universities with a full range of baccalaureate programs, awarding at least 50 Ph.D. degrees annu-

1. Subsequent to the survey of faculty at research universities and comprehensive universities and colleges, a question series on undergraduate teaching objectives was added to the survey form. This item, originally designed for the 1972–73 national survey of college and university faculty conducted by the American Council on Education (Bayer, 1973), included two sets of responses for fourteen teaching goals. One response set was for rating the importance of specific teaching goals for the responding faculty member; the second set represented the faculty members' perception of the importance of the same goal by their institution. Major variations have been found in the endorsement of these various teaching goals, particularly in association with academic discipline (Liebert and Bayer, 1975). Thus, the item was incorporated in some of the surveys for later analysis. This survey question is not, however, used in the context of this book.

ally, and placing a high priority on research with at least $35.5 million in annual federal support, and comprehensive colleges and universities II (CUC-II), that is, institutions with enrollment of 2,500 or fewer students and offering both bachelor's and master's degrees. This survey was conducted during the spring semester of 1989.

Survey II: Liberal arts colleges I (LAI), that is, highly selective undergraduate colleges that award more than half of their baccalaureate degrees in arts and sciences, and liberal arts colleges II (LAII), that is, less selective undergraduate colleges that award more than half of their baccalaureate degrees in arts and sciences. This survey was conducted during the spring semester of 1993.

Survey III: Two-year community, junior, and technical colleges (2YR), that is, institutions offering certificate or degree programs through the associate of arts level. This survey was conducted during the fall semester of the 1994–95 academic year.

Sampling of Disciplines

For each of the three surveys, an equal number of faculty members were selected from the same four disciplinary areas. These four disciplines were picked to be representative of each category in two of the dimensions of the Biglan (1973a, 1973b) classification scheme for subject matter specialties. Biglan's classification sorts academic subject matter areas into eight categories using three dimensions: hard-soft, pure-applied, and life-nonlife (1973a, 1973b). The hard-soft dimension pertains to the extent of paradigmatic development exhibited by a subject matter area. The pure-applied dimension arrays subject matter areas according to their orientation to pure or applied academic pursuits. The life-nonlife dimension categorizes academic subject matter areas according to whether living organisms are a focus of a given subject matter area.

We used the hard-soft paradigmatic development and life-nonlife dimensions of Biglan's classification scheme, and the disciplines selected are biology (hard/life), mathematics (hard/nonlife), psychology (soft/life), and history (soft/nonlife). All four of these disciplines are classified as pure disciplines according to Biglan's classification system.

The Biglan typology was employed because research using this classification scheme for academic subject matter areas indicates that individual academic disciplines differ in the amount of time spent on teaching, the style of teaching, and the preference for or amount of importance attached to teaching (Creswell and Roskens, 1981; Becher, 1989; Braxton and Hargens, 1996). Thus, faculty in different subject matter areas may differ on the degree of importance accorded to the deviant teaching-related behaviors we list in the CTBI. Selection of these representative subject matter areas allows the testing of differences in the degree of impropriety associated with these teaching norms by faculty members affiliated with these disparate disciplines.

Selection and Administration Procedures

For each of the three surveys, a random selection of institutions fitting our criteria was drawn. For each survey, 800 faculty members were drawn from these institutions, with a quota of 200 from each of the four specified disciplines. The mailing procedures were identical for each of the three surveys. An initial mailing to each addressee by name to institutional departmental addresses was composed of a cover letter, the eight-page survey instrument, and a postage-paid reply envelope. Approximately one week after the initial mailing, a postcard reminder was sent to all sample members. Approximately three to five weeks later, a second mailing including a revised cover letter, another copy of the instrument, and another postage-paid reply envelope was sent to all nonrespondents from the first mailing. All three surveys employed a cluster sampling approach. Specific colleges and universities constituted the clusters, and these clusters were, in turn, used to identify the names of faculty members at these randomly selected institutions in each of the four academic disciplines represented in this research. Details on the sampling and response rates to each of the three surveys is described below.

Survey I. From the population of 70 institutions classified as research universities I, 11 universities were randomly selected; 25 institutions were randomly drawn from the population of 171 comprehensive universities and colleges II. To construct the faculty sample, the specific names of faculty were derived from the most recent university and college catalogs or bulletins of the randomly chosen colleges and universities. All faculty holding the rank of assistant professor or higher and listed under one of the four academic departments represented in this research were eligible for selection.

Eight lists of faculty were formed, one list for each of the four academic subjects at the two institutional types. From each list, a random sample of 100 faculty members was drawn. This sample was comprised of 200 faculty members from each of the four subject areas, or 400 faculty members from each of the two types of colleges and universities included in this study.

A total of 356 individuals responded with a completed survey form. Thus, a response rate of 44.5 percent was realized.

Survey II. A total population of 144 liberal arts colleges I and 545 liberal arts colleges II was identified from the Carnegie Foundation report (1987). From each list, a random sample of institutions was selected, college catalogs were obtained, and a sampling of catalogs continued until a list of 100 faculty members was generated for each of the four academic disciplines. All 144 liberal arts colleges I were selected, whereas 131 liberal arts colleges II were randomly drawn.

These lists were combined to create a sample of 200 faculty members from each of the four subject areas, or 400 faculty members from each of the two categories of liberal arts colleges.

A total of 382 individuals returned a completed survey form. Thus, a response rate of 47.8 percent was obtained.

Survey III. As with the other two surveys, a two-stage design was employed for the study of community college faculty. From the list of 1366 two-year colleges in the Carnegie Foundation report (1987), 137 institutions were randomly selected. A microfiche copy of the current (1993–95) catalogs was obtained for each selected institution. In the second stage, individual faculty members were selected from these institutions.

From the catalogs of the randomly selected institutions, all faculty members clearly in one of the four disciplines was noted for possible inclusion in the sample of faculty. Since the number of faculty associated with each of these fields varies, sampling continued until the least-occurring discipline reached 200. Inasmuch as these persons were listed in the institutions' catalogs, they may be assumed to be the more permanent members of the faculty at these two-year colleges. When part-time or adjunct faculty could be distinguished in the college catalog, they were excluded from the sample. Those individuals who were similarly identified in the other three fields were then randomly selected until 200 were picked from each discipline. This yields a total sample size of 800 individuals. A total of 265 usable replies were received. This represents a response rate of 33.1 percent.

Despite the response rates for the three surveys conducted, a minimal degree of bias exists in the samples obtained. Appendix B describes the results of the procedures used to determine the extent of respondent bias in each of the three surveys.

The Aggregated Sample

The research questions pursued in this project were addressed by aggregating the three surveys for statistical analyses. This aggregated sample is made up of 949 faculty respondents.[2] More specifically, this aggregated sample is composed of 140 faculty members from research universities I, 204 faculty members from comprehensive universities and colleges II, 174 faculty members from liberal arts colleges I, 180 faculty members from liberal arts colleges II, and 251 faculty members from two-year colleges. Of these 949 faculty, 259 individuals are biologists, 222 are mathematicians, 231 are psychologists, and 237 are historians.

With the five selected faculty demographic and career characteristics, the profile of the aggregated sample takes the following form. Male academics constitute 72.3 percent of this sample, whereas women faculty make up 27.7 percent. Full professor, the rank of high intrainstitutional professional status (see Chapter 7), constitutes 47.2 percent of this sample, and 52.8 percent of the aggregated sample hold an academic rank other than full professor. Academic tenure is held by 46.0 percent of this sample, whereas 54.0 percent of this faculty sample is untenured. Moreover, almost two-thirds (65.0 percent) of faculty in the aggregated sample have never been dean or department chairperson, and 35.0 percent of this sample has had such administrative experience. During the past three years prior to the focal survey, faculty in the aggregated sample averaged 1.79 publications (journal articles and books/monographs combined). Slightly more than one-third (36.3 percent) of faculty in the aggregated sample had no articles or books published during the past three years prior to their completion of the CTBI.

Concluding Comments

Data collection for this project spanned a period of just under six years. Three separate surveys were conducted, focusing on faculty in different segments of the population of higher education institutions. The first mail survey was launched in April 1989, and data collection for the third survey ran until January 1995.

2. The number of faculty in the aggregated sample is less than the sum of respondents to the three surveys (n = 1003), because only faculty for whom an institutional and academic discipline were identified were included in the aggregated sample.

For some comparative research purposes, such a span of time might be assumed to "contaminate" results. That is, populations may change sufficiently over time that it would be difficult to identify differences resulting from institutional variation as opposed to differences resulting from different time periods. But our focus is on the normative system(s) in academe and it is a sociological truism that norms generally change only very slowly over time within a social system. Therefore, the time span reflected in the data collected for this study has negligible effect on the results and conclusions.

Finally, it should be noted again that we did not sample higher education faculties from all types of disciplines and all types of institutions. The disciplines were selected on the basis of a proven robust classification system (Biglan, 1973a, 1973b), and so they can be assumed to be approximately representative of a broader array of similar academic specialty fields.

Similarly, the survey samples include faculty from selected types of higher education institutions, but not from *all* types as classified by the Carnegie Foundation (1987). Nevertheless, the sample ranges from the most prestigious and very large doctoral-granting research universities (RUI) to the community colleges whose mission is almost exclusively teaching and whose students often terminate their postsecondary education with a two-year associate's degree or a certificate for a technical field. In addition, a variety of institutions that fall within this range are included. Smaller comprehensive colleges and universities that offer master's degree programs as their highest level (CUC-II) are included, along with a sample of the full span of liberal arts institutions (LAI and LAII) that emphasize teaching heavily and concentrate on offering baccalaureate programs.

The survey instrument—the CTBI—is generally applicable across disciplines, across institutional settings, and over time. The analysis of results reported in the following chapters attests to the utility and viability of the CTBI. More specifically, the next two chapters describe the normative structure of undergraduate college teaching identified through faculty responses to the CTBI.

THREE

Inviolable Norms

Faculty members differ in their assessments of a breach of various proscribed behaviors. Norms vary in their intensity: violations of some are largely ignored or dismissed as personal eccentricities, whereas violations of others are seen as demanding the most severe sanctions available to social agents. This interpretation is consistent with Durkheim's observation that norms are best identified through the degree of moral outrage or anger their violation elicits from others (1995 [1912]). Consequently, some norms are inviolable because of the extreme severity of the sanctions believed to fit transgressions of such norms. This chapter addresses the research question: What inviolable patterns comprise the normative structure of undergraduate college teaching? This chapter describes seven inviolable norms.

Specific behaviors are defined as being an inviolable norm if their mean values were 4.00 or higher on the sanctioning action scale described in Chapter 2. Appendix C displays the mean values of the 126 behaviors of the CTBI. Of these 126 behaviors, a total of 33 behaviors met this criterion for an inviolable norm.

A factor analysis using the principal components approach was used to discern the underlying pattern of meaning of these 33 proscribed behaviors. A scree test was used to determine that a seven-factor solution was appropriate. These seven factors were rotated using the varimax method. The seven patterns of inviolable proscribed norms identified, in alphabetical order, are: *condescending negativism, inattentive planning, moral turpitude, particularistic grading, personal disregard, uncommunicated course details,* and *uncooperative cynicism.*

Each of the seven inviolable proscribed norms are described in this chapter. Fictional vignettes are presented for each of the normative transgressions.

Condescending Negativism

This normative pattern proscribes the treatment of both colleagues and students in a condescending and demeaning way. Transgressions oc-

TABLE 3.1. Factor Loadings of Specific Behaviors of the Inviolable Proscriptive Norm against Condescending Negativism

CTBI Item	Loading
F5. An instructor makes condescending remarks to a student in class.	.737
F3. The instructor expresses impatience with a slow learner in class.	.679
H3. A faculty member criticizes the academic performance of a student in front of other students.	.662
H9. An advisee is treated in a condescending manner.	.644
G9. A faculty member makes negative comments about a colleague in public before students.	.493
C8. Instructions and requirements for course assignments are not clearly described to students.	.433

Note: Percent of explained variance = .29; Cronbach alpha = .82. Extent of consensus against condescending negativism at the level 4.00 and higher = 70.9%; at the level 3.99 and lower = 29.1%.

cur both in and out of class. Such a lack of civility is regarded as unprofessional (Callahan, 1982) and as an example of poor teaching (Hook, 1994).

The prohibited behaviors in this normative cluster violate the ethics of teaching. Nisbet (1977) asserts that tyrannical behavior toward students is unethical. Condescending negativism also breaches the principle of student development contained in *Ethical Principles for College and University Teaching* developed by the Society for Teaching and Learning in Higher Education in Canada. In this report, Murray and his associates (1996) note that "derogatory comments toward students" detract from student development. In addition, condescending negativism clearly violates the norm of "respect for persons" (Smith, 1996), or the principle of "respect for students as individuals" (Reynolds, 1996; Svinicki, 1994).

The inviolable status of condescending negativism stems from the formal power faculty have over students. Wilson (1982) calls this relationship an "asymmetry of power." Because such power is unmonitored, abuses of this "asymmetry of power," such as condescending negativism toward students, can be problematic. The treatment of students in a condescending and demeaning way by a faculty member negatively affects learning. Markie (1994) asserts that such faculty behavior discourages learning and intellectual risk-taking because students view their questions as mistakes or "personal failures." Svinicki (1994) contends that disrespect for students discourages their learning.

Six prohibited behaviors comprise this normative configuration (Table 3.1). The behaviors having the highest loadings on this normative factor are: "the instructor makes condescending remarks to a student in class"; "the instructor expresses impatience with a slow learner"; "a faculty member criticizes the academic performance of a student in front of other students"; and "an advisee is treated in a condescending manner."

A considerable degree of consensus exists among faculty on the inviolability of condescending negativism. More specifically, 70.9 percent of faculty respondents agreed about the seriousness (rated 4.00 or higher) of this normative pattern.

CASE: Condescending Negativism

Jackson Barkley came to Hidden Valley Community College with outstanding references and his graduate degree from a university known to offer one of the strongest mathematics programs in the region. Nevertheless, he has been informed that his contract with HVCC would not be extended.

His termination is directly attributable to his abrasive interpersonal style. Other faculty members in the Department of Mathematical Sciences have grown estranged from Barkley. All have heard comments from their students of demeaning and embarrassing remarks he has made to classmates in his courses. Stories abound of student tears and abrupt departures by students from his classes.

He is severely judgmental of other faculty members in the department. No one has been spared his criticisms—even to the point of derogatory remarks about the universities where each of them received their degrees. Not infrequently, he will interrogate individual students in the middle of his class session about who taught their prerequisite HVCC course for his class. He will then proceed to criticize those individual instructors for not adequately teaching the material one would expect his students to know before they enrolled in his class.

His approach to students within class is even less kind. Besides criticizing students' other teachers for inadequately preparing them for his calculus and advanced algebra classes, he assails students in front of the rest of the class members for their poor academic performance. Throughout the semester he expresses impatience and criticism of anyone who is slow to grasp a solution to a problem or a proof to a theorem.

Barkley's intimidating classroom demeanor is well-known around campus. Unfortunately, for many of those students in the academic track at least one class "experience" with him is virtually impossible to avoid. If anyone should not be familiar with Barkley when they begin the semester, by the end of the first class session his "style" is clear. Survival is best obtained by rarely or never speaking in class. Even nontraditional students who are considerably older in age and maturity than Barkley quickly adopt a passive classroom demeanor.

Those few students who seek Barkley's out-of-class help on homework or seek some advising assistance seldom return a second time to visit him during his office hours. He is as critical and condescending in the confines of his office as he is in his classroom.

The departmental program coordinator has sought out Barkley on several occasions to discuss his departmental demeanor and offer constructive suggestions. At other times, she's been quite harsh and direct in her criticism of him. In response, Barkley has totally ignored her attempts to help and instead has simply become more hostile toward her.

"Barking Barkley" is the target of many comments behind his back. Students talk of starting a fund-raising campaign to hire a mafia hit man. Faculty members talk of pitching in to pay his tuition to "Miss Manner's School for the Humble" or joke about the administration needing to hire a team of psychiatrists to treat Barkley on an around-the-clock basis.

HVCC will soon no longer have its tyrant on its faculty. Moreover, his replacement will surely be scrutinized well beyond a reading of reference letters and appraisal of the prominence of the degree-granting institution. The Department of Mathematical Sciences will soon be a better place— for both the faculty and the students.

Inattentive Planning

A lack of attention to the planning of a course by a faculty member constitutes the normative cluster censuring inattentive planning. Cahn (1986) asserts "no responsible instructor ever enters the classroom without careful planning" (p. 17). Markie (1994) concurs by indicating that faculty have an obligation to share a course syllabus with their students. Thus, inattentive planning represents a failure to uphold this professorial obligation.

Recently, some proponents of what has come to be called feminist pedagogy (Lather, 1991; Hooks, 1994; Maher and Tetreault, 1994; Cohee et al., 1998; Ropers-Huilman, 1998) reject detailed planning and preparation of a formal syllabus, including specification of criteria for awarding grades, before first meeting with one's classes. To some, a formal syllabus prepared before a class begins is viewed as an archaic remnant of the male

TABLE 3.2. Factor Loadings of Specific Behaviors of the Inviolable Proscriptive Norm against Inattentive Planning

CTBI Item	Loading
A1. Required texts and other reading materials are not routinely ordered by the instructor in time to be available for the first class session.	.765
A2. A course outline or syllabus is not prepared for a course.	.692

Note: Percent of explained variance = .03; Cronbach alpha = .54. Extent of consensus against inattentive planning at the level 4.00 and higher = 78.6%; at the level 3.99 and lower = 21.4%.

power perspective. From this particular feminist perspective, it is imperative that course content, class projects, grading criteria, and other aspects of a class that might be assumed to be contained in a syllabus available on the first day of class is negotiated in an egalitarian classroom environment. Advocates of this approach deny that this represents inattentiveness. They view development of a course as reflected in a syllabus as an interactive process between students and their instructor, and they claim that this too takes careful planning.

This perception that a syllabus should be available on the first day of class springs from the notion that a syllabus is a student's guide to the course (Markie, 1994). More specifically, students need information to make informed decisions about a course (Markie, 1994). Moreover, students learn better if they know where a course is headed and the reasons for the course's direction (Markie, 1994).

Two specific prohibited behaviors constitute the normative configuration of inattentive planning (Table 3.2). These behaviors are: "required texts and other reading materials are not routinely ordered by the instructor in time to be available for the first class session"; "a course outline or syllabus is not prepared for the course."[1]

Consensus exists on the inviolability of this norm. More than three-fourths (78.6 percent) of faculty respondents espouse the need for sanctioning action (rated 4.00 or higher) suggestive of a norm that must not be violated.

1. In lieu of a hardcopy syllabus, college and university faculty members are increasingly using an electronic web site for conveying class material traditionally on syllabi. Our discussion of syllabi hereafter equally refers to the alternative of an Internet homepage including the same information.

CASE: Inattentive Planning

It is almost the beginning of another semester. Assistant Professor Karen Willburn has full capacity enrollment in the four classes she will be teaching: two sections of Principles of Economics, one of Microeconomic Theory, and another of Labor Economics. Yet no syllabi have been submitted for preparation by departmental staff nor any textbook orders placed with the bookstore for any of Dr. Willburn's classes.

Once again Professor Virginia Ordcutt, chair of the Department of Economics and Labor Studies at Mount Hollybrook College, will have to visit Karen Willburn and address her procrastination every semester in preparing for her new classes. But this time Ordcutt will have to plan a firmer rebuttal to Willburn's usual excuses. The litany will be familiar: too busy counseling students, too overloaded meeting with student organizations as their adviser, several manuscripts to review for professional journals, committed to finish a commissioned book chapter before the new term begins, important committee assignments with her professional associations, committed to presentations to local civic and labor organizations, and so on. Ordcutt has heard the endless list time and again.

Of course, all of those other activities are important and Willburn has certainly kindled broader recognition of the Department of Economics and Labor Studies, and indeed to Hollybrook itself. But this time Ordcutt is not going to be thrust in a defensive position because Willburn is doing so much. Karen Willburn will either have to drop some of her other laudable professional activities, or at least not always accumulate them to be done just before a new semester begins. This time, she will be told in no uncertain terms that her teaching *and* advance planning must take first priority above all else. Hollybrook prides itself on the quality of its teaching and on its first-rate teaching faculty. Wilburn must be persuaded to give top priority to this institutional mandate.

Ordcutt will plan this time also to make the point that appraisal of teaching performance includes not only student evaluations, but course planning, course content (especially focusing on the syllabus—a crucial item that Willburn seldom generates), and collegial evaluation of *all* aspects of her teaching. She'll emphasize that without strong teaching performance, assistant professors cannot get tenure at Hollybrook.

The meeting, however, must be handled with all the tact that can be mustered. Other than her frustration with Willburn's unresponsiveness to their previous discussions of procrastination in planning her courses, Ordcutt genuinely admires Willburn. Moreover, Willburn is viewed by the

Table 3.3. Factor Loadings of Specific Behaviors of the Inviolable Proscriptive Norm against Moral Turpitude

CTBI Item	Loading
H7. A faculty member has a sexual relationship with a student enrolled in the course.	.757
H6. A faculty member makes suggestive sexual comments to a student enrolled in the course.	.646
C21. While able to conduct class, the instructor frequently attends class while obviously intoxicated.	.585

Note: Percent of explained variance = .03; Cronbach alpha = .61. Extent of consensus against moral turpitude at the level 4.00 and higher = 98.5%; at the level 3.99 and lower = 1.5%.

administration as a rising star and Hollybrook ambassador. Ordcutt *must* convince Willburn to change, but tenure and promotion will have to be dealt with carefully. Ordcutt must not let it be perceived as a threat that would prompt Willburn to search for a position elsewhere. On the other hand, the emphasis on teaching in the promotion and tenure criteria needs to be used firmly as an incentive to alter Willburn's behavior and ensure that in the future there will be no lapses in preparation for upcoming teaching assignments.

Moral Turpitude

The normative pattern regarding moral turpitude prohibits depraved, unprincipled acts by faculty members. The three condemned behaviors loading on this factor are: "a faculty member has a sexual relationship with a student enrolled in the course"; "a faculty member makes suggestive sexual comments to a student enrolled in the course"; and "while able to conduct class, the instructor frequently attends class while obviously intoxicated" (Table 3.3).

Moral turpitude represent proscribed behaviors that Cahn (1986) calls "an egregious abuse of authority." Sexual exploitation, in particular, constitutes extreme egregious perversion of authority in the context of the asymmetry of power that exists between faculty and students (Murray et al., 1996; Svinicki, 1994).

Moreover, Cahn (1986) and Markie (1994) assert that faculty have a fundamental obligation to give equal consideration to all students. Faculty cannot give equal consideration to all students in their teaching, advising, and assessment if they are having a sexual relationship with a student (Markie, 1994). Like condescending negativism, the principle of "respect for students as individuals" is also breached by the normative pattern of moral turpitude (Svinicki, 1994).

Whicker and Kronenfeld (1994) imply that only these activities—norms regarding sexual harassment—are ethically clear with regard to the teaching role of the professoriate; they suggest that all other possible norms of behavior regarding teaching are "fuzzy." Their contention finds support in the nearly unanimous accord that exists on the norm of moral turpitude. Almost all faculty (98.5 percent) believe in the inviolability (rated 4.00 or higher) of this particular proscribed pattern of behavior.

CASE 1: Moral Turpitude

"You girls may not like this one, but you've gotta hear it . . ." For as many years as anyone could remember, old Professor Hasselmann would zing in at least one offensive off-color joke a week to the staff in the department's main office. Years ago, the women would laugh politely at his jokes. But now he seldom receives even a courteous smile from the office staff, yet he "doesn't get it" and continues to relate his sexual and sexist jokes.

Humor of poor taste is not the only offense, however. Despite his years, sex seems forever on his mind. (Behind his back, many of his male colleagues call him "Old Letcher"; his female colleagues prefer other epithets). He has bragged to some of his faculty friends about sexual affairs with several of his students over the years, although there's no record of any formal complaints from these women.

His off-color remarks and jokes in class have, however, evoked numerous complaints to his department chair over the years. Chairman Ostrick has also received four allegations over the past seven years by women undergraduates that Hasselmann has touched them inappropriately and sexually propositioned them.

Ostrick has never discussed these complaints with Professor Hasselmann. Nor has he dealt very sympathetically with the students' complaints: he tells them to put their complaints in writing and take them to the director of personnel. Until this month, Ostrick never heard anything further on these cases. But now one of the students has followed through with his suggestion.

The director of personnel, who is also the affirmative action officer, has scheduled a meeting with Ostrick. Ostrick expects the worst—paperwork, proceedings, bad publicity for the department. He has never liked the concept of affirmative action in the first place, and he considers the director to be too committed to the letter of the law and overly aggressive in enforcing it on campus. Ostrick feels that his obligations include defending Hasselmann and attacking what he views as obtrusive federal legislation and distorted overreaction by college officials.

CASE 2: Moral Turpitude

Jake Kennedy knew that as a full professor his job opportunities at a new institution would be sparse, but he felt it was time for a move. His numerous papers and grants on polymer research, together with his year as an interim chair of his department and several years as the associate dean for undergraduate studies in his college, afforded good credentials for his application for the outside search for the departmental chair in chemistry at A&M University.

Kennedy was a finalist and had a superb interview at A&M. It was a good match, and the Search Committee gave clear signals that he was the preferred candidate. But the interview visit ended in an unusual way: the three senior chemists who were members of the Search Committee arranged to meet privately with him at the conclusion of his visit. Bad news. They indicated the most difficult dilemma in the department regarded Professor James Lesher; Jake knew Lesher's work well and he considered him the departmental senior "star." The three indicated that they supported Jake for the position, but that if he came they expected him to "solve" the problem of Lesher's alcoholism—a problem of long standing that was extremely disruptive to the department and affected all areas of Lesher's performance, particularly teaching. Dealing with an alcoholic tenured star chemist was not an attractive prospect, but Jake started the new position the following fall.

With the exception of his predecessor, every faculty member—tenured and untenured—mentioned to Chairperson Kennedy the need to deal with Lesher. But at the same time many of the same persons were enablers for Lesher's alcoholism. The former department chair would repeatedly spirit Lesher out of the building when he came in intoxicated, and Jake learned that he would also buy groceries to bring to Lesher when he was on a binge. On those occasions, Jake even learned that one of the three persons on the Search Committee who had first alerted him to the problem would sometimes quietly reassign his graduate assistant to teach one of Lesher's classes.

Kennedy's predecessor denied being aware of any drinking problems with Lesher, except, on occasion, he might have "a few too many at a professional meeting." So there was no paper trail of any prior problems with Lesher, and most of the faculty were reticent to put complaints in writing. But gradually Jake got agreement from some faculty members to document incidents in writing. This became easier as student delegations complained to his office of Lesher's drunkenness and incoherence in class and spokespersons were willing to put complaints in writing.

Jake routinely wrote summaries of the complaints and presented them to Jim Lesher (a procedure suggested to him by A&M's dean of faculty and by the director of the personnel office). Denial and anger would follow each encounter. It was a year and three documented incidents before Lesher acknowledged that he had a drinking problem. Subsequently, he entered a 28-day in-patient detox program three times, but each was followed by a mid-semester binge recurrence over the next year and a half.

Consequently, with advice of the university attorney, Kennedy prepared a letter of dismissal for cause. Lesher immediately countered by engaging his own attorney. All of the tenured faculty, including those who had been on the Search Committee, protested that Kennedy was taking inappropriate action against a colleague who was suffering from an illness. Few of them accepted that there was any "dereliction of duty" by Lesher, despite the fact that almost all of these same persons had insisted that Kennedy "do something."

Jake Kennedy had quickly soured on his enthusiasm for A&M and his respect for the faculty in his department. Jim Lesher's future was still not resolved. Moreover, complaints about Lesher had quickly been transformed by some faculty to criticism of Kennedy's "heavy-handedness" and "lack of respect for the tenure system." It was going to be another long hard year for Jake Kennedy.

Particularistic Grading

Particularistic grading condemns the uneven or preferential treatment of students in the awarding of grades. Indeed, issues of testing and grading may be an area requiring special attention, given its pervasiveness. Scriven (1982, p. 313) asserts: "the largest area of ethical malfeasance in postsecondary instruction probably concerns testing."

To be more specific, particularistic grading breaches Smith's (1996) norm of fairness. This norm stipulates that objectivity should prevail in both faculty dealings with students and in the assessment of student achievement. Murray and his associates (1996) as well as Reynolds (1996) posit the fair assessment of students as an ethical principle of college teaching. Strike (1994) provides more concrete guidance to this principle by maintaining that faculty have a duty to students to use relevant criteria in the assessment of their achievement.

Particularistic grading also transgresses the principle of equal treatment of students (Markie, 1994). Scriven (1982), Cahn (1986), and Murray and his associates contend that faculty should avoid demonstrating favoritism toward some students. Favoritism erodes academic standards (Murray et al., 1996) and hinders the learning process (Cahn, 1986). Svinicki (1994) also asserts that favoritism prevents all students from having an equal chance to exhibit their academic capabilities.

The normative cluster prohibitive of particularistic grading parallels the research-oriented norm of universalism described by Merton (1942, 1973). Universalism prescribes that research should be assessed on the basis of merit rather than on the basis of particularistic criteria such as race, nationality, class, personal relationships, or individual qualities. Like particularistic grading, violations of universalism negatively affect the advancement of knowledge and of careers (Merton, 1942, 1973; Braxton, 1986).

The proscriptive normative pattern of particularistic grading consists of eight denounced behaviors (Table 3.4). The prohibited behaviors with the highest loadings on this particular normative factor are: "social, personal, or other nonacademic characteristics of students are taken into account in the awarding of student grades"; "the instructor allows personal friendships with students to intrude on the objective grading of their work"; "stated policies about late work and incompletes are not universally applied to all students"; and "individual students are offered extra-credit work in order to improve their final course grade *after* the term is complete."

The vast majority of faculty assent to particularistic grading as a completely unacceptable pattern of behavior. To be specific, 82.7 percent of faculty respondents agree with the extreme severity of sanctions befitting violations of this norm.

CASE: Particularistic Grading

To the general academic community at Western Rock State College, Dr. Pierce appears to be an exemplary and dedicated teacher. She teaches two sections of English literature each semester and holds forth with some of her students at the WRSC Student Center after every class. Through these routine coffee klatches, Pierce brings together six or eight students who regularly discuss their class materials and are encouraged by Pierce simply to socialize.

TABLE 3.4. Factor Loadings of Specific Behaviors of the Inviolable Proscriptive Norm against Particularistic Grading

CTBI Item	Loading
E14. Social, personal, or other nonacademic characteristics of students are taken into account in the awarding of student grades.	.740
E12. The instructor allows personal friendship with a student to intrude on the objective grading of his or her work.	.689
F1. Stated policies about late work and incompletes are not universally applied to all students.	.585
E9. Individual students are offered extra-credit work to improve their final course grade after the term is completed.	.537
F2. Students are not permitted to express viewpoints different from those of the instructor.	.434
H1. Office hours scheduled for student appointments are frequently not kept.	.378
E4. Individual student course evaluations, where students can be identified, are read prior to the determination of final course grades.	.315
H12. A faculty member neglects to send a letter of recommendation that he or she had agreed to write.	.314

Note: Percent of explained variance = .05; Cronbach alpha = .76. Extent of consensus against particularistic grading at the level 4.00 and higher = 82.7%; at the level 3.99 and lower = 17.3%.

Other faculty from around campus have noticed the clockwork gatherings and frequently mention their favorable impressions to their colleagues in the English Department. After all, it is laudatory that Carolyn Pierce clearly goes well beyond the bounds of typical accessibility to students—at least as far as one can see. In fact, she frequently misses scheduled office appointments with other students in order to continue her gatherings at the Student Center.

Her "hospitality" and attention to these select students is also manifested in her little "rule-bending" for special cases. For example, to assure quality emphasis on student writing, the department has a cap of 25 students enrolled in each English literature class. Pierce's classes are always full and popular, particularly to members of the basketball team, and she frequently makes cap exceptions to enroll additional team members in her classes inasmuch as she believes that their sports practice sessions and game schedules allow them less latitude for course times than other students. (The Athletic Department also sends her free game passes every season, which she enjoys using and which she believes are not related to her self-appraised "compassionate" consideration of the special circumstances of WRSC basketball players.)

These "little exceptions," however, are also manifested in her grading of students. Sometimes she lowers her cut-off point for high letter grades on tests or papers in order to ensure that her basketball player and coffee klatch students receive better scores. Alternatively, she sometimes adds a few points to individuals' test scores because of the study time she presumes was lost to basketball practice or because of regular attendance and voluntary participation in the after-class sessions at the Student Center.

Of course, she does not mention these little extra criteria in her class or on her syllabus. Indeed, her syllabus proposes stringent criteria, even stressing that assignments that are not submitted on time will be given an F and that there will be no offering of extra-credit work in order to improve class grades. For most students in her class, she is quite rigid in adherence to these policies. Yet for those sycophants she has come to know well from the coffee sessions and for the basketball players that seem to migrate regularly to her classes, exceptions are made because of most any "special circumstances" these students may claim.

Sometimes, for these students, she allows extra-credit work, even after she has submitted final course grades for the semester and despite the fact that she will need to process change-of-grade paperwork. For those she knows well, she is sympathetic to the need to increase one's grade point average in order to maintain sports eligibility or because parents may be disappointed in their student's academic performance. (And she believes they are also "deserving" because she knows them personally from the Student Center sessions—and she intuitively knows as well that they really are better students than their grades sometimes reflect.)

Sullivan, the English Department chair, knows of the positive impressions of Pierce's teaching dedication that are held by many WRSC faculty members as well as by the athletic program staff. But Sullivan has also received complaints from some of Pierce's students who allege that she plays favorites in grading and makes exceptions to her own course policies for some students but not for others. Other departmental faculty members have likewise heard these student complaints and have told Sullivan that they think she should take some action to correct Pierce's apparent and overt favoritism for some students over others. One English professor insists that her acceptance of complimentary game tickets is tantamount to bribery by the Athletic Department. Sullivan knows she must meet with Pierce, but she worries how to approach the situation to correct the inappropriate practices without putting Pierce on the defensive. Pierce will likely insist that grading policy is a professional prerogative predicated on the principles of professional autonomy and academic freedom and is a component of the sanctity of the classroom, which should not be breached by administrators.

Personal Disregard

A disrespect for the needs and sensitivities of students is censured by the normative factor proscribing personal disregard.

This normative array, like condescending negativism, unquestionably transgresses the norm of "respect for persons" (Smith, 1996) and the principle of "respect for students as individuals" (Reynolds, 1996; Svinicki, 1994).

Six prohibited behaviors underlie personal disregard (Table 3.5). The behaviors with the highest factor loadings are: "the instructor practices poor personal hygiene and regularly has offensive body odor"; "the instructor frequently uses profanity in class"; and "the class is usually dismissed early."

Some consensus exists on this particular configuration of unacceptable behaviors. Of faculty responding to the College Teaching Behaviors Instrument, 69.1 percent of them concur with the inviolability (rated 4.00 or higher) of the prosciptive norm of personal disregard.

CASE: Personal Disregard

The compilation from the end-of-semester students' evaluations of their class and instructor just arrived through the campus mail system. As usual, Brad McLaughlin's scores rank at the bottom of all of the faculty members in his department. Hopeful that his decision to give easier tests and higher grades would make him more popular with students and improve his evaluation scores, McLaughlin is more than just mildly frustrated. He has been told that he needs to improve his teaching. But at his institution, while increasing emphasis is being placed on teaching performance, it's measured most heavily by standardized form scores from student evaluations. Yet his easing of class standards has not produced the positive evaluations he expected.

Brad has not been perceptive of what is really wrong with his classes. By midsemester, his average class attendance is only about 40 percent of enrollment. So he assumes that his students don't care much about learning, but care only about grades.

It is actually his jaundiced view of students and his disregard for them in his cavalier approach to his classes that is the problem. He is invariably

TABLE 3.5. Factor Loadings of Specific Behaviors of the Inviolable Proscriptive Norm against Personal Disregard

CTBI Item	Loading
C19. The instructor practices poor personal hygiene and regularly has offensive body odor.	.633
C4. The instructor frequently uses profanity in class.	.627
C5. Class is usually dismissed early.	.625
C12. The instructor is routinely late for class meetings.	.478
C6. The instructor meets the class without having reviewed pertinent materials for the day.	.457
E7. An instructor lowers course standards in order to be popular with students.	.434

Note: Percent of explained variance = .04; Cronbach alpha = .77. Extent of consensus against personal disregard at the level 4.00 and higher = 69.1%; at the level 3.99 and lower = 30.9%.

late for class, and he often cuts class short. He assumes that students are not there to learn (as long as they get good grades) so that they don't care if the classes start late and end early.

He further shows his disregard for students by coming to class poorly prepared. The classroom presentations are disorganized and repetitive, interspersed with long pauses while he tries to think out what he wants to say. Students are ignored: he discourages class discussion, scarcely asks a question, and rarely acknowledges raised hands.

By the end of the first two weeks of class, students have learned not to request clarifications or ask questions. They also are aggravated by their long wait for his arrival to class and soon become haphazard about their own class attendance. McLaughlin expresses no concern or threats about students skipping class; therefore few attend class regularly.

Others don't attend class because they are personally offended by the instructor's frequent profanity—often interspersed with irreverent contempt for students' personal moral beliefs. His disregard and disrespect for others is not only oral but also olfactory. He practices poor personal hygiene, and his body odor can be almost overwhelming.

Those who attend class regularly, despite these offenses and frustrations with the teacher, complain to each other that they're "not getting their money's worth." Even some of those who have given up regular attendance make the same complaint. But none registers this complaint to

Mr. McLaughlin (nor would he believe their complaint was genuine if he did hear it) or to any other faculty members or administrators.

Those in charge have little basis—not even hearsay—on which to address Brad McLaughlin's poor teaching performance, except for consistently poor scores on standardized forms used for students' evaluations. Both he and the administrators know the many arguments against the utility and credibility of student evaluations of teaching. So any correction of McLaughlin's disregard for students or of his classroom habits, based on evaluation scores, is unlikely. Until the administration is perceived by students as more receptive to their concerns, and additional methods to evaluate teaching performance are instituted, one individual faculty member will have a disproportionate influence on students' disaffection with teaching at their college.

Uncommunicated Course Details

The normative pattern condemning uncommunicated course details denounces the failure of a faculty member to inform students of important particulars about a course during the first day of class. Cahn (1986) views such behaviors as irresponsible. He regards careful course planning prior to the first day of class as an important professorial activity. Thus, this normative cluster resembles the norm of inattentive planning.

The three specific behaviors (Table 3.6) proscribed by this norm are: "the instructor changes classroom location to another building without informing students in advance"; "the instructor changes class meeting times without consulting students"; and "students are not informed of the instructor's policy on missed or make-up examinations." These three prohibited behaviors show a solid degree of internal consistency.

The overwhelming majority of faculty concur with the proscribed nature of the norm regarding uncommunicated course details. More specifically, 83.3 percent of faculty completing the CTBI offer such an appraisal (rated 4.00 or higher) of this cluster of behaviors.

CASE: Uncommunicated Course Details

Cheryl Matherson is a generally superb classroom teacher—at least after a hectic and confusing first week of classes. She has a good repertoire of courses she has taught for her department over the years and has not had to do a complete new course preparation for many semesters. Moreover, she is consistent in keeping her class content current, keeping up with journal reading on new research pertinent to her classes, and rou-

TABLE 3.6. Factor Loadings of Specific Behaviors of the Inviolable Proscriptive Norm against Uncommunicated Course Details

CTBI Item	Loading
B4. The instructor changes classroom location to another building without informing students in advance.	.757
B5. The instructor changes class meeting time without consulting students.	.753
B6. Students are not informed of the instructor's policy on missed or make-up examinations.	.577

Note: Percent of explained variance = .04; Cronbach alpha = .69. Extent of consensus against uncommunicated course details at the level 4.00 and higher = 83.3%; at the level 3.99 and lower = 16.7%.

tinely bringing relevant newspaper and news magazine clippings in for class discussion.

Matherson is respected and often emulated by her colleagues. She is a master of the Socratic method of teaching. Junior colleagues from her department, and occasionally faculty members from other programs around campus, will request visits to observe her classes and learn her style of teaching.

A contrasting view of Dr. Matherson is held by the departmental office staff. Like clockwork, the beginning of every semester finds the departmental office in chaos. Students come in panicked because they cannot find her class. Others are angry because they have to redo their class schedule when Matherson announces a conflicting time change on the first class meeting. The office staff members are both embarrassed and angry. They are not informed of her rescheduling of class meeting times and room changes so they cannot properly direct students to Matherson's classes. They also bear the brunt of student frustration because the students assume that the staff have made errors on the published timetable of classes from which they and their advisers had designed their class schedule for the term.

While she is aware of the confusion she creates, she is not sympathetic with the office staff or the student complaints. She believes that her heavy teaching load, particularly her heavy load of grading near the end of a term, doesn't allow her to make the course arrangements she wants for the next term. She ignores all advanced course scheduling matters. Her course syllabi for the new term are typically only a single page, stating nothing about weekly class topics or even her general instructional policy regarding such matters as class attendance or procedures for making up missed exams or quizzes. She prefers to make last minute changes to accommodate her own immediate personal preferences and plans.

David White, the chairperson of her department, is aware of the chaos Cheryl Matherson creates. An occasional student might approach him each term or two to complain about Cheryl's ad hoc changes in classroom locations and class times. The office staff will complain a little more vehemently but always indirectly by intentionally grumbling when White is present.

But White sees little use in attempting to deal directly with Matherson. She's been doing things much the same ever since before he arrived on campus. It is little wonder that he's stymied by low office staff morale. Yet he fails to see how his inaction with Matherson on what he calls a "minor routine transitory problem" is contributing to low morale and regular office staff turnover in his department.

Uncooperative Cynicism

Uncooperative cynicism describes the refusal to participate in departmental matters as part of the role of college teaching. Kerr (1996) gives more specific form to this obligation by asserting that faculty should not gain from the benefits offered by a college or university without doing one's fair share. Uncooperative cynicism represents both a failure to uphold one's responsibility to the university and to participate equally in institutional governance by not taking part in departmental matters and shunning some of the major aspects of the role of college teaching.

This normative pattern includes five proscribed behaviors (Table 3.7). The behaviors with the highest factor loadings are: "a faculty member refuses to advise departmental majors"; "a faculty member refuses to participate in departmental curricular planning"; and "a cynical attitude toward the role of teaching is expressed by an instructor."

Significant consensus on this particular proscriptive norm exists. Specifically, 71.9 percent of faculty concur with the severity (rated 4.00 or higher) of behaviors evocative of uncooperative cynicism.

CASE: Uncooperative Cynicism

Marilyn Hoffman, chair of the Accounting Department at the University of the Southwest, is thinking through how to begin discussion of her "personnel problem" in the upcoming meeting she has arranged with

TABLE 3.7. Factor Loadings of Specific Behaviors of the Inviolable Proscriptive Norm against Uncooperative Cynicism

CTBI Item	Loading
H13. A faculty member refuses to advise departmental majors.	.797
G16. A faculty member refuses to participate in departmental curricular planning.	.698
H14. A cynical attitude toward the role of teaching is expressed by an instructor.	.552
H15. A faculty member's involvement in research is so great that he or she fails to prepare adequately for class.	.466
E8. The standards for a course are set so high that most of the class receives failing grades for the course.	.356

Note: Percent of explained variance = .04; Cronbach alpha = .71. Extent of consensus against uncooperative cynicism at the level 4.00 and higher = 71.9%; at the level 3.99 and lower = 28.1%.

the dean of the Business College and the university vice president for Academic Affairs. To characterize Truman Moore's behavior as "insubordination" sounds too militaristic. She decides to start her meeting by simply asserting that Moore is a difficult and uncooperative "departmental citizen" and one who engenders low morale among his colleagues.

She has also made copies of the several letters and memos of reprimand that she has written to Moore over the past two years. She will give copies to both the dean and the vice president to show that she has tried her best to remedy the situation on her own. She will also mention the several private conversations she has had with Moore that have been unsuccessful in resolving her difficulties with him.

Dr. Truman Moore has been at USW for fifteen years. He is a full professor with two successful textbooks in accounting and a continuing record of publication of articles in the top journals in the field. There have been no student complaints about his classes, but he is no star in teaching.

Indeed, despite the recent administrative efforts at USW to emphasize quality teaching, Moore continues his cynicism toward the role of teaching. He spends as little time as possible in preparing for his classes, preserving as much time as possible for his professional writing. He has rebutted Hoffman's expressions of concern about his teaching by admonishing her for trying to "homogenize the faculty" in the Department of Accounting. He reminds her that he is the most productive scholar in the department. He suggests she recognize differentiation in expectations, meaning that the bulk of all teaching-related activities should go to all the other faculty members who are less productive scholars than he is.

Moore carries this argument for his nonparticipation to all teaching-related service roles in the department. He vehemently declines to be assigned any undergraduate majors as advisees. He refuses to consent to serving on the departmental curriculum committee. In fact, last year Hoffman put him on the committee anyway, but he would not attend a single meeting.

Hoffman thinks that Truman Moore is intentionally trying to undermine her. She knows he voiced strong objections to her as a candidate for departmental chairperson when she was being considered for that appointment two and a half years ago. It is difficult not to take his intransigence as a personal vendetta against her.

But she also feels rebuffed by her dean in her attempts to correct Moore's uncooperativeness. In addition to documenting his refusal to serve on departmental committees or to advise students, she recommended no salary increase for him in the last round of salary review. Yet the dean ignored her recommendation and processed an above-average salary increase, which he justified on the basis of Moore's continuing publication activity and widely adopted accounting textbooks.

Hoffman feels that her last hope is in the upcoming meeting with the dean and vice president. She plans to appeal to them to meet with her and Moore to address his cynical and uncooperative behavior—his poor "departmental citizenship." If the present meeting is a failure—and especially if the dean indicates that he will not fully support her next recommendation to hold Truman Moore's salary at the present level—she is convinced that she has no recourse but to resign the chair in protest.

Although she is unaware, at this point her colleagues would generally be pleased to hear of her resignation. They know nothing of Marilyn's contact with the higher administration about Truman, but they feel that his incivility, uncooperativeness, and unwillingness to do his equal share in the department should have been resolved long ago. No longer is it only Truman Moore but also Marilyn Hoffman whom the faculty view as contributing to their low morale and sense of unfairness in the USW Department of Accounting.

Conclusion

This chapter described seven empirically obtained proscribed normative clusters: condescending negativism, inattentive planning, moral turpitude, particularistic grading, personal disregard, uncommunicated course details, and uncooperative cynicism. Each of these seven proscribed behavior patterns demand severe sanctions. Thus, these seven patterns of prohibited behaviors are inviolable by faculty.

These seven inviolable normative configurations also provide empirical support for espoused ethical principles. The norms of condescending negativism, moral turpitude, and personal disregard embody violations of the principle of "respect for persons" (Smith, 1996) and its corollary "respect for students as individuals" (Reynolds, 1996; Svinicki, 1994). Moreover, the normative clusters of moral turpitude and particularistic grading empirically portray breaches of the principle of equal consideration of students in advisement, teaching, and grading (Cahn, 1986; Markie, 1994). In addition, the proscribed normative patterns of inattentive planning and uncommunicated course details afford empirical validation for the professorial obligation to plan for courses thoroughly, as espoused by Cahn (1986). Uncooperative cynicism empirically grounds the obligation faculty members have to their departments and colleges and to their colleagues to do one's share in governance related to teaching and in other teaching-related activity (Kerr, 1996).

The next chapter describes nine admonitory norms. These, too, are strongly held beliefs by the professoriate regarding inappropriate behaviors in the teaching role. But admonitory norms are behavioral proscriptions which, when violated, elicit less outrage or expectation of formal sanction and intervention than inviolable norms.

FOUR

Admonitory Norms

Admonitory norms are proscriptions that evoke less indignation when violated than inviolable norms. Faculty response to infractions of such norms is uncertain. Because of this uncertainty, individual faculty are cautioned not to violate them. This chapter concentrates on the research question: What admonitory clusters of inappropriate behaviors comprise the proscriptive normative structure of undergraduate college teaching? Nine such patterns were identified and are described in this chapter.

Admonitory norms are those specific prohibited behaviors that register a mean value between 3.00 and 3.99 on the sanctioning action scale. This range of mean values falls between "mildly inappropriate, generally to be ignored" behavior (3.0) and "inappropriate behavior, to be handled informally by colleagues or administrators suggesting change or improvement" (4.0) on the sanctioning action scale. Such a range implies a negative but uncertain type of response to a given transgression. A total of 53 such specific behaviors satisfy this criterion as evidenced by the mean values of the 126 behaviors of the CTBI shown in Appendix C.

These 53 prohibited behaviors were submitted to a principal components factor analysis to identify an undergirding configuration of meaning to these censured behaviors. A nine-factor solution was chosen using the scree test. The varimax method was used to rotate these nine factors. The nine clusters of admonitory norms delineated are, in alphabetical order, advisement negligence, authoritarian classroom, inadequate communication, inadequate course design, inconvenience avoidance, instructional narrowness, insufficient syllabus, teaching secrecy, and undermining colleagues.

Each of the nine admonitory norms are described in this chapter. Vignettes of fictional violations of each of these norms are presented.

TABLE 4.1. Factor Loadings of Specific Behaviors of the
Admonitory Proscriptive Norm against Advisement Negligence

CTBI Item	Loading
H11. A faculty member refuses to write letters of reference for any student.	.682
H10. A faculty member avoids giving career or job advice when asked by students.	.511
H16. Scholarly literature is not read for the purpose of integrating new information into one's courses.	.476
H8. A faculty member does not refer a student with a special problem to the appropriate campus service.	.352

Note: Percent of explained variance = .02; Cronbach alpha = .67. Extent of consensus against advisement negligence at the level 3.00 and higher = 85.6%; at the level 2.99 and lower = 14.4%.

Advisement Negligence

This admonitory norm cluster involves the failure of faculty to serve the advising needs of students. Kerr (1996) cites the obligation to advise students conscientiously as a tenet of his ethics of knowledge.

Four specific prohibited behaviors comprise this normative pattern (Table 4.1). These behaviors are: "a faculty member refuses to write letters of reference for any student"; "a faculty member avoids giving career or job advice when asked by students"; "scholarly literature is not read for the purpose of integrating new information into one's courses"; and "a faculty member does not refer a student with a special problem to the appropriate campus service."

Considerable consensus exists on the admonitory status of advisement negligence. To be specific, 85.6 percent of faculty respondents to the CTBI assess the severity of preferred sanctions as 3.00 or higher on the sanctioning action scale of this inventory.

CASE: Advisement Negligence

It has been a great career start since Susan Baker-Harrison received her Ph.D. two years ago. She has had several papers published, a grant from NSF to extend her dissertation fieldwork on plant life in the Antarctic, and exceptional teaching evaluations from her students. Moreover, she loves her first faculty position as assistant professor of biology at Northern Atlantic University. All of the faculty have been cordial and supportive, and she has already formed close friendships with two colleagues, Elizabeth and Carole.

Her classes have gone exceptionally well, even the very large sections of general biology that she has taught each semester. The graduate students who have been assigned to her to assist in the lab sections have been extraordinary and cooperative. Even the two new courses in plant biology and plant taxonomy that she prepped and taught received outstanding student evaluations.

Now in her third year at NAU, she's been assigned as an undergraduate adviser—to almost 100 biology majors. Until now, she had never thought much about this particular role as part of academic life. And she is not approaching it as a particularly important one.

No one has discussed the advising role with her. Nor is she aware that there is an *NAU Faculty Adviser's Handbook.*

In her first round of advising for course scheduling for the next semester, she devised the following advice for each student:

"Check the University Catalogue for requirements. Then fill out the class registration form for whatever you want. Bring it by my office and I'll sign it."

When students approached her about other advising matters, she was equally flippant. Several students, for example, had asked her about career opportunities in biology and about applying to graduate programs. In these cases she merely suggested they go ask a full professor, any of whom, she claims, would know more about those matters than she. Similarly, when asked to write letters of reference she would consistently demur and suggest they ask tenured faculty.

Even more problematic were those students who approached her seeking advice on personal problems. Her response was generally that she was "only a biologist" and she then might offer an almost useless advice snippet. For example, for a student distressed about a pregnancy, she said "go talk it over with your mother." For another student who disclosed she was having a problem with bulimia, Baker-Harrison's curt reply was "just stop eating junk food and only eat healthy low calorie meals."

One evening when she was out with Elizabeth and Carole, Susan mentioned that students seemed to expect too much from their advisers. After some further discussion, both Elizabeth and Carole explained how important they thought this role was and how central it was as an extension to teaching and to performance expectations of a faculty member. They told her about the *NAU Adviser's Handbook,* the campus career center, and the outstanding walk-in counseling services that were available at NAU.

Elizabeth related that when she first arrived at NAU, she read the *Un-*

dergraduate Catalogue and the department's own description of academic program requirements. She visited the University's career center, counseling center, financial aid office, and the health services center. Carole noted that there was a rape crisis center, an eating disorders support group, and a local branch of Planned Parenthood. She noted that each had relevant literature, and she suggested that Susan call each of these and request a supply of flyers from them that she could then share with students as appropriate.

Susan thanked them both for their helpful suggestions. She said she would follow through on their advice. But it didn't happen. Advising preparation never seemed to have enough priority. The NSF project and class preparation took precedence.

Elizabeth and Carole continued hearing complaints from students. Clearly, their suggestions and advice had been ignored. They began to withdraw from Susan. They were at a loss to know what else they might do. Susan Baker-Harrison's biology advisees were no less perplexed.

Authoritarian Classroom

The normative cluster of authoritarian classroom deals with faculty classroom demeanor reflecting a rigid and closed approach to course content and different points of view espoused by students. Faculty prohibited behaviors indicative of authoritarian classroom violate key ethical principles: content competence, neutrality, and objectivity.

The principle of content competence requires that representative points of view on topics be included and that differences of opinion and of interpretation be acknowledged. This principle is espoused in *Ethical Principles for College and University Teaching* generated by the Canadian Society of Teaching and Learning in Higher Education (Murray et al., 1996). Kerr (1996) offers a similar view, as he holds that an openness to alternative explanations and a tolerance of views other than one's own are among his ethics of knowledge.

Authoritarian classroom also breaches the ethical principles of neutrality and objectivity. Both Baumgarten (1982) and Churchill (1982) regard neutrality in teaching as an ethical precept. Thus, indoctrination is regarded as unethical teaching behavior (Cahn, 1986; Callahan, 1982; Churchill, 1982; Nisbet, 1977; and Svinicki, 1994).

Five specific behaviors in this normative pattern are criticized (Table 4.2). The censured behaviors with the highest factor loadings are: "the instructor does not include pertinent scholarship of women and minorities in the content of the course"; "the instructor insists that students take one

TABLE 4.2. Factor Loadings of Specific Behaviors of the Admonitory Proscriptive Norm against Authoritarian Classroom

CTBI Item	Loading
D5. The instructor does not include pertinent scholarly contributions of women and minorities in the content of the course.	.687
D2. The instructor insists that students take one particular perspective on course content.	.463
E22. Sexist or racist comments in students' written work are not discouraged.	.437
F7. A clear lack of class members' understanding about course content is ignored by the instructor.	.409
E11. Written comments on tests and papers are consistently not made by the instructor.	.356

Note: Percent of explained variance = .03; Cronbach alpha = .67. Extent of consensus against authoritarian classroom at the level 3.00 and higher = 90.5%; at the level 2.99 and lower = 9.5%.

particular perspective on course content"; and "sexist or racist comments in students' written work are not discouraged."

This normative pattern garners overwhelming consensus among faculty: 90.5 percent of faculty responding to the CTBI favored a severity of action of 3.00 or higher on the sanctioning action scale of this inventory.

CASE: Authoritarian Classroom

Pinegrove Hills College is nationally recognized as one of the finest liberal arts colleges in the nation. It is known for its innovative pedagogy, its distance learning opportunities, its superior teaching faculty, and its outstanding curriculum, which includes a study abroad component and three-week minimesters where students design their own independent study programs in conjunction with a member of the faculty. In its publications, Pinegrove consistently highlights its fine teaching as a central core of its "educational philosophy."

The Department of Religion at Pinegrove likewise prides itself in its emphasis on outstanding teaching. Or, more precisely, three of the four members of the departmental faculty are clearly dedicated to their students' learning, both in and out of the classroom. But L. V. Singh, the senior faculty member of the department, has let the rising eminence and teaching reputation of Pinegrove pass him by.

Over the years, Singh has held a comfortable niche at Pinegrove and in his department. He is the only faculty member among the four who does not teach the department's courses on Old and New Testament biblical studies or on western religion. He specializes in eastern religions and teaches the only overview courses addressing the historic and philosophic systems of Hinduism, Buddhism, Confucianism, Taoism, and Shintoism. Students majoring in several of the liberal arts programs at Pinegrove are required to take one of his courses on eastern religions. Thus many students cannot escape Singh during their stay at the institution.

Despite the high enrollment each term in his courses, Singh is one of the few faculty members on campus that students gripe about. Students see him as unsympathetic to class questions seeking clarification of the material he presents. He is also dogmatic about students taking his particular view on his interpretation of religious perspectives. He is quick to chastise students for introducing what he calls their "western Christian-Judeo biases."

He expresses disdain as well for any student comments expressing feminist or liberation theology. Indeed, he often trivializes any relevant works written by women or by African-Americans. He is known not to discourage criticism of women or African-Americans, even on those occasions when comments are transparently sexist or racist.

Nevertheless, students are hesitant to complain to campus authorities about Singh's authoritarianism, bigotry, and intolerant demeanor. Informally, however, Singh's teaching stance is well-known across campus. Faculty advisers often hear grumbles and groans when their advisees must sign up for Singh's required course. This has prompted many curious faculty members to make probing inquiries to the students for more details.

Faculty have come to believe Singh is anathema to the vision of teaching preeminence enjoyed by Pinegrove Hills College. Individually and confidentially, several have appealed for action by Althea Jackson, who came to Pinegrove just this past September as the new chairperson of the department. Althea has heard no student complaints about Singh but agrees to speak with him "off the record."

The meeting was unexpectedly catastrophic and brief. Jackson had barely begun to review what she understood as a classroom problem, when Singh interrupted with a tirade. Immediately he wrongly assumed that Jackson had solicited criticism from some students. He admonished her for listening to "whining spoiled children." He reminded her that he was a full professor with many more years of experience than she and that she had no right to inquire about matters pertaining to his "privacy in the classroom."

As soon as the meeting terminated, Althea knew she would have to try

TABLE 4.3. Factor Loadings of Specific Behaviors of the Admonitory Proscriptive Norm against Inadequate Communication

CTBI Item	Loading
B2. The instructor does not introduce her/himself to the class.	.655
A13. The instructor does not request necessary audiovisual materials in time to be available for class.	.634
B12. The first reading assignment is not communicated to the class.	.624
A14. Assigned books and articles are not put on library reserve by the instructor on a timely basis for student use.	.623
B14. The instructor does not ask students if they have any questions regarding the course.	.603
B3. Office hours are not communicated to students.	.597
B7. Students are not informed of extra credit opportunities which are available in the course during the term.	.508
E3. Graded tests and papers are not promptly returned to students by the instructor.	.420
C18. The instructor does not follow the course outline or syllabus for most of the course.	.419
A12. In-class activities are not prepared and anticipated in advance, but are developed while the class is in session.	.401
C7. The instructor routinely allows one or a few students to dominate class discussion.	.396
E10. Explanation of the basis of grades given for essay questions or papers is not provided to students.	.383

Note: Percent of explained variance = .03; Cronbach alpha = .87. Extent of consensus against inadequate communication at the level 3.00 and higher = 91.2%; at the level 2.99 and lower = 8.8%.

again. This first meeting had ended with her apologizing to L. V.! She had been both unprepared and intimidated. It was a lesson learned, and an incident that Althea would not allow to be repeated. She decided to have a few days for a cooling-off period, but then she would drop in to L. V.'s office to admonish him. This time she would be as aggressive as necessary and not again be intimidated by his arrogance and self-righteousness.

Inadequate Communication

Failure to convey course details to students is proscribed by the normative pattern of inadequate communication. This normative pattern is composed of 12 behaviors (Table 4.3). Those with the highest loadings on this normative factor are: "the instructor does not introduce herself or himself to the class"; "the instructor does not request necessary audio-visual materials in time to be available for class"; "the first reading assignment is not communicated to the class"; "assigned books and articles are not put on library reserve by the instructor on a timely basis for student use"; and "the instructor does not ask students if they have questions regarding the course."

The level of agreement on the normative cluster of inadequate communication is quite consistent: 91.2 percent of faculty responding to the CTBI concurred with the severity (rated 3.00 or higher) of this normative pattern.

CASE: Inadequate Communication

It is only the second week of the new academic year and John Kindler, chair of the Psychology Department, is experiencing déjà vu. Last year was Becky Desmond's first year at McKinley & Wilson College, and her first position after receiving her Ph.D. Almost from the beginning, John had heard Becky characterized by colleagues as "unprepared," "disorganized," "haphazard," "confused," and even "flaky." He chose largely to disregard the epithets and give Becky "time to settle in" to her new environment.

However, he was beginning to hear the same derogatory labels again at the onset of a new school year. Now they were from students as well as from colleagues. Kindler knew that Desmond was often late and unprepared for departmental and committee meetings. But he wasn't aware until now how these same behaviors might be carrying over to her classroom. Kindler decided that this year he would take each occasion when he heard a critical labeling of Desmond to probe and question students to get more information about precisely what Desmond was doing or not doing. He felt he had to be armed with more then generalities before he discussed the matter with her.

Over time, a dismal picture emerged—particularly for her introductory experimental psychology and psychology of learning courses. This was especially confounding because these were the disciplinary areas for which she was expressly hired to teach at M&WC.

Classroom disaster started on the first day of Desmond's classes. She inadequately communicated necessary information about her courses. Her syllabi were grossly incomplete. She failed to give her name, office location, or office hours on the syllabi. Only general course topics were listed for each week. Specific reading assignments and activities related to each topic were not on the syllabus for any of her courses. To complicate matters, she simply handed out the syllabus and took no time on the first day to discuss it or even to encourage questions about it or of the course generally.

Class content is often disorganized as well. She does not fully prepare in advance of class. During the semester she substantially deviates from even her rough course outline on the syllabus. When she assigns library readings to her students, she often has forgotten to ask that the library reserve them in time to be available to her students. She waits until the last minute to order and pick up slides or videos that she wants to use for the day, and so she sometimes cannot get them in time for her class.

Oversights and communication failures even extend to testing and grading. She forgets to mention extra credit opportunities she had planned to offer to students. Graded exams and term papers are not returned to students in timely fashion. Moreover, she rarely communicates any written explanations for the grades she assigns on students' papers and essay exams.

As this concrete evidence accumulates in support of the epithets, Kindler cannot resist wondering how he and the Search Committee had not uncovered any of these characteristics about Desmond before she was hired. When he retrieves her letters of reference and rereads them, he can now see veiled allusions that he and the Search Committee should have followed up on. While Kindler has learned a lesson for future faculty recruiting processes, he ponders how he might now best approach Desmond regarding the information he has ascertained about her teaching.

Inadequate Course Design

The transgressions associated with inadequate course design involve poor preparation for teaching a course. Markie (1994) asserts that faculty have an obligation to prepare for their courses. Cahn (1986) echoes this perspective; he holds that a concern for detail in course preparation is an essential component of serious teaching. Inadequate course design breaches this obligation of thorough preparation.

The three reproved behaviors (Table 4.4) comprising this admonitory normative pattern are: "required course materials are not kept within reasonable cost limits as perceived by students"; "the course is designed without taking into account the needs or abilities of students enrolling in the course"; and "new lectures or revised lectures which reflect advancements in the field are not prepared."

Considerable agreement among faculty exists on the admonitory status of this particular normative cluster. To be specific, 89.7 percent of fac-

TABLE 4.4. Factor Loadings of Specific Behaviors of the
Admonitory Proscriptive Norm against Inadequate Course Design

CTBI Item	Loading
A10. Required course materials are not kept within reasonable cost limits as perceived by students.	.635
A8. The course is designed without taking into account the needs or abilities of students enrolling in the course.	.614
A11. New lectures or revised lectures that reflect advancements in the field are not prepared.	.578

Note: Percent of explained variance = .02; Cronbach alpha = .61. Extent of consensus against inadequate course design at the level 3.00 and higher = 89.7%; at the level 2.99 and lower = 10.3%.

ulty completing the CTBI endorse an assessment of 3.00 or higher on the sanctioning action scale for this pattern of norms.

CASE: Inadequate Course Design

Associate Professor Ronald Lastowski has never much enjoyed teaching the large mass sections of lower division family and child development courses. Until the general faculty of his department voted two years ago to rotate teaching assignments so that all members share in the teaching of these large undergraduate courses, Lastowski principally taught small upper-division specialty courses together with a disproportionate number of the graduate program courses. He enjoyed the small seminars, the stimulation of enthusiastic graduate students, and the lack of responsibility to design, administer, and grade large numbers of tests. Now things were different. He found himself regularly looking at a sea of faces and teaching material unrelated to any of his present specialty interests within the area of child development and family studies.

His lack of enthusiasm infected his students. The undergraduate family and child development courses were among the most popular electives among students across the university. But Lastowski had quickly developed a campuswide reputation as one to be avoided. His class attendance would quickly dwindle early in the semester. Students joked that Professor Lastowski made sex sound boring.

Lastowski decided that diverse heavy reading assignments could compensate for his lack of interest in preparing for topical areas of little interest to him. Hence he required that students purchase not only the standard textbooks used by most instructors of these courses, but two different books of readings and, typically, one or two technical research monographs. Together, the students' costs for books for his single course were the highest of any course on campus with the exception of two or three upper-division engineering and architecture courses. Many of the readings from these materials were difficult for the students to absorb. In fact, some of the required books were the same as Lastowski used in his graduate courses.

So, too, was much of his class lecture materials. He favored those specialty areas with which he was familiar and simply presented outdated material on other topics, or simply showed the class a video on the topics and then dismissed the class without discussion, or relied solely on the out-of-class assignments from the text and supplemental course readings.

Exams were difficult and Lastowski was a hard grader. Most students felt lucky to survive his course with a C. For many students, the high point of the course was to have it over and to get back some money by selling their used FCD textbooks.

If it were not for the poor grades he gave and the excessive cost of textbooks for his course, few students would probably have complained. But these two factors gave rise to frequent complaint to other FCD faculty members who had established good rapport with undergraduates. In the course of these discussions, several faculty members concluded that Ron was simply not preparing adequately for his undergraduate introductory courses.

While Ron was a congenial colleague, none of the other faculty members felt comfortable about discussing his undergraduate teaching performance with him. When the departmental Performance Evaluation Committee convened for its annual review of all faculty members, however, all of the committee members had been approached by others and asked to scrutinize Ron's undergraduate course grading patterns, closely analyze student instructional rating form scores, and compare his course outlines to university catalog descriptions, which appeared to stress aspects of family and child development different from those that he emphasized in his courses.

The committee reported to the departmental chair and recommended that Ron Lastowski not be awarded a salary increase for the next year. The committee stressed that Lastowski gave inadequate attention to designing his lower division courses. Rather, he appeared to employ the same material he used in his generally good graduate and upper division specialty courses. This strategy failed, however, to cover the content and breadth of the courses as described in the catalog. Also noted was his low student instructional rating scores, bolstered by anecdotal accounts from various faculty members who had discussed his teaching with students.

The department chair dreaded taking the recommended salary action and discussing the reasons with Lastowski. Apart from the undergraduate teaching problems, Ron Lastowski was a productive scholar, a good departmental citizen, and an affable colleague. Hence, the chair scheduled a luncheon at which Ron was told of the severe negative teaching assessment provided by the Performance Evaluation Committee and the salary recommendation made by the committee. The chair expressed confidence that Ron would make considerable improvements in his undergraduate courses in the future. Thus, the chair was going to take the action of not implementing the committee's salary recommendation yet. But it was also made clear that if the same committee recommendation was made again, the chair would have to concur and act accordingly. They finished lunch on friendly terms and parted with Ron assuring the chair that he would "consider changes" in his "teaching situation" next year.

Inconvenience Avoidance

Faculty efforts to escape inconvenience related to the courses they teach are the focus of the normative cluster inconvenience avoidance. This normative factor consists of four prohibited behaviors (Table 4.5): "graded papers and examinations are left in an accessible location where students can search through to get back their own"; "final examinations are administered during a regular class period rather than at the official examination period"; "the instructor frequently introduces opinion on religious, political, or social issues clearly outside the realm of the course topic"; and "the instructor routinely holds the class beyond its scheduled ending time."

A particular facet of inconvenience avoidance violates the principle of student-faculty confidentiality (Markie, 1994; Murray et al., 1996). Confidentiality is breached, and indeed federal law is violated, when faculty leave graded papers and examinations in such a way that students are able to learn the grades of their classmates. Murray and his associates (1996) contend that violations of this principle lead to distrust of faculty by students that can, in turn, reduce student motivation to learn. Student-faculty confidentiality is as essential to the professorial role as physician-patient and lawyer-client confidentiality.

The degree of consensus on the normative array of inconvenience

TABLE 4.5. Factor Loadings of Specific Behaviors of the
Admonitory Proscriptive Norm against Inconvenience Avoidance

CTBI Item	Loading
E25. Graded papers and examinations are left in an accessible location where students can search through to get back their own.	.639
E15. Final examinations are administered during a regular class period rather than at the official examination period.	.516
D4. The instructor frequently introduces opinion on religious, political, or social issues clearly outside the realm of course topics.	.494
C13. The instructor routinely holds the class beyond its scheduled ending time.	.448

Note: Percent of explained variance = .02; Cronbach alpha = .52. Extent of consensus against inconvenience avoidance at the level 3.00 and higher = 90.6%; at the level 2.99 and lower = 9.4%.

avoidance is also strong. Of faculty respondents to the CTBI, 90.6 percent of them agreed with the severity (rated 3.00 or higher) of this group of proscribed behaviors.

CASE 1: Inconvenience Avoidance

Like most other faculty members at his college, Chuck Waldron genuinely enjoys teaching. After a particularly good session, in which he has inspired a dynamic dialogue among students in his class, he will enjoy the residual "glow" of a good classroom experience for the remainder of the day. While he has been at the college for more than thirty years, the "glows" haven't diminished.

Despite his enthusiastic teaching and good classroom involvement in learning, like some of his other colleagues he dislikes the process and the inconvenience of evaluating, testing, and grading his students. He's been known to expound at length on his belief that there is no learning value in taking exams; that administering tests takes away from the opportunity for classroom learning; and that grading is not an integral part of the "art of teaching," as he calls it.

He recognizes, however, that testing and grading are "necessary evils" at his institution. A short midterm and final is the extent of his testing in all of his classes. Very short. Often he'll devise two or three essay questions just before he is to meet the class. No test handouts, just brief questions written on the blackboard after he enters the classroom.

Waldron believes the grading of exams is as inconvenient as the necessity to administer them. He hastily reads them and generally just writes "pass" on them (with an occasional P+ or P– and a *very rare* F).

His contempt for tests and grading and his annoyance at the inconvenience they cause him are reflected in his means of returning the exams to students. He doesn't wish to "waste valuable learning time," so he simply piles the exams in the hallway by his office door. Students can retrieve them at their convenience.

In recent years, Chuck Waldron has also decided to avoid the inconvenience of staying on campus an extra few days at the end of the term in order to administer finals during the designated period. Rather, it's more convenient to administer finals on the last regularly scheduled class day. He knows it is against college policy, but many of his students appear to be pleased to get this final exam over with sooner.

His colleagues are well aware of his feelings about exams. More than one general faculty meeting has been occasion for Waldron to declare his "philosophy" on the basic "incompatibility of teaching students versus exercising power over them through testing and grading." Since he is perceived as a reasonably good teacher, seldom has anyone challenged his "philosophy."

The lack of challenge has lead Waldron to believe that, first, most everyone is in agreement with him, and, second, no one is aware of his "shortcuts" on exams. He is therefore quite surprised one morning when he finds two documents attached to his door, with bright yellow highlighting of particular passages.

One of these documents is a copy of the college president's directive, dated four years earlier, stating that it is the policy of the institution that no final exams may be administered before the scheduled time during the final examination period. The other document, an even older one, had been circulated to all faculty members many years ago. It contained wording of the Federal Privacy Act and some college administrator's listing of some specific examples of prohibited acts, including such things as publicly posting grades with students names, and (highlighted with a yellow marker) leaving graded exams with students' names in a publicly accessible place for retrieval by students.

Waldron was furious. His anger increased when he found an additional set of highlighted documents in his mailbox, and yet a third set prominently posted on the bulletin board in the faculty lounge. There were no "glows" for Waldron on this day. He vowed to get to the bottom of the matter and find out who the perpetrator or perpetrators might be. He had a few hunches.

CASE 2: Inconvenience Avoidance

Professors using ancient yellowed notes may be a cliché. If so, Professor Stevenson is a living cliché. His lecture notes are, in fact, yellowed and tattered. Ironically, he teaches early American history. His students joke that his notes are original documents prepared by Thomas Jefferson.

From unsolicited student comments, all of his departmental colleagues are aware of his outdated lectures. Little new historical research, and no new perspectives and interpretations, appear to be incorporated into his lecture content. Yet students evaluate his courses as good although below the departmental average on standardized teaching evaluation measures. In his annual departmental performance review, his teaching is characterized as "adequate" year in and year out.

For Stevenson, an "adequate" annual evaluation on his teaching is fine. There are more important things these days, from which he doesn't want distractions by his teaching. He's been elected to the faculty senate, which he takes as a mandate to increase his attacks on the university administration and what he believes to be its top-heavy staff and excessive budget. Moreover, he is an officer in the university's collective bargaining unit, and that work absorbs a substantial portion of his time each week.

So he considers his teaching to be little more than a nuisance that takes time away from his other campus activities. He's taught all of the history courses in his repertoire numerous times, so they require little out-of-class time and, he thinks, no need for updating. Moreover, he makes little effort to revise his tests. It is more expedient to use virtually the identical multiple choice exams each semester. Classes and teaching are an inconvenience to what he considers his "important" campus work but a tolerable inconvenience so long as he can avoid any reworking of his old lectures and exams.

Over time, however, the "staleness" of his lectures is becoming more apparent to students. But he holds fast to his old notes for his daily units. Sometimes, he'll run short of material in his notes and dismiss class early. More often he'll run the class five or ten minutes over in order to complete the day's unit. He asserts that the material he presents after the normal class ending time will be on the exam, thereby decreasing the number of students who walk out, but increasing the number who are consequently late in arriving for their next class. While he is aware that this frustrates his students (and other faculty members), he feels this is less costly than his time to rework his notes to correspond with designated class times.

Stevenson unwittingly exacerbates student frustration by frequently going off on tangents. Worse yet, these digressions are not relevant tales of historical episodes related to his course. Rather, they are sometimes discourses on his opinion about the recent actions of Congress or the U.S. president. Even more frequently, they are thinly veiled tirades on his views about the ineptness of various university administrators, their inappropriate micromanagement of the faculty, their financial mismanagement, and the unnecessary top-heavy administrative structure of the university.

Word of Professor Stevenson's classes has spread throughout the student body. Whenever possible, students will invariably sign up for any history course not taught by him. While overall enrollment in history has been increasing annually, Stevenson's courses are generally undersubscribed. His departmental chairperson has made a mental note of this "trend" but he has yet to decide what interpretation and action to take in response to this observation. Is it because of Stevenson's renowned outdated material? Should the chairperson reconsider his annual "adequate" rating of Stevenson's teaching? Should he approach Stevenson to discuss the reasons for the chronic undersubscription to his classes each semester?

Instructional Narrowness

Narrowness in the assessment of students and in the use of teaching methods is the focus of this particular admonitory normative cluster, which consists of 10 censured behaviors (Table 4.6). Those with the highest factor loadings are: "examination questions do not tap a variety of educational objectives ranging from the retention of facts to critical thinking"; "memorization of course content is stressed at the expense of analysis and critical thinking"; "connections between the course and other courses are not made clear by the instructor"; and "a faculty member avoids reading literature on teaching techniques or methods."

Narrowness in the use of teaching methods embodied by the avoidance of literature on teaching techniques or methods depicts a transgression of various ethical formulations. Narrowness of this sort is unprofessional, as knowledge of new teaching methods is an index of professionalism (Scriven, 1982). Such an avoidance also violates the principle of pedagogical competence contained in the *Ethical Principles for College and University Teaching* developed by the Canadian Society of Teaching and Learning in Higher Education (Murray et al., 1996). Pedagogical competence entails being aware of alternative instructional methods or strategies.

This facet of the normative array of instructional narrowness also represents a failure to meet the professorial obligation to engage in the scholarship of teaching. Markie (1994) holds that faculty have an obliga-

TABLE 4.6. Factor Loadings of Specific Behaviors of the
Admonitory Proscriptive Norm against Instructional Narrowness

CTBI Item	Loading
E21. Examination questions do not tap a variety of educational objectives ranging from the retention of facts to critical thinking.	.655
D6. Memorization of course content is stressed at the expense of analysis and critical thinking.	.649
D7. Connections between the course and other courses are not made clear by the instructor.	.611
H17. A faculty member avoids reading literature on teaching techniques or methods.	.580
F4. The instructor does not encourage student questions during class time.	.560
H18. A faculty member avoids professional development that would enhance his or her teaching.	.539
E5. Examination questions do not represent a range of difficulty.	.476
C20. The instructor wears a sloppy sweatshirt and rumpled blue jeans to class.	.441
E20. The final course grade is based on a single course assignment or a single examination.	.437
E1. The instructor does not give assignments or examinations requiring student writing skills.	.424

Note: Percent of explained variance = .05; Cronbach alpha = .87. Extent of consensus against instructional narrowness at the level 3.00 and higher = 72.6%; at the level 2.99 and lower = 27.4%.

tion to keep abreast of journals devoted to different teaching strategies. Such scholarship informs the choices faculty make about their teaching.

A noteworthy level of consensus exists on the status of the behaviors associated with the proscriptive normative factor of instructional narrowness. More specifically, 72.6 percent of faculty respondents concur with the severity (rated 3.00 or higher) of this normative pattern.

CASE: Instructional Narrowness

His baggy sweatshirt with polyester trousers and worn-out sneakers fit the worst caricature of a public university professor. But his sloven and unkempt appearance hardly fits the stereotype of a professor of nutrition. Herbert Walcott is out of touch with the prevailing social mores in his department. Worse, he is out of touch with advancements in his field.

Walcott hasn't done any research and writing in the field for more than a decade. Nor has he put much effort into his teaching. He consistently ignores any opportunities for professional development for his teaching. Learning new pedagogical techniques is of no interest. Recent applications of computer technology to teaching nutrition have been ignored.

Consequently, he has been put in the backwaters of course offerings at the undergraduate level. None of his courses is required for either nutrition track: dietetics or community nutrition. He is resigned to the fact he no longer teaches any courses in the department's active master's program.

At an earlier time, Walcott's approach in the college classroom was perhaps little less than routine practice. But times have changed and yet he continues to teach with essentially the same style and content. Rote learning and passive students are Walcott's standard and preference. Indeed, Walcott quickly trains his students not to ask questions. He intentionally ignores raised hands. When he occasionally acknowledges a raised hand and receives a question, his response inevitably is "we'll get to that in another lecture."

Seldom does a class go by that Walcott doesn't at least once suggest that students memorize something (often something outdated), followed by a reminder that it might be on a test. Little of his course content requires analytical thinking, and he never encourages critical thinking.

Not surprisingly, his exams parallel his classroom style. They are literally a regurgitation of "facts" and lists from his lectures and assigned readings. There is little range of difficulty in his examination questions. There are no questions requiring writing skills or critical thinking.

His colleagues are at best merely tolerant of Herbert Walcott. In fact, he is largely socially and intellectually ostracized by his peers, but he seems oblivious to it.

Similarly, both his chair and his dean had exercised mostly unspoken tolerance or avoidance of Walcott. Recently, however, Walcott has been a regular topic of discussion between the dean and the chair of the Department of Nutrition. The word is that the state legislature will soon be approving an attractive buy-out policy for early retirement. Walcott will be one of those who will be eligible for the buy-out incentive. His dean and chair are considering ways to sweeten the incentive for what will already be an attractive prospect.

Insufficient Syllabus

The normative proscriptions related to insufficient syllabus concern the failure of faculty to provide students with an adequate syllabus for a course. This normative factor resembles the inviolable norm of inattentive

TABLE 4.7. Factor Loadings of Specific Behaviors of the Admonitory Proscriptive Norm against Insufficient Syllabus

CTBI Item	Loading
A4. A course outline or syllabus does not contain dates for assignments and/or examinations.	.685
B13. A course outline or syllabus is not prepared and passed out to students.	.524
D1. The instructor does not have students evaluate the course at the end of the term.	.431
A5. Objectives for the course are not specified by the instructor.	.424

Note: Percent of explained variance = .02; Cronbach alpha = .68. Extent of consensus against insufficient syllabus at the level 3.00 and higher = 78.1%; at the level 2.99 and lower = 21.9%.

planning described in Chapter 3. Like inattentive planning, the normative cluster of insufficient syllabus violates the duty faculty have to share their plan for the course with students (Markie, 1994). It is also a mark of poor teaching given that Hook (1994) regards the preparation of a syllabus as characteristic of good teaching.

Four specific proscribed behaviors comprise this normative pattern (Table 4.7). Those behaviors having the highest loadings on this normative factor are: "a course outline or syllabus does not contain dates for assignments and/or examinations"; and "a course outline or syllabus is not prepared and passed out to students."

The level of consensus on this particular pattern of censured behaviors is substantial. Specifically, more than three-fourths (78.1 percent) of faculty completing the CTBI assent to the preferred severity of action (rated 3.00 or higher) for this admonitory norm.

CASE: Insufficient Syllabus

Whether it is squeezing in one more end-of-summer vacation or just taking a last-minute holiday after completing grading of final exams from the preceding semester, Alberto Chavez routinely finds himself without time to be fully prepared for the beginning of a new semester. Indeed, it seems to him that he simply jumps from one high-paced exhausting semester to the next. He feels that only the short vacation breaks he makes for himself allow any opportunity for him to "recharge his batteries."

He often returns to campus only the day before classes begin. With good intentions to use that precious time for class preparation, he often is diverted by his accumulation of e-mail and snail-mail. If not that, it's colleagues stopping by his office to socialize for a while and talk about their vacations.

As a result he often does not have a syllabus prepared for his classes. Even when he manages to rough one out, or when he just cannibalizes a syllabus used earlier, there is insufficient time for the departmental clerical staff to prepare it and get copies run off for distribution on the first class day.

Often it is the second or third week of classes before he distributes syllabi. Even so, they are predictably incomplete. He consistently does not attempt to state any course objectives on them. Nor does he explain how students' work will be graded, when various topics will be covered, or even what readings he expects students to complete for a particular class session.

Chavez does not like to take class time for "housekeeping." He will not volunteer to provide orally what might otherwise be on a syllabus. But if a student asks a specific housekeeping question, he will try to answer it as directly as possible.

Syllabi are prepared largely to placate some of the students who request them. Chavez doesn't feel that classes need syllabi. In fact, he sees them as overorchestrated constraints to his "free style of teaching" or as an obstacle that must inevitably be disregarded in order to allow the classes to "flow."

Students often feel they are floundering at the onset of the term. They have little idea what they'll find as the class topic in upcoming sessions. They are frustrated generally in not being able to plan more than a class session in advance for when their exam or quiz will be given.

Much of the students' frustration with insufficient class structure could be rectified by a syllabus like the ones that practically all other instructors pass out at the beginning of the semester. Remarkably, however, Chavez appears to compensate for the problem through his dynamic classroom teaching. Students find his lectures interesting, he engages them in enlightening debates and dialogues among themselves, and his use of everything from music and dance to computer animation makes his class fun.

Consequently, students eventually appear to accept the lack of a syllabus—or at least a detailed useful one. The class is enjoyable and enlightening. So, they think, maybe a comprehensive syllabus is discretionary for teachers (despite the fact that they have never encountered any other class without a syllabus). The class would be a lot better, especially at the beginning, but now it doesn't seem fair to complain because Mr. Chavez is a good teacher. Besides, as students, who would you complain to?

Teaching Secrecy

The normative factor dealing with teaching secrecy involves faculty refusal to provide colleagues with information and materials relevant to the role of college teaching. This normative cluster resembles the norm of communality, a norm governing research conduct identified by Merton (1942, 1973). Communality ordains that research findings be made public, as they are the property of the research community (Merton, 1942, 1973). Thus, research secrecy constitutes a violation of this norm.

Teaching is also the collective responsibility of faculty, given Callahan's (1982) contention that faculty should assist one another with teaching. Thus, teaching secrecy constitutes an abrogation of this collective responsibility.

Teaching secrecy consists of seven reproved behaviors (Table 4.8). Those with the highest loadings on this factor are: "a faculty member refuses to share a syllabus with colleagues"; "a faculty member avoids sharing ideas about teaching methods with colleagues"; "a faculty member refuses to allow colleagues to observe his or her classroom teaching"; and "a faculty member avoids talking about his or her academic specialty with departmental colleagues."

Substantial consensus on teaching secrecy as a censured pattern of behaviors exists among faculty. More specifically, 70.5 percent of academics answering the CTBI are in accord with the severity (rated 3.00 or higher) of this normative cluster.

CASE: Teaching Secrecy

There is no evidence for her colleagues to believe that Professor Blackstone is anything but a solid teacher. Indeed, her student evaluation scores are quite good—generally her courses score above the departmental average. Yet, inexplicably, she refuses to discuss her teaching with anyone in the department. She is adamant that no peers observe her classroom teaching. Even with her departmental chair she is cautious and evasive about discussing any details having to do with her classes or her teaching.

She is not entirely comfortable in disclosing information about her present research and writing either. She just doesn't seem to have a level of trust with others that all of her colleagues tend to enjoy with each other. Some try to just pass off Blackstone's reluctance as "a touch of paranoia,"

TABLE 4.8. Factor Loadings of Specific Behaviors of the
Admonitory Proscriptive Norm against Teaching Secrecy

CTBI Item	Loading
G4. A faculty member refuses to share course syllabi with colleagues.	.794
G5. A faculty member avoids sharing ideas about teaching methods with colleagues.	.744
G6. A faculty member refuses to allow colleagues to observe his or her classroom teaching.	.694
G13. A faculty member avoids talking about his or her academic specialty with departmental colleagues.	.623
G3. A faculty member does not tell an administrator or appropriate faculty committee that a colleague's course content largely includes obsolete material.	.582
G7. A faculty member assumes new teaching responsibilities in the specialty of a colleague without discussing appropriate course content with that colleague.	.533
D9. A cynical attitude toward the subject matter is expressed by the instructor.	.310

Note: Percent of explained variance = .03; Cronbach alpha = .83. Extent of consensus against teaching secrecy at the level 3.00 and higher = 70.5%; at the level 2.99 and lower = 29.5%.

but other members of the faculty interpret her secrecy, particularly in regard to teaching, as raw uncollegiality and unprofessionalism.

A number of the lower division courses that Blackstone teaches are multisection courses, so there are several other faculty members with similar teaching assignments and teaching interests. On several occasions one or two of these other teachers have suggested that all of those who teach the same course get together informally to share their evaluations of various possible texts, exchange syllabi, discuss different pedagogical techniques that each has found useful, and generally to discuss course objectives. Consistently, Blackstone has declined to provide her syllabus or any information about her teaching techniques to her colleagues. Regardless of when gatherings are planned, Blackstone will predictably withdraw with some weak excuse at the last minute.

Even when Blackstone has been scheduled to teach a new course that was formerly taught by other colleagues, she maintains her complete isolationist stance. She will not seek advice about course objectives and instructional materials from anyone. Often the other teachers will feel slighted. They feel that their prior familiarity in teaching the course gives them some valuable experiential expertise. It is exasperating that they are not approached as potential "resources" for preparing for a class. Indeed, it is difficult not to feel as if one has been rejected by Blackstone, and sometimes the emotional response borders on overt anger.

To an outside observer, Blackstone's "blind spot" regarding sharing discussion about teaching might appear as a mere trivial idiosyncrasy. Certainly her attitude would be within the range of autonomy and independence normally accorded to a college faculty member. Yet when one is in regular contact with such a person, it becomes not just a trivial matter but a constant source of irritation and disparagement.

Blackstone's "touch of paranoia" is infecting the morale of the entire department. It is only because of her peculiar degree of secrecy that it has even occurred to her colleagues that some sort of breach of teaching ethics —or at least violated collegial courtesies—is an ever-present threat to departmental well-being. They wonder, however, whether anyone from "outside" could appreciate their situation or understand why they cannot just proceed with their own departmental activities and simply disregard one of their departmental members.

Undermining Colleagues

This particular admonitory normative array centers on faculty efforts to demean or belittle courses offered by colleagues. The proscribed behavior of undermining colleagues represents a clear-cut violation of the principle of respect for colleagues delineated by Murray and his associates (1996) in *Ethical Principles for College and University Teaching* developed by the Society of Teaching and Learning in Higher Education in Canada.

In their elaboration on the principle of respect for colleagues, Murray and his associates (1996) state that disagreements about teaching should be discussed in private. This principle of respect for colleagues mirrors the rules of professional etiquette described by Freidson (1975), which stipulate that colleagues should not be criticized in public by another colleague.

Four unacceptable behaviors comprise the normative pattern of undermining colleagues (Table 4.9). The three behaviors most indicative of this normative array are: "a faculty member makes negative comments in a faculty meeting about the courses offered by a colleague"; "a faculty member aggressively promotes enrollment in his or her course at the expense of the courses of departmental colleagues"; and "the requirements in a course are so great that they prevent enrolled students from giving adequate attention to their other courses."

Academics demonstrate overwhelming agreement on the extent of

TABLE 4.9. Factor Loadings of Specific Behaviors of the
Admonitory Proscriptive Norm against Undermining Colleagues

CTBI Item	Loading
G8. A faculty member makes negative comments in a faculty meeting about the courses offered by a colleague.	.684
G10. A faculty member aggressively promotes enrollment in his or her courses at the expense of the courses of departmental colleagues.	.643
G11. The requirements in the course are so great that they prevent enrolled students from giving adequate attention to their other courses.	.492
C3. Joke-telling and humor unrelated to course content occurs routinely in class.	.334

Note: Percent of explained variance = .03; Cronbach alpha = .59. Extent of consensus against undermining colleagues at the level 3.00 and higher = 88.3%; at the level 2.99 and lower = 11.7%.

condemnation for behaviors reflective of this normative pattern. Of faculty responding to the CTBI, 88.3 percent concur with the severity of censure (rated 3.00 or higher) for this configuration of behaviors.

CASE: Undermining Colleagues

As a sociologist specializing in social psychology, Karen Littlefield dedicates at least an afternoon every few weeks to perusing relevant psychology and sociology journals in the campus library. Today an article title caught her eye and led her to read a series of psychology articles by the same author.

She was excited about what she learned and immediately called her best friend and departmental colleague, Lisa Swelland, when she arrived home from the library. No answer. Just Lisa's answering machine.

Karen said: "Hi, Lisa. It's me. Call when you get in. We're wrong about that bastard Boutwell. He's no Machiavellian. He's an asp."

Lisa called back in 15 minutes. "Hi. Got your message. What do you mean Boutwell isn't a Machiavellian but an ass?"

Karen laughed. "Not ass. Asp. A-S-P. But not the snake, although that might apply too. It stands for Aberrant Self-Promoter. I just ran into the term in a series of articles by a clinical psychologist by the name of Gustafson. She identifies ASP as a psychopathology involving a self-serving narcissistic personality. Her work sounds like a clinical case study of Boutwell. We've been wrongly calling him a Machiavellian. 'Machs' are exploitive and operate in self-interest. ASP's are similar, but they are also more likely to subvert the organization for their own self-interest and be aggressively hostile toward others who might stand in their way. That sounds like the jerk to me. I think we now have a precise psychological label for Boutwell."

Lisa responds: "Yes, it sounds like it fits Boutwell to a 'T.' But I guess I wasn't that far off when I thought you said on my answering machine that you discovered Boutwell was an 'ass.'"

Both laughed.

Doug Boutwell views himself as the epitome of the expert college teacher, particularly as regards the introductory sociology course. He doesn't hesitate to criticize others personally at faculty meetings. His critiques include attacks on both Swelland and Littlefield, among others, for the intro texts they use, their disorganized course content, which he claims he hears about constantly from "many" students, alleged poor exams, and on and on.

Despite rejection several times, he regularly volunteers to be the "co-ordinator" of all those who teach intro. He says he can provide needed "quality control." His colleagues think: "control, yes; quality, no."

Boutwell continually attempts to transform the introductory course into an exercise in self-aggrandizement. He constantly promotes his course, even encouraging undergraduates to drop their enrollment in another faculty member's section and add his instead.

A few years ago Boutwell reviewed an introductory sociology textbook manuscript for a publisher. He suggested only minor revisions, and he recommended a couple of his published articles on the sociology of health be cited and discussed in the text. He also aggressively pursued the publisher to commission him to write the preface. The textbook author capitulated.

Of the 20 or so best-selling intro textbooks on the market, this is one of the weakest, but it is the only one that cites anything written by Boutwell. Since its publication he has regularly used it as the required text for his course. He constantly promotes it for adoption by others, but he has been successful with only one of the untenured members of the faculty. He even made a motion at a faculty meeting that the faculty vote to use the text as a standard for all intro sections. The proposal was roundly defeated, much to his obvious consternation and disgust.

In addition to the textbook, Boutwell has a local photocopying company compile a book of readings, composed of reprinting eight of his own articles on the sociology of health, as required reading for his introductory course. His colleagues recognize it as a manifestation of his narcissism and far too narrow a selection of readings for an undergraduate overview course, but no one wants to risk challenging it.

He is also a self-promoter of teaching awards. He virtually insists that colleagues and his department chair routinely nominate him for teaching awards. One year it was rumored that he even passed out teacher-of-the-year nomination forms to every student in his classes. He has received several certificates of excellence in teaching from the College of Social Sciences and even a universitywide teaching award. All of the certificates are displayed in oversized frames on his office wall.

Yet he seems insatiable in seeking more teaching awards, often even undermining nominations for teaching excellence awards to others in the Sociology Department. While the dean of Social Sciences respects confidentiality, he thinks Boutwell quite presumptuous. Over recent years, Boutwell has written confidential letters to the dean criticizing the teaching of three different departmental colleagues who, he discovered, had been nominated for teaching awards. With the exception of one teaching award to Karen Littlefield, Doug Boutwell is the only other faculty member in his department to have received any teaching awards.

Now Boutwell has positioned himself as a member of both the college and the university Teaching Awards Committees. He's now feeling quite smug that no one else in his department, including Littlefield, will receive awards anytime soon.

Conclusion

This chapter delineated nine empirically derived proscribed normative arrays: advisement negligence, authoritarian classroom, inadequate communication, inadequate course design, inconvenience avoidance, instructional narrowness, insufficient syllabus, teaching secrecy, and undermining colleagues. These unacceptable behaviors are admonitory norms; that is, they elicit indignation when violated, although less so than inviolable norms. Nevertheless, individual faculty are cautioned not to violate them.

Various ethical principles gain empirical grounding through these admonitory normative patterns. Only one principle, however, receives some empirical confirmation by more than one admonitory norm: the obligation of course preparation. The proscriptive normative clusters of inadequate course design and insufficient syllabus offer such confirmation. The norm condemning inadequate communication is not addressed in the literature on the ethics of teaching.

There are, however, ethical precepts empirically grounded by admonitory normative patterns: content competence (authoritarian classroom), content neutrality and objectivity (authoritarian classroom), student-faculty confidentiality (inconvenience avoidance), teaching scholarship (instructional narrowness), collective responsibility for teaching (teaching secrecy), and respect for colleagues (undermining colleagues).

Institutional type (Ruscio, 1987) and academic discipline (Storer and Parsons, 1968; Ruscio, 1987) are distinguishing features of the structure of the academic profession. Given their differences, several basic questions emerge: Do faculty in different types of colleges and universities vary in their level of espousal of the seven inviolable norms and the nine admonitory norms? Do faculty in different academic disciplines vary in their level of espousal of the seven inviolable norms and the nine admonitory norms? Are there norms that cut across different types of colleges and universities and across different academic disciplines? These three questions are pursued in the next two chapters.

FIVE

Institutional Type
and Norm Espousal

In Chapter 1, we noted that institutional type plays a strong role in the structural differences that impinge on the members of the academic profession (Braxton, 1989; Ruscio, 1987). The Carnegie Classification System reflects the great variability in missions among institutions in the U.S. system of higher education (1987). Missions range from the two-year colleges, which provide lower-division teaching solely, to the universities, which stress graduate education, research, and scholarship, as well as public service. Such missions exert a strong influence on institutional structures, which, in turn, influence the way professorial roles are performed (Ruscio, 1987). Thus, the relative emphasis placed on teaching and research is a major differentiating factor among various types of colleges and universities in the structure of the academic profession.

As a consequence of such varying degrees of emphasis on teaching and research, the work styles, attitudes, beliefs, reference groups, and professorial roles vary across different types of colleges and universities (Blackburn and Lawrence, 1995; Ruscio, 1987; Fulton and Trow, 1974). Although most faculty teach, the level of publication productivity (Blackburn and Lawrence, 1995; Finkelstein, 1984; Fulton and Trow, 1974) and compliance with Mertonian research-oriented norms of science (Braxton, 1989) vary across different types of colleges and universities. Because of such differences, Fulton and Trow (1974) postulate a "fault line" in the structure of the academic profession. Below this "fault line," faculty may espouse attitudes and values that differ from those of their counterparts above this demarcation. Blackburn and Lawrence (1995) and Light (1974) posit that the academic life of faculty vary by institutional type.

The types of institutions represented in this study vary in terms of their institutional missions. Two-year colleges and less selective liberal arts colleges are at one extreme, oriented predominantly toward teaching. Research universities I are at the other extreme, oriented toward research. More selective liberal arts colleges and comprehensive universities and colleges II occupy middle ground, oriented toward both teaching and research (McGee, 1971; Finnegan, 1993).

Given such differences in the structure of the work settings of the academic profession, we might also expect the normative structure for undergraduate college teaching to differ by institutional type. The set of seven inviolable norms and nine admonitory norms described in Chapters 3 and 4 comprise the normative structure of undergraduate college teaching. Are any of these normative clusters similar in their level of espousal across the five types of colleges and universities represented in this study? Or are there different core norms for different types of collegiate institutions? Are any of these normative arrays more strongly endorsed by faculty in some types of colleges and universities than in others? Are there inviolable and admonitory norms that are differentiated by institutional type? These questions are pursued in this chapter.

The statistical technique used to address the guiding questions of this chapter was a 5 × 4 analysis of variance conducted for each of the seven inviolable norms and each of the nine admonitory norms. The two factors of these analyses of variance were institutional type and academic discipline. Five levels of institutional type were used: two-year colleges, liberal arts colleges II (less selective), liberal arts colleges I (more selective), comprehensive universities and colleges II and research universities I. Biology, history, mathematics, and psychology constituted the four levels of academic discipline.[1]

The level of faculty disapproval was measured using composite scales developed for each of these 16 norms. The composite scales were computed by summing faculty assessments of the severity of action that should be meted out for the specific behaviors of a given normative orientation and then dividing this sum by the number of specific behaviors composing that normative pattern.[2] Faculty members' assessments of the severity of action befitting each of the specific behaviors were measured using the five-point scale described in Chapter 2. These 16 composite

1. Prior to executing each of the analyses of variance, the homogeneity of variance assumption was tested. Detected heterogeneous variances are noted only for those analyses yielding statistically significant variation.
2. Although factor loadings of .40 or higher are recommended for the computation of factor-based scores (Kim and Mueller, 1978), the specific behaviors meeting normative criteria below .40 were included in the construction of some of these composite scales so that all 33 behaviors meeting the criterion for inviolable norm status and all 53 behaviors meeting the criterion for admonitory norm status could be subsumed under one of the 16 normative orientations.

scales were also used to address the research questions pursued in Chapters 6 and 7.

Because this chapter concentrates on possible similarities and differences among faculty in the espousal of inviolable and admonitory norms across five types of colleges and universities, only the findings for institutional type are presented. These findings are, however, independent of the effects of academic discipline on faculty espousal of inviolable and admonitory norms.[3] The .05 probability level was used to identify statistically significant differences in norm espousal across the five types of colleges and universities.[4]

Inviolable Norm Espousal and Institutional Type

Table 5.1 exhibits the results of the analyses of variance conducted for each of the seven inviolable norms. Where statistically significant results are observed, Table 5.1 also displays the results of post hoc mean comparisons between the five types of colleges and universities represented in this study.

Core Inviolable Norms

The proscribed normative patterns of moral turpitude and particularistic grading constitute a set of core norms for research universities I, comprehensive universities and colleges II, more and less selective liberal arts colleges, and two-year colleges. As evidenced by Table 5.1, faculty across all five types of colleges and universities espouse parallel degrees of disapproval for such acts as making sexual comments to students, having sexual relationships with students enrolled in a class, or attending class while intoxicated. Such uniformity in levels of agreement supports Whicker and Kronenfeld's (1994) contention that among unethical behaviors sexual harassment is clearly one of the most condemned.

As they did with moral turpitude, members of the professoriate in research universities I, comprehensive universities and colleges II, more and less selective liberal arts colleges, and two-year colleges see relatively equal degrees of impropriety in the preferential treatment of students in the

---

3. The effects of the interaction between institutional type and academic discipline were tested in each of the 16 analyses of variance conducted. None of these interactions, however, was statistically significant at the .05 level.

4. Where statistically significant variation across institutional types was observed (the F-ratio for the main effect of institutional types), the Scheffe method of post hoc group mean comparisons was used to identify those institutional types which were different from one another in their level of norm espousal.

TABLE 5.1. Results of Analyses of Variance of the Seven Inviolable Proscribed Normative Patterns by Institutional Type

Normative Pattern	F-Ratio	Normative Pattern Means by Institutional Type					Post Hoc Mean Comparisons
		RU	CUCII	LAI	LAII	2YR	
Condescending negativism	7.06***	3.98	4.19	4.15	4.22	4.24	RU less than CUCII, LAII, & 2YR*
Inattentive planning	7.04***	3.94	4.21	4.11	4.31	4.29	RU less than LAII & 2YR**
Moral turpitude	1.71	4.85	4.86	4.93	4.88	4.89	
Particularistic grading	1.03	4.28	4.36	4.35	4.37	4.37	
Personal disregard	7.91***	4.03	4.22	4.08	4.24	4.27	RU less than 2YR**
Uncommunicated course details	8.69***	4.16	4.38	4.21	4.35	4.46	RU less than CUCII & 2YR*
							LAI less than 2YR*
Uncooperative cynicism	12.45**	3.94	4.27	4.25	4.29	4.06	RU less than CUCII, LAI & LAII**
							2YR less than CUCII & LAII**

Note: F-ratio for institutional type is independent of the F-ratio for academic discipline. *p. < .05, **p. < .01, ***p. < .001.

awarding of grades. This pattern of agreement with the severity of particularistic grading resembles the similar level of conformity to the research norm of universalism found across different types of colleges and universities (Braxton, 1989).

Inviolable Norm Response by Institutional Type

The differences in response to the transgression of inviolable norms by institutional type take two forms. First, although faculty in different types of institutions may differ in their level of disapproval, they nevertheless regard a particular normative cluster as inviolable. Second, academic professionals in one or more types of institutions view a normative array as evoking less indignation than a pattern of behaviors befitting inviolable norm status.

Although viewed as inviolable, the proscribed norms personal disregard and uncommunicated course details vary across different types of collegiate institutions in the faculty's level of disapproval. More specifically, personal disregard receives comparable levels of condemnation from academics in comprehensive universities and colleges II (mean = 4.22), more selective liberal arts colleges (mean = 4.08), less selective liberal arts colleges (mean = 4.24), and two-year colleges (mean = 4.27). But faculty in research universities I express, in a statistically reliable way, less disapproval (mean = 4.03) for faculty associates who ignore the needs and sensitivities of their students than do their colleagues in two-year collegiate institutions.[5]

Research university I faculty members also tend to express a statistically significant lower level of censure (mean = 4.16) over the failure of colleagues to inform students of important details about a course during the first class meeting than do their counterparts in comprehensive universities and colleges II (mean = 4.38) and two-year colleges (mean = 4.46). But academics in research universities I and more selective liberal arts colleges (mean = 4.21) accord similar levels of disapproval of uncommunicated course details. Moreover, academic professionals in two-year colleges, less selective liberal arts colleges and comprehensive universities and colleges II confer comparable levels of criticism to this normative pattern.

The remaining three inviolable norms evoke an ambiguous response from academic professionals in research-oriented universities. To elaborate, academics in research universities I (mean = 3.98) register less offense

---

5. Heterogeneous variances were detected for this normative array. To reduce the probability of committing a type I error due to such variances, the .01 level of statistical significance was used.

over condescending and demeaning treatment of colleagues and students by faculty members than do their counterparts in two-year colleges (mean = 4.24), less selective liberal arts colleges (mean = 4.22), and comprehensive universities and colleges II (mean = 4.19). Given such an average level of disapproval expressed by such faculty, condescending negativism tends to be regarded by research university faculty as an admonitory norm rather than as an inviolable norm.

Academics in two-year colleges (mean = 4.24), more selective liberal arts colleges (mean = 4.15), less selective liberal arts colleges (mean = 4.22), and comprehensive universities and colleges II (mean = 4.19), however, assign comparable degrees of disapproval to condescending and demeaning treatment of both colleagues and students. Although academic professionals in more selective liberal arts colleges do not differ in a statistically significant way from research university faculty, these individuals as well as their counterparts in the other three types of collegiate institutions accord inviolable norm status to condescending negativism.

Faculty in research universities also view, on average, inattentive planning as admonitory and not as inviolable: academics in research universities I (mean = 3.94) tend to accord a statistically significant lesser degree of indignation toward faculty colleagues who demonstrate a lack of attention to course planning than do their counterparts in both two-year colleges (mean = 4.29) and less selective liberal arts colleges (mean = 4.31).[6] Nevertheless, faculty in two-year colleges (mean = 4.29), both more (mean = 4.11) and less selective (mean = 4.31) liberal arts colleges, and comprehensive universities and colleges II (mean = 4.21) ascribe similar levels of impropriety to the proscribed behaviors of inattentive planning.

Uncooperative cynicism joins the ranks of condescending negativism and inattentive planning as admonitory norms in the eyes of research university I academic professionals. More specifically, academics in universities emphasizing research espouse, in a statistically significant manner, less severe sanction (mean = 3.94) over the shunning of college teaching and departmental activities by faculty associates than do their colleagues in comprehensive universities and colleges II (mean = 4.27) and more selective (mean = 4.25) and less selective (mean = 4.29) liberal arts colleges.[7]

6. Heterogeneous variances were detected for this normative array. To reduce the probability of committing a type I error due to such variances, the .01 level of statistical significance was used.
7. Heterogeneous variances were detected for this normative array. To reduce the probability of committing a type I error due to such variances, the .01 level of statistical significance was used.

Moreover, such research university academic professionals accord, on average, admonitory, not inviolable, normative status to uncooperative cynicism.

In addition, faculty in two-year colleges tend to express a statistically significant lower level of sanctioning (mean = 4.06) for uncooperative cynicism by colleagues than do their faculty counterparts in either less selective liberal arts institutions or comprehensive universities and colleges II.

Summary

Faculty across different types of colleges and universities agree on the level of impropriety accorded two inviolable norms: particularistic grading and moral turpitude. Thus, these two norms constitute core inviolable norms for the five categories of colleges and universities represented here. But the remaining five normative clusters are differentiated by institutional type through some disagreement on the level of appropriate sanctioning response registered for condescending negativism, inattentive planning, personal disregard, uncommunicated course details, and uncooperative cynicism. Faculty in research-oriented universities tend to express less indignation toward these proscribed behavior patterns than do academic professionals in other types of collegiate institutions. Furthermore, research university faculty tend to hold ambivalent views regarding the severity of action suitable for condescending negativism, inattentive planning, and uncooperative cynicism given that such faculty accord admonitory, not inviolable, status to these normative arrays.

Admonitory Norm Espousal and Institutional Type

Next we will focus on whether there is a set of core admonitory norms and whether various admonitory norms are differentiated by institutional type. Table 5.2 displays the results of the analyses of variance conducted for each of the nine admonitory norms and the results of post hoc mean comparisons between each of the five types of colleges and universities for those normative patterns that yielded statistically reliable analysis of variance results.

Core Admonitory Norms

Three proscribed behavioral patterns emerge as core admonitory norms for the five groupings of colleges and universities. Specifically, faculty across the five types of institutions tend to agree on their level of indignation at the proscribed normative behaviors reflective of an authori-

TABLE 5.2. Results of Analyses of Variance of the Nine Admonitory Proscribed Normative Patterns by Institutional Type

Normative Pattern	F-Ratio	Normative Pattern Means by Institutional Type					Post Hoc Mean Comparisons
		RU	CUCII	LAI	LAII	2YR	
Advisement negligence	12.32**	3.43	3.79	3.67	3.75	3.47	RU less than CUCII, LAI & LAII* 2YR less than CUCII, LAI & LAII*
Authoritarian classroom	2.52	3.63	3.77	3.74	3.79	3.65	
Inadequate communication	5.88***	3.47	3.67	3.58	3.70	3.73	RU less than CUCII, LAII & 2YR*
Inconvenience avoidance	10.45**	3.59	3.84	3.56	3.80	3.87	RU less than CUCII & 2YR* LAI less than CUCII, LAII & 2YR*
Inadequate course design	2.69*	3.53	3.72	3.69	3.75	3.72	RU less than CUCII, LAII & 2YR*
Instructional narrowness	20.86**	2.99	3.48	3.19	3.48	3.49	RU less than CUCII, LAII & 2YR* LAI less than CUCII, LAII & 2YR*
Insufficient syllabus	6.62***	3.26	3.55	3.50	3.67	3.46	RU less than CUCII & LAII*
Teaching secrecy	1.75	3.21	3.36	3.34	3.41	3.29	
Undermining colleagues	9.53***	3.36	3.69	3.58	3.74	3.61	RU less than CUCII, LAI, LAII & 2YR*

Note: F-ratio for institutional type is independent of the F-ratio for academic discipline. *p. < .05, **p. < .01, ***p. < .001.

tarian classroom; that is, academic professionals espouse a similar level of disapproval for colleagues who demonstrate a rigidity toward course content and against different points of view expressed by students. Academics also accord comparable degrees of reproach for inadequate course design across the five types of colleges and universities represented in this study. Put differently, faculty view faulty course design with similar degrees of disapproval regardless of their institutional affiliations.

In Chapter 4, we found that teaching secrecy proscribes the refusal of colleagues to share information and materials pertinent to the role of college teaching. This normative pattern is analogous to the research-oriented norm of communality (Merton, 1942, 1973). Academic professionals in all five types of colleges and universities regard teaching secrecy with similar degrees of denunciation. This pattern of findings is consistent with Braxton's (1989) finding that faculty conformity to the norm of communality is invariant across different types of collegiate institutions.

Admonitory Norm Response by Institutional Type

Although six admonitory norms engender various degrees of contempt across different types of colleges and universities, faculty contempt for five of these normative orientations does not dip below that of an admonitory norm.

Advisement negligence. The failure of faculty to serve the advisement needs of students evokes, to a statistically significant extent, more condemnation from academics in both more (mean = 3.67) and less selective liberal arts colleges (mean = 3.75) and comprehensive universities and colleges II (mean = 3.79) than their counterparts in research universities I (mean = 3.43). Although two-year college faculty (mean = 3.47) differ little in a statistically reliable way from research university faculty, they attach statistically significant less importance to advisement negligence than their colleagues in the other three types of colleges and universities.

Inadequate communication. Members of the professoriate in two-year colleges (mean = 3.73), more selective liberal arts colleges (mean = 3.58), less selective liberal arts colleges (mean = 3.70), and comprehensive universities and colleges II (mean = 3.67) express comparable levels of reproval for faculty colleagues who fail to convey course details to students. But academics in research universities I view less harshly (mean = 3.47), in a statistically significant manner, inadequate communication than do their counterparts in two-year colleges, less selective liberal arts colleges, and comprehensive universities and colleges II. Nonetheless, both more selective liberal arts college and research university faculty hold corresponding levels of condemnation for this proscribed normative cluster.

Inconvenience avoidance. Faculty who avoid personal inconvenience at the expense of students are similarly reproved by their colleagues in two-year colleges (mean = 3.87), less selective liberal arts colleges (mean = 3.80), and comprehensive universities and colleges II (mean = 3.84). Academics in both more selective liberal arts colleges (mean = 3.56) and research I universities (mean = 3.59), however, ascribe a statistically significant lesser degree of severity to the normative pattern of inconvenience avoidance than do two-year colleges and comprehensive universities and colleges II faculty. More selective liberal arts college academic professionals also indicate a statistically significant lower degree of disapproval of this normative cluster than their counterparts in less selective liberal arts colleges.

Instructional narrowness. Academics in two-year colleges (mean = 3.49), less selective liberal arts colleges (mean = 3.48), and comprehensive universities and colleges II (mean = 3.48) view the proscribe normative orientation of instructional narrowness with comparable disapproval. However, faculty members in more selective liberal arts colleges (mean = 3.19) and research-oriented universities (mean = 2.99) rebuke to a lesser extent, in a statistically significant manner, narrowness in the instruction of students than do their counterparts in the other three types of institutions of higher learning. Moreover, research university faculty fall slightly below ascribing admonitory status to this particular normative array.

Insufficient syllabus. The proscriptive normative cluster insufficient syllabus is viewed with similar degrees of reproval by faculty in comprehensive universities and colleges II (mean = 3.55), in more (mean = 3.50) and less selective liberal arts colleges (mean = 3.67), and in two-year colleges (mean = 3.46). Academics in research universities (mean = 3.26), however, ascribe, in a statistically reliable way, less condemnation to the failure of colleagues to provide students with an adequate course syllabus than do their counterparts in less selective liberal arts colleges and comprehensive universities and colleges II.

Undermining colleagues. Academics in two-year colleges (mean = 3.61), more (mean = 3.58) and less (mean = 3.74) selective liberal arts colleges, and comprehensive universities and colleges II (mean = 3.69) view faculty who demean or try to harm the courses offered by their colleagues with comparable degrees of condemnation. Their academic counterparts in research-oriented universities, however, view the proscriptive norm pattern of undermining colleagues with statistically significant less contempt (mean = 3.36) than do faculty in these other four types of institutions of higher learning.

Summary

Faculty members across all five types of colleges and universities share similar disapproval of three admonitory norms: authoritarian classroom, inadequate course design, and teaching secrecy. Hence, these three proscribed behavioral arrays constitute core admonitory norms for the five categories of colleges and universities represented. Members of the professoriate in research universities, however, tend to voice less contempt for five admonitory norms: advisement negligence, inadequate communication, inconvenience avoidance, insufficient syllabus, and undermining colleagues. Moreover, research university faculty marginally fail to ascribe admonitory norm status to instructional narrowness. In addition, academics in more selective liberal arts colleges also express less disapproval of two proscriptive normative arrays: inconvenience avoidance and instructional narrowness.

Concluding Comments

Five proscribed behavior patterns constitute a set of core norms for the five types of colleges and universities represented in this study. These core normative orientations are the inviolable norms of particularistic grading and moral turpitude, as well as the admonitory norms of authoritarian classroom, inadequate course design, and teaching secrecy. But the espousal of the remaining inviolable and admonitory norms are differentiated by institutional type. The existence of these five core norms across institutional type raises the question of whether they also constitute a set of core proscriptions for the four academic disciplines. The question of whether the various inviolable and admonitory norms are differentiated by academic disciplines is explored in Chapter 6.

Academic Disciplines
and Norm Espousal

Academic disciplines differentiate the structure of the academic profession just as institutional types do. And the level of paradigmatic development, that is, the extent of consensus on theoretical orientation, appropriate research methods and techniques, and the importance of research questions to the advancement of the discipline (Kuhn, 1962, 1970; Lodahl and Gordon, 1972; Biglan, 1973a, 1973b) differs from discipline to discipline.

Braxton and Hargens (1996) concluded from an extensive review of research that the differences among academic disciplines are "profound and extensive." More specifically, disciplinary paradigmatic development affects the emphasis faculty place on teaching and research activities. Academics in disciplines of high paradigmatic development experience lower journal rejection rates, have higher levels of publication productivity, comply more with research-oriented norms, and exhibit little or no relationship between their research and teaching activities (Braxton and Hargens, 1996). In contrast, faculty in disciplines of low paradigmatic development receive higher course evaluations and show complementarity between the roles of teaching and research (Braxton and Hargens, 1996). Moreover, academic professionals in disciplines of low paradigmatic development also evince an affinity for teaching practices designed to improve undergraduate education (Braxton, 1995).

The four academic disciplines represented in this study vary in their level of paradigmatic development. Biology and mathematics are high in their level of paradigmatic development, whereas history and psychology are low in theirs (Biglan, 1973a).

Such differences in teaching role performance between disciplines of high and low paradigmatic development strongly suggest that the normative structure of undergraduate college teaching may also be differentiated by academic disciplines. Accordingly, this chapter addresses two questions: Are there inviolable and admonitory normative clusters that constitute a set of core norms for the disciplines of biology, mathematics, history, and psychology? Are any of the inviolable and admonitory normative patterns more strongly subscribed to by members of some of these academic disciplines than others?

Analysis of variance was the statistical procedure used to address the guiding questions of this chapter. A total of 16 analyses of variance were conducted, one for each of the seven inviolable norms and one for each of the nine admonitory norms.[1] Composite scales were developed to assess the level of faculty espousal of each of the seven inviolable and nine admonitory normative clusters. The factors of these 5 × 4 analyses of variance were academic discipline and institutional type.[2] Biology, history, mathematics, and psychology comprised the four academic disciplines, whereas two-year colleges, less selective liberal arts colleges, more selective liberal arts colleges, comprehensive universities and colleges II and research universities I constituted the five institutional types.

The findings in this chapter for academic discipline are independent of the effects of institutional type on faculty espousal of inviolable and admonitory norms. The .05 probability level was employed to identify statistically significant differences in norm espousal across the four academic disciplines.[3]

Inviolable Norm Espousal and Academic Discipline

Table 6.1 exhibits the results of the seven analyses of variance conducted. Where statistically significant results are identified, Table 6.1 also shows the results of post hoc mean comparisons made among the four academic disciplines.

Core Inviolable Norms

Two inviolable norms emerge as core norms for the academic disciplines of biology, mathematics, history, and psychology. Faculty across all four academic disciplines view the lack of attention to course planning with comparable degrees of disfavor. Therefore, the level of paradigmatic development possesses little or no association with espousal of this nor-

1. The homogeneity of variance assumption was tested before running each of the 16 analyses of variance. For those analyses of variance yielding statistically significant variation, detected heterogeneous variances are noted.
2. Interactions between academic discipline and institutional type were tested in each of the 16 analyses of variance executed. None of these interactions were statistically significant at the .05 level.
3. When statistically significant variation across academic disciplines was observed, the Scheffe method of post hoc group mean comparisons was used to identify the academic disciplines that differ from one another in their level of norm espousal.

TABLE 6.1. Results of Analyses of Variance of the Seven Inviolable Proscribed Normative Patterns by Academic Discipline

Normative Pattern	F-Ratio	Normative Pattern Means by Academic Discipline					Post Hoc Mean Comparisons
		Bio	Hist	Math	Psych		
Condescending negativism	5.33***	4.27	4.09	4.18	4.14		Biology greater than history*
Inattentive planning	2.53	4.25	4.24	4.24	4.18		
Moral turpitude	1.91	4.92	4.86	4.89	4.87		
Particularistic grading	3.93**	4.43	4.31	4.34	4.31		Biology greater than history & psychology*
Personal disregard	14.44**	4.32	4.12	4.23	4.04		Biology greater than history & psychology* mathematics greater than psychology**
Uncommunicated course details	4.05**	4.40	4.35	4.33	4.24		Biology greater than psychology*
Uncooperative cynicism	7.41***	4.31	4.13	4.12	4.13		Biology greater than history, mathematics & psychology**

Note: F-ratio is independent of the effects of the F-ratio for institutional type. *p < .05, **p < .01, ***p < .001.

mative cluster. Thus, inattentive planning constitutes a core inviolable norm for biology, history, mathematics, and psychology.

Like inattentive planning, the proscribed normative cluster of moral turpitude evokes equal levels of condemnation from faculty in the four academic disciplines. Given such similarities, moral turpitude also constitutes a core inviolable norm for both hard and soft academic disciplines.

Inviolable Norms Differentiated by Academic Discipline

Five inviolable norms are differentiated by academic discipline: condescending negativism, particularistic grading, personal disregard, uncommunicated course details, and uncooperative cynicism. More specifically, academic professionals in the disciplines of history, mathematics, and psychology share similar reactions to the proscriptive normative cluster of condescending negativism. Academic biologists (mean = 4.27), however, espouse a statistically significant greater degree of disapproval for demeaning treatment of students and colleagues than do faculty in the discipline of history (mean = 4.09). Thus, high paradigmatic development appears to be positively associated with greater dislike for condescending negativism than low discipline paradigmatic development.

Statistically reliable differences between academic disciplines also obtain for the proscribed normative array of particularistic grading. More specifically, faculty members in the discipline of biology (mean = 4.43) express a greater degree of disapproval for this normative pattern than their counterparts in the disciplines of history (mean = 4.31) and psychology (mean = 4.31).

Academic biologists (mean = 4.32) also espouse a statistically reliable greater degree of disapproval for behaviors indicative of a disrespect for the needs and sensitivities of students than do their counterparts in both psychology (mean = 4.04) and history (mean = 4.12). Moreover, academic mathematicians (mean = 4.23) also accord a higher degree of disapproval to this normative cluster than do faculty in the discipline of psychology (mean = 4.04).[4] Thus, high disciplinary paradigmatic development tends to be identified with greater distaste for personal disregard than low paradigmatic development.

Moreover, biology faculty also ascribe a statistically meaningful greater degree of condemnation (mean = 4.40) for the failure to inform

---

4. Heterogeneous variances were observed for this normative cluster. To reduce the probability of committing a type I error because of such variances, the more conservative .01 level of statistical significance was applied.

TABLE 6.2. Results of Analyses of Variance of the Nine Admonitory Proscribed Normative Patterns by Academic Discipline

| Normative Pattern | F-Ratio | Normative Pattern Means by Academic Discipline | | | | Post Hoc Mean Comparisons |
		Bio	Hist	Math	Psych	
Advisement negligence	7.85***	3.79	3.57	3.58	3.54	Biology greater than history, mathematics & psychology*
Authoritarian classroom	1.41	3.75	3.75	3.65	3.72	
Inadequate communication	3.92**	3.73	3.59	3.58	3.53	Biology greater than psychology*
Inconvenience avoidance	8.22***	3.85	3.72	3.82	3.61	Biology & mathematics greater than psychology**
Inadequate course design	5.69***	3.81	3.59	3.81	3.62	Biology greater than history**
Instructional narrowness	5.43***	3.46	3.28	3.42	3.28	Biology greater than history & psychology*
Insufficient syllabus	12.91**	3.67	3.53	3.26	3.50	Biology, history & psychology greater than mathematics*
Teaching secrecy	17.40**	3.51	3.12	3.44	3.22	Biology & mathematics greater than history & psychology*
Undermining colleagues	4.99**	3.72	3.59	3.58	3.53	Biology greater than psychology*

Note: F-ratio for academic discipline is independent of the F-ratio for institutional type. *p. < .05, **p. < .01, ***p. < .001.

students of important course details during the first day of class than faculty in psychology (mean = 4.24). However, academic professionals in the disciplines of mathematics, psychology, and history hold comparable degrees of disapproval for the proscribed normative pattern of uncommunicated course details.

Academics in the disciplines of mathematics, psychology, and history look at colleagues who shun teaching and departmental matters with comparable degrees of disfavor. Academic biologists (mean = 4.31), however, ascribe a statistically significant higher degree of objection to uncooperative cynicism than academic mathematicians (mean = 4.19), psychologists (mean = 4.13), and historians (mean = 4.13) do.[5]

Summary

Two inviolable normative patterns are central to the four academic disciplines: inattentive planning and moral turpitude. Academic biologists voice the greatest degree of disapproval for the remaining five proscribed normative patterns: condescending negativism, particularistic grading, personal disregard, uncommunicated course details, and uncooperative cynicism.

Admonitory Norm Espousal and Academic Discipline

The guiding questions of this chapter are next pursued for the nine admonitory normative patterns. Table 6.2 exhibits the results of the nine analyses of variance conducted and the results of post hoc mean comparisons between the four academic disciplines where statistically reliable analysis of variance results are discerned.

Core Admonitory Norm

Only the pattern authoritarian classroom arises as a core proscriptive norm for the academic disciplines of biology, mathematics, history, and psychology. To be specific, a rigid and closed approach to teaching and course content provokes comparable degrees of contempt from academic professionals across all four academic disciplines.

Admonitory Norms Differentiated by Academic Discipline

Differences among the four academic disciplines exist for eight admonitory norms. Varying degrees of disapproval obtain for advisement

---

5. Heterogeneous variances were observed for this normative cluster. To reduce the probability of committing a type I error because of such variances, the more conservative .01 level of statistical significance was applied.

negligence, inadequate communication, inconvenience avoidance, inadequate course design, instructional narrowness, insufficient syllabus, teaching secrecy, and undermining colleagues. These differences are described below.

Advisement negligence. The failure to serve the advisement needs of students elicits similar disapproval from faculty in the disciplines of history, mathematics, and psychology. But the normative array of advisement negligence evokes a statistically reliable greater degree of condemnation from academic biologists (mean = 3.79) than from their counterparts in the other three disciplines.

Inadequate communication. As they do for advisement negligence, academic biologists (mean = 3.73) exhibit a statistically significant greater degree of concern for inadequate communication than faculty in psychology (mean = 3.53). But academics in history, mathematics, and psychology share relatively equal levels of disapproval of the failure to convey course details to students.

Inconvenience avoidance. Faculty aversion to inconvenience arouses similar degrees of disfavor from academic professionals in the disciplines of history (mean = 3.72) and psychology (mean = 3.61). Academic biologists (mean = 3.85) and mathematicians (mean = 3.82), however, voice a statistically significant greater degree of contempt for inconvenience avoidance than their counterparts in psychology (mean = 3.61) do.[6]

Inadequate course design. The normative array inadequate course design provokes comparable degrees of disapproval from faculty members in mathematics, history, and psychology. Biologists (mean = 3.81) express a statistically significant greater degree of disapproval for unsatisfactory preparation for teaching a course than academic historians (mean = 3.59).

Instructional narrowness. Faculty in the disciplines of mathematics, history, and psychology subscribe to similar unfavorable views of colleagues who use a narrow range of teaching methods and ways of assessing students. Academic biologists (mean = 3.46), however, express statisti-

---

6. Heterogeneous variances were observed for this normative cluster. To reduce the probability of committing a type I error because of such variances, the more conservative .01 level of statistical significance was applied.

cally meaningful greater degrees of disapproval for the normative pattern of instructional narrowness than do psychologists (mean = 3.28) and historians (mean = 3.28).

Insufficient syllabus. As previously indicated, disciplinary difference exists for the proscribed behavioral configuration of insufficient syllabus. Faculty in the disciplines of psychology and history assign similar levels of disapproval for this proscribed behavioral pattern, whereas academic biologists (mean = 3.67), historians (mean = 3.53), and psychologists (mean = 3.50) voice a greater degree of condemnation, in a statistically significant way, for the failure of a faculty member to provide students with an adequate course syllabus than do their academic colleagues in mathematics (mean = 3.26).

Teaching secrecy. In comparison to academic psychologists (mean = 3.22) and academic historians (mean = 3.12), faculty in the disciplines of biology (mean = 3.51) and mathematics (mean = 3.44) express a statistically significant greater degree of contempt for faculty who refuse to share teaching information and materials with their colleagues. Moreover, faculty in psychology and history hold comparable degrees of disapproval for the normative cluster teaching secrecy.

Undermining colleagues. Academics in the disciplines of mathematics, history, and psychology ascribe comparable degrees of objection to the proscribed behavior pattern undermining colleagues. Biologists (mean = 3.72) express, in a statistically reliable manner, a higher degree of disapproval of faculty members who demean the courses of their colleagues than do academic psychologists (mean = 3.53).

Summary

Authoritarian classroom represents a core admonitory norm for the academic disciplines of biology, history, mathematics, and psychology. Moreover, academic biologists express a greater degree of concern for the remaining eight admonitory normative patterns than faculty in the other three academic disciplines.

Concluding Comments

Three core norms for the four academic disciplines were identified: two inviolable and one admonitory. The core admonitory norm is authoritarian classroom, whereas the two inviolable core proscribed behavior patterns are inattentive planning and moral turpitude. Two of these core normative clusters are also core proscriptions for the five types of colleges and universities: authoritarian classroom and moral turpitude. Thus, these two proscribed patterns of behavior constitute a set of universal core norms for college and university faculty.

The characteristics of individual faculty may also influence the espousal of the seven inviolable norms and the nine admonitory norms. Chapter 7 focuses on such possible influences.

SEVEN

Individual Faculty Characteristics and Norm Espousal

Chapters 5 and 6 demonstrate that institutional type and academic discipline differentiate the normative structure of undergraduate college teaching. Institutional type and academic discipline also represent sources of social control that render norms effective (Reiss, 1951). Personal control exists in addition to such social controls. Reiss defines personal control as "the ability of the individual to refrain from meeting needs in ways which conflict with the norms and rules of the community" (p. 196). Accordingly, personal control may also affect faculty espousal of the seven inviolable and nine admonitory norms.[1]

Administrative experience, gender, professional status, research activity, and tenure are five faculty characteristics that may influence norm espousal and constitute personal control.

Administrative Experience

Administrative experience is defined herein as whether or not a faculty member currently serves or has served as either a dean or department chairperson.[2] Deans and department chairpersons are members of the administrative structure of colleges and universities and therefore possess some degree of formal authority (Leslie, 1973; Tucker, 1981). Their responsibilities include dealing with inadequate performance and unethical behavior of faculty (Tucker, 1981).

Chairpersons also occupy a position between the faculty of their departments and the administration, given that they might be termed "first among equals" (Leslie, 1973). Consequently, faculty members with such

---

1. Although Reiss's formulations pertain most directly to influences on conformity with norms, it is reasonable to argue that personal controls that induce conformity are also indices of the degree to which an individual subscribes to a particular normative behavioral pattern.
2. This variable was measured using the following survey item common to all three studies: "Are you, or have you ever been, a department head/chair or a dean?" The following response categories were provided: no; yes, but not now; and yes, and am currently. Administrative experience was defined by using the last two categories.

administrative experience may likely have observed teaching wrongdoing and have had to address it. Thus, they are likely to have more clearly formed views on appropriate teaching conduct as well as stronger opinions about the type of action that should be taken against norm transgressions. Hence, faculty with administrative experience may more severely denounce the inviolable and admonitory norms of undergraduate college teaching than their faculty colleagues who lack such administrative experience do.

Gender

Women faculty members express a greater commitment to teaching than their male counterparts do (Bayer and Astin, 1975; Boyer, 1990; Boice, 1992; Finkelstein, 1984; Tierney and Rhoads, 1993). Blackburn and Lawrence (1995) surmise that women prefer teaching because they view it as a nurturing activity. Moreover, men and women academics also differ in their perceptions of the characteristics of good teaching (Goodwin and Stevens, 1993). For example, women academics tend to view concern for student self-esteem as more characteristic of good teaching than their male counterparts do (Goodwin and Stevens, 1993). Women faculty also tend to believe to a greater extent than male faculty that competition for grades should be minimized (Goodwin and Stevens, 1993). Consequently, men and women faculty may differ on the severity of their reactions to the seven inviolable and nine admonitory normative orientations.

Professional Status

Research indicates that professional status is related to espousal of and compliance with ethical principles (Abbott, 1983; Carlin, 1966; Handler, 1967). Professional status also influences the formality of actions individuals are willing to take for personally known incidents of scientific wrongdoing (Braxton and Bayer, 1996; Knight and Auster, 1999). Because the visibility of an individual faculty member increases with their professional status, their professional behavior possesses symbolic significance (Carlin, 1966). Accordingly, the professional conduct of faculty with high status is more likely exemplary and beyond reproach (Carlin, 1966).

Because teaching is an activity done for the institution (Light, 1974) and carries little recognition outside of the employing college or university (Fox, 1985), academic rank serves as an indicator of intrainstitutional professional status. As a consequence, academic rank is likely to influence faculty espousal of undergraduate teaching norms. More specifically, the rank of full professor provides an index of such high intrainstitutional professional status. Thus, full professors may differ from faculty of lower academic ranks in their judgments about the inviolable and admonitory norms comprising the structure of undergraduate college teaching.

Research Activity

Indignation and outrage are possible reactions to transgressions of inviolable and admonitory teaching norms. Such reactions reflect the social significance of such normative orientations (Durkheim, 1995 [1912]; Braxton, Bayer, and Finkelstein, 1992; Sullivan, 1996). Thus, the greater the value placed on teaching, the greater the social significance that might be expected to be attached to violations of these normative configurations (Braxton, Bayer, and Finkelstein, 1992; Sullivan, 1996). Faculty who value research highly are, however, less likely to value teaching highly (Fulton and Trow, 1974; Smart, 1991; Fox, 1992; Creamer, 1998). Consequently, research activity is potentially inversely related to how seriously faculty view inviolable and admonitory norm transgressions in the teaching domain.[3]

Publication productivity during the past three years is used here as an indicator of research activity. This measure is an unweighted composite of journal articles, books, and monographs.[4]

Tenure

Faculty holding academic tenure are more likely to take seriously the normative orientations for undergraduate teaching than are faculty not holding tenure. Because they are more likely to have experienced various forms of teaching improprieties, faculty holding tenure are more likely to have more fully developed views on the types of teaching behaviors that are inappropriate and deserving of sanctioning action (Braxton, Eimers, and Bayer, 1996). Moreover, an allegation of teaching wrongdoing by a tenured faculty member is more likely to be seriously pursued than such

3. Sullivan (1996) found that publication productivity, a measure of research activity, is not associated with the five normative patterns identified by Braxton, Bayer, and Finkelstein (1992), but her research was conducted using only faculty in research universities I. Because the present study includes five types of colleges and universities, greater variability in publication productivity across the five types of institutions may result in statistically significant relationships between publication productivity and the seven inviolable and nine admonitory normative patterns. Moreover, the current study also focuses on 16 normative orientations rather than five.

4. This composite measure is created from a survey item common to all three studies that takes the following form: "during the past three years, how many of each of the following have you published: journal articles, books, and monographs." Respondents used the following categories: none, 1–2, 3–4, 5–10, 11 or more. These categories were assigned the following values to scale this measure: none = 1; 1–2 = 2; 3–4 = 3; 5–10 = 4, and 11 or more = 5.

an allegation by an untenured faculty member is (Black, 1976). Because they believe that their indignation will be heeded, tenured faculty are more likely to voice stronger disapproval of inviolable and admonitory normative patterns of proscribed behavior than are untenured academics. In addition, tenured faculty may be less fearful of being vulnerable and stigmatized as a whistleblower than their untenured counterparts are. Whistleblower stigmatization can not only damage the professional standing of an academic but also harm the chances for career advancement (Tangney, 1987). Academic professionals who fear being labeled a whistleblower are less likely to take formal action for personally known incidents of research wrongdoing (Braxton and Bayer, 1996). By extension, whistleblower stigmatization might also lead to less formal action for teaching impropriety.

These formulations indicate that the personal controls of administrative experience, gender, professional status, research activity, and academic tenure may be associated with the degree of disapproval academic professionals ascribe to the set of seven inviolable norms and the set of nine admonitory norms. As a consequence, this chapter attends to the question: Do faculty characteristics affect espousal of inviolable or admonitory normative patterns above and beyond the effects of institutional type and academic discipline? This general question was pursued through the following four aspects:

- Do these personal controls, or individual faculty characteristics, affect espousal of the core inviolable norm of moral turpitude and the core admonitory norm of authoritarian classroom?
- Do these personal controls affect faculty espousal of the remaining six inviolable norms and eight admonitory norms that are differentiated by either institutional type or academic discipline?
- Do these personal controls affect faculty espousal of the remaining six inviolable and eight admonitory norms above and beyond the effects of institutional type and academic discipline?
- Do institutional type and academic discipline account for more variance in the espousal of these teaching normative orientations than faculty individual characteristics do?

The first two questions were addressed using bivariate statistics: the t-test and Pearson's product-point correlation. The t-test was used to test for differences in norm espousal for administrative experience, gender, professional status, and tenure, whereas the Pearson's product-moment correlation was used to determine the relationship between research activity (publication productivity) and norm espousal. Questions three and four were simultaneously addressed using hierarchical linear multiple regression. Specifically, regression was employed to determine if individual faculty characteristics affect the espousal of the various inviolable and admonitory normative clusters above and beyond the influence of institutional type and academic discipline. Apportionment of the percent of variance explained by institutional type and academic discipline in contrast to individual faculty characteristics was also accomplished using multiple regression. A total of 16 regression equations were solved, one for each of the normative patterns. Each of these 16 normative arrays was measured using the composite scales developed for the seven inviolable and nine admonitory normative orientations described in Chapter 5. Each of the 16 normative orientations were regressed first on four variables representing institutional type—research universities I, comprehensive universities and colleges II, liberal arts colleges I, and two-year colleges—and three variables representing academic discipline—biology, history, and psychology—and then on the five individual characteristics. The first seven variables were measured as dummy variables.[5] All statistical tests were conducted at the .05 level of statistical significance.

Inviolable Norm Espousal and Individual Faculty Characteristics

Table 7.1 shows the bivariate relationships between the five faculty characteristics and the level of espousal for each of the seven inviolable normative behavioral patterns. The zero-order intercorrelations among the independent variables included in the multiple regression analyses are exhibited in Appendix D.[6] The multiple regression equations estimated for

---

5. The dummy variables used to represent institutional type were coded as follows: research universities I = 1, the other four types of institutions = 0; comprehensive universities and colleges II = 1, the other four types of institutions = 0; liberal arts colleges I = 1, the other four types of institutions = 0; two-year colleges = 1, the other four types of institutions = 0. A dummy variable for liberal arts colleges II was not created because multiple regression requires that one category of a group such as institutional type be dropped from dummy variable construction. Its variance is represented, however, in the other category of the four other dummy variables.

Disciplines were dummy coded as follows: biology = 1, the other three disciplines = 0; history = 1, the other three disciplines = 0; and psychology = 1, and the other three disciplines = 0. A dummy variable for mathematics was also not developed for the same reason described above.

6. An inspection of the zero-order intercorrelations among the independent variables included in each of the regression equations indicates that multicolinearity is not problematic for the interpretation of the regression coefficients obtained.

TABLE 7.1. Bivariate Relationships between the Seven Inviolable
Proscribed Normative Patterns and Five Faculty Characteristics

ADMINISTRATIVE EXPERIENCE

Normative Pattern	Mean Exp.	Mean No Exp.	t-value
Condescending negativism	4.16	4.17	0.22
Inattentive planning	4.23	4.15	1.51
Moral turpitude	4.86	4.87	0.52
Particularistic grading	4.37	4.33	1.07
Personal disregard	4.20	4.14	1.53
Uncommunicated course details	4.36	4.29	1.41
Uncooperative cynicism	4.22	4.14	1.93

GENDER

Normative Pattern	Mean Female	Mean Male	t-value
Condescending negativism	4.26	4.14	3.29***
Inattentive planning	4.17	4.25	1.45
Moral turpitude	4.92	4.87	2.66**
Particularistic grading	4.37	4.34	0.99
Personal disregard	4.26	4.15	2.85**
Uncommunicated course details	4.35	4.33	0.54
Uncooperative cynicism	4.19	4.17	0.61

PROFESSIONAL STATUS

Normative Pattern	Mean Higher	Mean Lower	t-value
Condescending negativism	4.18	4.16	0.54
Inattentive planning	4.22	4.17	1.16
Moral turpitude	4.89	4.88	0.43
Particularistic grading	4.36	4.33	0.99
Personal disregard	4.23	4.13	2.57*
Uncommunicated course details	4.37	4.29	1.81
Uncooperative cynicism	4.22	4.15	1.81

each of the seven inviolable normative orientations are displayed in Table
7.2.[7]

7. For some normative clusters, the results of the regression analyses differ from those of the
post hoc group mean comparisons made for institutional type and academic discipline.
These differences exist because individual faculty characteristics are controlled in the regression analysis but not in the analysis of variance and attendant post hoc mean comparisons.

TENURE STATUS

Normative Pattern	Mean Tenured	Mean Untenured	*t*-value
Condescending negativism	4.16	4.23	2.15*
Inattentive planning	4.20	4.16	0.73
Moral turpitude	4.88	4.89	1.11
Particularistic grading	4.34	4.36	0.45
Personal disregard	4.19	4.16	0.67
Uncommunicated course details	4.35	4.29	1.39
Uncooperative cynicism	4.18	4.16	0.51

RESEARCH ACTIVITY

Normative Pattern	Correlation Coefficient
Condescending negativism	−.14***
Inattentive planning	−.09*
Moral turpitude	−.09*
Particularistic grading	−.04
Personal disregard	−.11**
Uncommunicated course details	−.09**
Uncooperative cynicism	−.07*

*p. < .05, **p. < .01, ***p. < .001.

Core Inviolable Norm

As we concluded in Chapter 6, moral turpitude is a core inviolable norm to all five types of colleges and universities and to all four academic disciplines represented in this study. As indicated by Table 7.1, only gender and research activity show statistically significant bivariate relationships with the level of faculty disapproval voiced for moral turpitude. Women faculty (mean = 4.92) voice slightly more disapproval than men faculty (mean = 4.87) of such grossly unprincipled behavior as sexual relationships with students and holding class while intoxicated. A small negative relationship (r = −.09, p <.05) between research activity and the extent of disapproval of behaviors involving moral turpitude exists. These sources of faculty personal control become statistically nonsignificant, however, when institutional type, academic discipline, and the other three faculty characteristics are simultaneously controlled. Moreover, the statistically

TABLE 7.2. Regression of the Seven Inviolable Proscribed Normative Patterns on Academic Discipline, Institutional Type, and Five Faculty Characteristics

	Condescending Negativism	Inattentive Planning	Moral Turpitude	Particularistic Grading	Personal Disregard	Uncommunicated Course Details	Uncooperative Cynicism
Biology	.16*	.10	.00@	.10	.14*	.10	.20**
	(.14)	(.06)	(.03)	(.09)	(.12)	(.08)	(.16)
History	.04	.17	-.05	.02	-.04	.03	.01
	(.03)	(.10)	(-.06)	(.02)	(-.03)	(.02)	(.01)
Psychology	.02	.10	-.03	-.03	-.20**	-.09	.05
	(.01)	(.06)	(-.04)	(-.03)	(-.15)	(-.06)	(.04)
RU	-.20	-.41**	.03	-.12	-.18	-.12	-.23*
	(-.14)	(-.21)	(.04)	(-.10)	(-.13)	(-.08)	(-.15)
CUCII	.03	-.13	.01	-.03	.06	.07	.04
	(.02)	(-.08)	(.01)	(-.02)	(.05)	(.05)	(.03)
LAI	-.04	-.28*	.04	-.01	-.16*	-.16	-.01
	(.08)	(-.14)	(.05)	(-.01)	(-.11)	(-.09)	(-.01)
2YR	.03	-.13	.01	-.01	.08	.07	-.25**
	(.02)	(-.07)	(.01)	(-.01)	(.06)	(.05)	(-.17)

Administrative experience	.04 (.04)	-.01 (-.01)	.06 (.10)	.06 (.06)	.12* (.11)	.05 (.04)	.02 (.02)
Gender	-.12* (-.10)	-.11 (-.07)	-.06 (-.08)	-.03 (-.03)	-.14** (-.12)	-.01 (-.01)	-.02 (-.02)
Professional status	.02 (.02)	.02 (.02)	.04 (.06)	.01 (.01)	.10 (.09)	.00@ (.00)@	.04 (.04)
Tenure status	-.09 (-.08)	.13 (.08)	-.09 (-.12)	-.03 (-.03)	-.07 (-.06)	.05 (.04)	.02 (.02)
Research activity	-.01 (-.04)	-.01 (-.02)	-.01 (.08)	.01 (.03)	-.00@ (-.00)@	-.02 (-.05)	-.02 (-.06)
Constant	4.48	4.23	5.07	4.41	4.38	4.24	4.14
R² (type+discipline)	.05	.04	.01	.02	.09	.04	.07
R² (faculty characteristics)	.02	.01	.01	.00@	.03	.01	.01
Total R²	.07***	.05**	.02	.02	.12***	.05*	.08***

Note: Standardized regression coefficients are in parentheses. *p < .05, **p < .01, ***p < .001. @, coefficient < ±.004.

nonsignificant regression equation displayed in Table 7.2 indicates that faculty espousal of the normative pattern of moral turpitude is uniform across the five types of colleges and universities, the four academic disciplines, and the five faculty characteristics. Thus, the status of moral turpitude as an ultimate core inviolable norm is firmly established.

Differentiated Inviolable Norms

Condescending negativism, inattentive planning, particularistic grading, personal disregard, uncooperative cynicism, and uncommunicated course detail are proscribed inviolable normative clusters that are differentiated by either institutional type or academic discipline. So the questions to be addressed in this section of this chapter take the form: Do personal controls affect faculty espousal of these six inviolable norms? Do personal controls affect faculty espousal of these six inviolable norms above and beyond the effects of institutional type and academic discipline? Do institutional type and academic discipline account for more variance in the espousal of these six inviolable normative orientations than the individual characteristics of faculty?

Condescending negativism. Faculty disapproval of condescending negativism is related in a statistically reliable way to gender, tenure, and level of research activity. Women academics (mean = 4.26) express slightly more antipathy for colleagues who treat their students and colleagues in a demeaning manner than their male (mean = 4.14) faculty counterparts do. Tenured faculty (mean = 4.16) voice less contempt for a condescending and demeaning attitude toward students than their untenured counterparts do (mean = 4.23). Moreover, a slight negative relationship between faculty research activity ($r = -.14$, $p < .001$) and level of contempt for this proscribed pattern of behavior also exists.

Research activity, however, becomes statistically nonsignificant, but gender ($b = -.12$, $p < .05$) remains statistically significant when institutional type, academic discipline, and the three other individual faculty characteristics are controlled in the multiple regression equation estimated for this normative cluster (see Table 7.2). Moreover, faculty membership in the discipline of biology ($b = .16$, $p < .05$) exerts a statistically significant influence on the level of disapproval voiced for the condescending treatment of students and colleagues.

This regression equation accounts for 7 percent of the variability in faculty espousal of this particular inviolable norm. Of this total percent of variance explained, institutional type and academic discipline jointly contribute 5 percent and individual faculty characteristics provide 2 percent.

Inattentive planning. The proscribed normative behavioral pattern of inattentive planning appears to be unaffected by administrative experience, gender, professional status, and tenure as the *t*-tests conducted demonstrate statistically nonsignificant mean differences for each of these individual faculty characteristics (see Table 7.1). Faculty research activity (r = −.09, p <.05), however, exhibits a small negative, but statistically significant, relationship with the level of reproof voiced for the lack of attention to course planning matters by faculty colleagues.

With institutional type, academic discipline, and the other four faculty characteristics held constant, the relationship between research activity and disregard for inattentive planning becomes statistically nonsignificant. Consequently, none of the five faculty characteristics wields an independent influence on the espousal of this particular normative array. Nevertheless, holding an appointment in a research university I (b = −.41, p <.01) or a liberal arts college I (b = −.28, p <.05) exerts a statistically reliable influence on faculty disapproval of the failure to attend to matters important to course planning above and beyond the influence of the other variables controlled in this particular regression analysis (see Table 7.2).

In addition, 5 percent of the variability in faculty disapproval of inattentive planning is accounted for by the variables included in this regression equation. Of this total explained variance, academic discipline and institutional type together explain 4 percent, and 1 percent is accounted for by individual faculty characteristics.

Particularistic grading. None of the five individual faculty characteristics possess a statistically reliable bivariate relationships with the condemnation of preferential treatment of students in the awarding of grades (see Table 7.1). In addition, none of the five characteristics wields an independent influence on particularistic grading above and beyond the influence of institutional type and academic discipline given the failure to obtain a statistically significant regression equation (see Table 7.2).

Personal disregard. Of the five personal sources of control, only administrative experience and tenure appear unrelated to disapproval of the inviolable normative configuration of personal disregard. Women academics (mean = 4.26) espouse a statistically significant slightly greater degree of contempt for faculty who fail to respect the needs and sensitivities of students than male (mean = 4.15) members of the professoriate do. Academic professionals possessing high intrainstitutional professional status (mean = 4.23) also accord a statistically reliable greater degree of distaste for these proscribed behaviors that violate the principle of "respect for students as individuals" (Reynolds, 1996; Svinicki, 1994) than do their counterparts (mean = 4.13) with lower intrainstitutional professional status. In addition, faculty research activity ($r = -.11$, $p < .01$) is inversely related to disapproval of this normative orientation in a statistically significant way.

Intrainstitutional professional status and research activity become statistically nonsignificant, however, when institutional type, academic discipline, and the other three individual faculty characteristics are simultaneously held constant in the regression equation solved for this normative pattern. Nonetheless, gender ($b = -.14$, $p < .01$) remains statistically meaningful and administrative experience achieves statistically reliable status ($b = .12$, $p < .05$). Thus, female academics and academics with administrative experience tend to ascribe a greater degree of disapproval of colleagues who disregard the needs and sensitivities of students than their faculty counterparts do.

Academic biologists ($b = .14$, $p < .05$) tend to accord a higher degree of censure for violations of this normative pattern than their colleagues in other academic disciplines do. In contrast, academic psychologists ($b = -.20$, $p < .01$) ascribe a lower degree of contempt. In addition, faculty in liberal arts colleges I ($b = -.16$, $p < .05$) voice lower degrees of disapproval of personal disregard.

The 12 variables in this regression equation account for 12 percent of the variability in faculty espousal of this particular normative configuration. Faculty characteristics contribute 3 percent, and academic discipline and institutional type jointly explain 9 percent of this variability.

Uncooperative cynicism. Of the five faculty characteristics, only research activity demonstrates a statistically significant bivariate relationship to contempt for colleagues who shun departmental activities and the role of college teaching. Specifically, faculty research activity ($r = -.07$, $p < .05$) has a small negative relationship with the level of contempt expressed for this normative cluster.

This relationship reduces to statistical insignificance, however, when institutional type, academic discipline, and the other four faculty characteristics are controlled in the multiple regression equation solved for this particular normative configuration. Nevertheless, being an academic biologist (b = .20, p <.01) and having a faculty post in a two-year college (b = −.25, p <.01) exert statistically significant influences on the offensiveness of uncooperative cynicism. More specifically, biologists tend to ascribe more disdain for academic colleagues who fail to assume their responsibility for institutional governance and the teaching domain, whereas, two-year college faculty lean toward less disapproval for this particular inviolable normative cluster.

The variables included in this particular regression equation account for 8 percent of the variance in faculty disapproval of uncooperative cynicism. Of this total explained variance, academic discipline and institutional type account for 7 percent, whereas the remainder is explained by individual faculty characteristics.

Uncommunicated course details. Professorial censure of colleagues who fail to inform students of important course details on the first day of class appear to be related in a statistically significant manner to one of the five faculty characteristics. Specifically, faculty research activity has a slight negative relationship (r = −.09, p <.001) with espousal of this normative cluster.

This source of personal control fails to wield a statistically significant effect on uncommunicated course details, however, when institutional type, academic discipline, and the other four faculty characteristics are held constant in the solution of the multiple regression equation. Although the regression equation is statistically reliable (see Table 7.2), all of the variables contained in this regression equation are statistically insignificant.

Summary

Moral turpitude remains a core inviolable normative orientation since none of the five faculty characteristics wields an influence on the espousal of this proscribed pattern of behavior.

Moreover, faculty characteristics also exert little or no influence on the level of disapproval expressed for the normative clusters of inattentive planning, particularistic grading, uncooperative cynicism, and uncommunicated course details.

Faculty sources of personal control do, however, affect the level of contempt expressed for condescending negativism and personal disregard. Women faculty tend to voice stronger disapproval of both of these inviolable normative orientations. In addition, faculty with administrative experience also express strong sanctioning action for personal disregard. Moreover, faculty professional status, tenure, and research activity fail to demonstrate an independent influence on the level of contempt voiced for any of the inviolable norms.

Furthermore, academic discipline and institutional type jointly account for a larger proportion of the variance explained in faculty disapproval of condescending negativism, inattentive planning, personal disregard, and undermining colleagues than do individual faculty characteristics. But much variability in faculty espousal of these four inviolable norms remains unaccounted for given that the total explained variance ranges from a low of 5 percent for inattentive planning and uncommunicated course details to a high of 12 percent for personal disregard.

Admonitory Norm Espousal and Individual Faculty Characteristics

Table 7.3 exhibits the bivariate relationships between the five faculty characteristics and the level of espousal for each of the nine admonitory normative clusters. The zero-order intercorrelations among the independent variables included in the multiple regression analyses are exhibited in Appendix D.[8] The multiple regression equations estimated for each of the nine admonitory normative orientations are contained in Table 7.4[9]

Core Admonitory Norm

Chapter 6 concludes that the proscribed normative pattern authoritarian classroom is a core admonitory norm because its espousal is invariant across the five types of colleges and universities and the four academic disciplines represented in this study. Of the five sources of personal control, only gender demonstrates a statistically significant association with faculty subscription to this normative pattern. Women academics (mean = 3.85) tend to voice stronger disapproval of colleagues who have a rigid

---

8. The zero-order intercorrelations among the independent variables included in each of the regression equations indicate that multicolinearity is not problematic for the interpretation of the regression coefficients obtained.
9. For some normative clusters, the results of the regression analyses differ from those of the post hoc group mean comparisons made for institutional type and academic discipline. These differences exist because individual faculty characteristics are controlled in the regression analysis but not in the analysis of variance and attendant post hoc mean comparisons.

and closed approach to course content and different points of view held by students than their male faculty (mean = 3.67) counterparts do.

Moreover, the regression equation solved for this normative pattern indicates that gender (b = −.20, p <.01) wields an influence on the espousal of authoritarian classroom with the effects of institutional type, academic discipline, and the other four individual faculty characteristics held constant. In addition to gender, disciplinary membership in history also wields a statistically reliable effect on espousal of this normative cluster. More specifically, history faculty members (b = .19, p <.05) accord more severe sanctioning for this transgression of the ethical principle of neutrality in teaching (Baumgarten, 1982; Churchill, 1982) than their colleagues in the other three academic disciplines do. But only 4 percent of the variability in faculty reaction to authoritarian classroom is explained by institutional type, academic discipline, and individual faculty characteristics. Of this explained variability, equal proportions are accounted for by institutional type and academic discipline and by individual faculty characteristics. Thus, both social and personal sources of control modestly influence faculty espousal of this proscribed admonitory normative orientation. Consequently, the status of authoritarian classroom as a core admonitory norm is called into question.

Differentiated Admonitory Norms

As described in Chapters 5 and 6, eight admonitory normative behavioral patterns are differentiated by either institutional type or academic discipline. The admonitory norms are advisement negligence, inadequate communication, inconvenience avoidance, inadequate course design, instructional narrowness, insufficient syllabus, teaching secrecy, and undermining colleagues. Do faculty characteristics affect espousal of these eight admonitory norms above and beyond the effects of institutional type and academic discipline? Do institutional type and academic discipline account for more variance in the espousal of these eight admonitory normative clusters than the individual characteristics of faculty?

Advisement negligence. Only professional status demonstrates a statistically meaningful connection with faculty concordance with the admonitory status of advisement negligence. Faculty with high intrainstitutional professional status (mean = 3.69) express somewhat greater denunciation of colleagues who fail to serve the advising needs of their students than their counterparts with less status (mean = 3.59) do.

TABLE 7.3. Bivariate Relationships between the Nine Admonitory Proscribed Normative Patterns and Five Faculty Characteristics

ADMINISTRATIVE EXPERIENCE

Normative Pattern	Mean Exp.	Mean No Exp.	t-value
Advisement negligence	3.65	3.59	1.35
Authoritarian classroom	3.76	3.68	1.68
Inadequate communication	3.66	3.61	1.13
Inconvenience avoidance	3.81	3.69	2.38*
Inadequate course design	3.68	3.64	0.64
Instructional narrowness	3.36	3.33	0.45
Insufficient syllabus	3.53	3.43	1.62
Teaching secrecy	3.32	3.31	0.25
Undermining colleagues	3.66	3.55	2.31*

GENDER

Normative Pattern	Mean Female	Mean Male	t-value
Advisement negligence	3.62	3.62	0.01
Authoritarian classroom	3.85	3.67	4.01***
Inadequate communication	3.71	3.63	2.11*
Inconvenience avoidance	3.76	3.75	0.11
Inadequate course design	3.72	3.68	0.92
Instructional narrowness	3.44	3.33	2.38*
Insufficient syllabus	3.54	3.48	1.02
Teaching secrecy	3.35	3.31	0.75
Undermining colleagues	3.68	3.58	2.28*

PROFESSIONAL STATUS

Normative Pattern	Mean Higher	Mean Lower	t-value
Advisement negligence	3.69	3.59	2.24*
Authoritarian classroom	3.77	3.69	1.78
Inadequate communication	3.69	3.61	2.01*
Inconvenience avoidance	3.84	3.66	4.19*
Inadequate course design	3.74	3.66	1.86
Instructional narrowness	3.37	3.34	0.67
Insufficient syllabus	3.54	3.47	1.28
Teaching secrecy	3.32	3.32	0.14
Undermining colleagues	3.68	3.55	2.89*

TENURE STATUS

Normative Pattern	Mean Tenured	Mean Untenured	t-value
Advisement negligence	3.63	3.61	0.45
Authoritarian classroom	3.71	3.75	1.01
Inadequate communication	3.65	3.64	0.23
Inconvenience avoidance	3.79	3.64	3.16**
Inadequate course design	3.71	3.64	1.59
Instructional narrowness	3.36	3.38	0.38
Insufficient syllabus	3.49	3.52	0.54
Teaching secrecy	3.31	3.36	0.99
Undermining colleagues	3.61	3.62	0.14

RESEARCH ACTIVITY

Normative Pattern	Correlation Coefficient
Advisement negligence	−.03
Authoritarian classroom	−.01
Inadequate communication	−.08*
Inconvenience avoidance	−.09**
Inadequate course design	−.06
Instructional narrowness	−.17***
Insufficient syllabus	−.01
Teaching secrecy	−.06
Undermining colleagues	−.14***

*p. < .05, **p. < .01, ***p. < .001.

With the influence of institutional type, academic discipline, and the other four faculty characteristics controlled, professional status is reduced to a statistically insignificant relationship. As a consequence, none of the five faculty characteristics exerts an independent influence on the espousal of this normative behavioral array. Academic biologists (b = .20, p <.001), however, express more contempt than do those in other disciplines for such proscribed behaviors. Academics in two-year colleges (b = −.36, p <.001) tend to voice less disgust than faculty members in other institutional settings do.

TABLE 7.4. Regression of the Nine Admonitory Proscribed Normative Patterns on Academic Discipline, Institutional Type, and Five Faculty Characteristics

	Advisement Negligence	Authoritarian Classroom	Inadequate Communication	Inconvenience Avoidance	Inadequate Course Design	Instructional Narrowness	Insufficient Syllabus	Teaching Secrecy	Undermining Colleagues
Biology	.20*** (.13)	.10 (.07)	.08 (.06)	.07 (.05)	.07 (.05)	.08 (.05)	.38*** (.23)	.17* (.11)	.25*** (.18)
History	.10 (.04)	.19* (.12)	-.02 (-.01)	-.03 (-.02)	-.11 (-.07)	-.03 (-.02)	.28** (.16)	-.21* (-.13)	.17* (.11)
Psychology	.01 (.01)	.11 (.07)	-.08 (-.01)	-.13 (-.09)	-.04 (-.03)	-.10 (-.07)	.24** (.14)	-.14 (-.09)	-.01@ (-.00)@
RU	-.19 (-.11)	-.18 (-.11)	-.24* (-.16)	-.16 (-.09)	-.28 (-.17)	-.35** (-.21)	-.52*** (-.27)	-.19 (-.10)	-.36** (-.22)
CUCII	.17 (.11)	-.02 (-.01)	-.03 (-.02)	.08 (.05)	-.04 (-.03)	.08 (.05)	-.12 (-.07)	.01 (.01)	-.02 (-.01)
LAI	-.06 (-.03)	-.06 (-.03)	-.14 (-.09)	-.27** (-.15)	-.12 (-.07)	-.31** (-.17)	-.27* (-.13)	-.13 (-.07)	-.16 (-.09)
2YR	-.36*** (-.21)	-.07 (-.04)	.03 (.02)	.05 (.03)	-.09 (-.05)	.01 (.01)	-.27* (-.14)	-.18 (.01)	-.15 (-.10)

Administrative experience	−.06 (−.05)	.08 (.06)	.01 (.01)	.12 (.09)	.01 (.01)	.03 (.02)	−.01 (−.01)	.01 (.01)	.06 (.05)
Gender	−.06 (−.04)	−.20** (−.14)	−.13* (−.11)	−.07 (−.05)	−.11 (−.08)	−.11 (−.07)	−.10 (−.06)	−.08 (−.05)	−.13* (−.10)
Professional status	.09 (.06)	.07 (.05)	.08 (.07)	.14* (.11)	−.11 (−.08)	.02 (.01)	.05 (.04)	.01 (.00)@	.12 (.09)
Tenure status	.02 (.01)	−.10 (−.07)	−.01 (−.00)	.05 (.03)	.03 (.02)	−.00@ (−.00)@	−.02 (−.01)	−.04 (−.02)	−.01 (−.00)ᵈ
Research activity	−.03 (−.09)	.01 (.02)	.01 (.04)	−.01 (−.04)	.03 (.09)	−.02 (−.06)	.03 (.09)	−.01 (−.02)	−.02 (−.06)
Constant	3.66	4.03	3.78	3.61	3.86	3.64	3.54	3.65	3.69
R² (type+discipline)	.08	.02	.03	.06	.03	.10	.07	.07	.08
R² (faculty characteristics)	.01	.02	.02	.03	.00@	.01	.01	.00ᵈ	.02
Total R²	.09***	.04*	.05*	.09***	.03	.11***	8.0***	.07***	.10***

Note: Standardized regression coefficients are in parentheses. *p < .05, **p < .01, ***p < .001. @ , coefficient <±.004.

The regression equation explains 9 percent of the variance in faculty reactions to this particular pattern of proscribed behaviors. Of this explained variability, institutional type and academic discipline together account for 8 percent, whereas individual faculty characteristics contribute the remaining 1 percent.

Inadequate communication. Three faculty characteristics possess statistically reliable bivariate relationships to the espousal of this particular admonitory normative configuration. Specifically, male faculty (mean = 3.63) ascribe less disapproval of inadequate communication than their female colleagues (mean = 3.71) do. Faculty with lower intraprofessional status (mean = 3.61) also dislike inadequate communication less than their high stature colleagues (mean = 3.69) do. In addition, faculty research activity ($r = -.08$, $p <.05$) bears a small negative relationship with the espousal of this particular admonitory normative pattern.

Two of these sources of personal control—intrainstitutional professional status and research activity—fail to reach statistical significance, however, when the effects of institutional type and academic discipline are held constant. Gender ($b = -.13$, $p <.05$) remains the sole faculty characteristic that exerts any statistically reliable influence on faculty criticism of the failure of colleagues to communicate course information to students adequately. Moreover, academics in research universities I ($b = -.24$, $p <.05$) tend to express less disapproval of this normative behavioral configuration than their counterparts in other types of collegiate institutions do. In addition, 5 percent of the variability in faculty perceptions of inadequate communication are accounted for by this regression equation. Of this explained variance, individual faculty characteristics contribute 2 percent and academic discipline and institutional type jointly supply 3 percent.

Inconvenience avoidance. Four faculty characteristics show a statistically meaningful bivariate relationship with the response to behaviors regarding the proscribed norm of inconvenience avoidance. To be specific, faculty with administrative experience (mean = 3.81) voice slightly more disdain for colleagues who endeavor to avoid being personally inconvenienced by the courses they teach than faculty without administrative experience (mean = 3.69) do. Faculty with high intrainstitutional professional status (mean = 3.84) also express greater contempt for inconvenience avoidance than faculty with lower intrainstitutional professional status (mean = 3.66) do. Tenured faculty (mean = 3.79) also object more to transgressions of this proscribed normative pattern than untenured academics (mean = 3.64) do. But academics with high levels of research activity tend to object less to this set of behaviors (r = −.09, p <.01).

Of these four faculty characteristics, all of them but intrainstitutional professional status are reduced to statistical nonsignificance when institutional type and academic discipline are statistically controlled in the regression equation for this particular normative pattern (see Table 7.4). Professional status (b = .14, p <.05) exerts an independent influence on the severity of faculty reactions to those behaviors. That is, faculty high in such status tend to disapprove of such behaviors more than their colleagues of lower professional status do. Moreover, holding academic appointment in liberal arts colleges I (b = −.27, p <.01) leads to less faculty contempt for inconvenience avoidance.

The solution of this particular regression equation accounts for 9 percent of the variance in faculty espousal of this admonitory normative pattern. Academic discipline and institutional type together explain 6 percent, and individual characteristics account for 3 percent of this total explained variability.

Inadequate course design. None of the five faculty characteristics possesses a statistically reliable bivariate relationship with espousal of this particular admonitory norm. Moreover, the regression equation fails to attain statistical significance.

Instructional narrowness. Gender and research activity display statistically significant relationships with the level of faculty disapproval of behaviors exhibiting instructional narrowness. More specifically, women academics (mean = 3.44) express more contempt for colleagues who are constricted in their approaches to the assessment of students, type of classroom activities, and type of teaching methods than men (mean = 3.33) do. Faculty research activity (r = −.17, p <.001) is negatively correlated with the degree of criticism voiced for this admonitory normative pattern. In contrast, administrative experience, intrainstitutional professional status, and tenure bear insignificant statistical relationships.

Moreover, both gender and research activity become statistically insignificant when institutional type, academic discipline, and the other three faculty characteristics are controlled in a regression analysis (see Table 7.4). But faculty appointments in research universities I (b = −.35, p <.01) and in liberal arts colleges I (b = −.31, p <.01) lead to less faculty contempt for these proscribed behaviors.

Finally, 11 percent of the variability in faculty perceptions of behaviors involving instructional narrowness is explained by this multiple regression equation. Individual faculty characteristics contribute 1 percent, and institutional type and academic discipline furnish 10 percent of this total explained variance.

Insufficient syllabus. Administrative experience, gender, intrainstitutional professional status, research activity, and tenure fail to demonstrate a statistically significant relationship with espousal of this particular admonitory normative configuration. Moreover, none of these characteristics demonstrates such a relationship when institutional type and academic discipline are controlled in the regression analysis conducted for this particular normative pattern. Nevertheless, institutional type and academic discipline show a statistically significant influence on the level of disapproval faculty ascribe to the behaviors of this normative pattern. These influences are registered in the equation solved for this particular normative cluster. Specifically, holding an appointment in research universities I ($b = -.52$, $p < .001$), in liberal arts colleges I ($b = -.27$, $p < .05$), and in two-year colleges ($b = -.27$, $p < .05$) leads to less faculty disdain for colleagues who neglect to supply students with an adequate course syllabus. In contrast, being an academic biologist ($b = .38$, $p < .001$), historian ($b = .28$, $p < .01$), or psychologist ($b = .24$, $p < .01$) heightens faculty contempt for this infraction of the professorial duty to share plans for a course with students.

The regression equation accounts for 8 percent of the variability in faculty reactions to this admonitory norm. Of this explained variability, academic discipline and institutional type together contribute 7 percent and individual faculty characteristics provide 1 percent.

Teaching secrecy. None of the five personal sources of control—administrative experience, gender, intrainstitutional status, research activity, and tenure—has a statistically meaningful association with the espousal of this particular admonitory normative pattern. These characteristics also fail to show statistical significance when institutional type and academic discipline are held constant in a regression analysis carried out for this normative orientation. However, membership in the discipline of biology ($b = .17$, $p < .05$) increases faculty disapproval of colleagues who refuse to give other faculty members information and materials about college teaching and their courses, whereas disciplinary affiliation as a historian (b = −.21, p <.05) decreases contempt for this admonitory proscribed set of behaviors.

The regression equation explains 7 percent of the variability in faculty reaction to this particular norm. Academic discipline and institutional type account for all of this total explained variance.

Undermining colleagues. Of the five sources of personal control, four of them possess a statistically significant relationship with faculty reactions to behaviors reflective of this particular admonitory normative pattern. Specifically, faculty with administrative experience (mean = 3.66) rebuke undermining colleagues to a slightly greater extent than faculty with no administrative experience (mean = 3.55) do. Women faculty (mean = 3.68) also tend to express more disdain for colleagues who demean or try to harm the teaching reputation and courses offered by other faculty members than their male counterparts (mean = 3.58) do. Faculty professional status also relates to espousal of this normative cluster, as faculty with high intrainstitutional status (mean = 3.68) voice somewhat greater contempt for this violation of the principle of respect for colleagues (Murray, Gillese, Lennon, Mercer and Robinson, 1996) than faculty with less status (mean = 3.55) do. But faculty research activity (r = −.14, p <.001) has an inverse relationship with the level of disapproval expressed for undermining colleagues.

Nevertheless, administrative experience, professional status, and research activity are reduced to statistical nonsignificance when institutional type and academic discipline are held constant through regression analysis. Gender (b = −.13, p <.05), however, remains a statistically reliable source of influence on faculty responses to this proscribed normative pattern. Moreover, institutional type and academic discipline are not attenuated by sources of faculty personal control. More specifically, disciplinary affiliation as a biologist (b = .25, p <.001) leads to greater reproof of this normative cluster, whereas having an appointment in a research university I (b = −.36, p <.01) reduces faculty criticism of behaviors indicative of undermining colleagues.

This regression equation explains 10 percent of the variance in faculty response to this particular admonitory norm. Of this total explained variability, individual faculty characteristics account for 2 percent, and academic discipline and institutional type contribute 8 percent.

Summary

The core admonitory normative status of authoritarian classroom is questionable, given the tendency of both disciplinary affiliation as a historian and women academics to accord greater contempt for this proscribed configuration of behaviors. Thus, authoritarian classroom is affected by both disciplinary and personal sources of control.

Moreover, individual faculty characteristics exert some influence on three of eight remaining admonitory normative clusters. Specifically, women faculty express more disapproval of inadequate communication and undermining colleagues. Faculty having high intrainstitutional professional status also declare greater aversion to inconvenience avoidance.

Faculty characteristics wield little or no influence on the admonitory normative orientations of advisement negligence, inadequate course design, instructional narrowness, insufficient syllabus, and teaching secrecy. Moreover, administrative experience, research activity, and tenure fail to exert independent influences on any of these eight admonitory norms.

In addition, academic discipline and institutional type—two sources of social control—contribute the largest proportion of the variance explained for each of these eight admonitory normative clusters. Yet vast amounts of variability in faculty espousal of these admonitory normative patterns remain unexplained. The largest proportion of explained variance is 10 percent for undermining colleagues, whereas the lowest percentage of explained variability is the 4 percent registered for the proscribed normative pattern of authoritarian classroom.

Concluding Thoughts

The configuration of findings reported in this chapter strongly suggests that structural dimensions of the academic profession—institutional type and academic discipline—exert a greater influence on faculty espousal of inviolable and admonitory normative patterns than the individual and career characteristics of faculty do. Put differently, contextual sources—discipline and institution of employment—are more potent than personal sources of control. Nevertheless, vast proportions of variability in response to these proscriptive normative patterns remain unexplained. Chapter 10 will discuss possible explanations for this array of findings.

A normative structure must be buttressed by compliance with norms as well as by a set of mechanisms of deterrence, detection, and sanctioning of normative violations. Without such social control mechanisms, a normative structure remains a justification for professional autonomy to the lay public (Mulkay, 1976). In the next chapter, these mechanisms of social control are viewed from the perspective of misconduct in the teaching role. Theoretical formulations are advanced for explaining incidents of teaching misconduct, as well as the deterrence, detection, and sanctioning of misconduct in teaching.

EIGHT

The Social Control
of Teaching Misconduct

In order for the normative structure of undergraduate college teaching to be institutionalized and binding (Mulkay, 1976), faculty must avoid those behaviors reflective of the seven inviolable and nine admonitory normative clusters. These inviolable and admonitory normative patterns define teaching-related behaviors that faculty regard as inappropriate conduct toward students and colleagues vis-à-vis the teaching role. Thus, faculty behavior reflective of these proscriptive normative clusters constitute teaching misconduct.

With the exception of cases of sexual harassment of students, a facet of the proscribed normative pattern of moral turpitude, most forms of teaching misconduct remain largely invisible to the lay public and academic professionals alike. Whereas record-keeping activities of the Office of Inspector General of the National Science Foundation and the Office of Research Integrity of the Public Health Service have emerged to chronicle allegations of scientific wrongdoing (National Academy of Sciences, 1992), official record-keeping of incidents of teaching wrongdoing rarely occurs. To paraphrase Harriet Zuckerman (1988, p. 523), no "social epidemiology" of teaching wrongdoing exits. Consequently, the amount of teaching misconduct in higher education is not known.

Nevertheless, it cannot be assumed that misconduct is rare. As Zuckerman points out, "norms and behavior are never perfectly correlated" (1988, p. 516). Merton calls this disjuncture a "painful contrast" between normative expectations and actual behavior (Merton, 1976, p. 40). Thus, some teaching misconduct is both known and expected. Accordingly, the advancement of explanations for teaching wrongdoing is essential to our understanding of this phenomenon. Control theory provides a possible explanation for teaching misconduct.

Control Theory

Human behavior is normally regulated by social norms (Frazier, 1976), but people are free to deviate when social organizations fail to produce individuals compliant with such norms. Weak or ineffective social control results in deviance from social norms. These formulations spring from Durkheim's (1951 [1897]) contention that individuals acting according to their own preferences is the natural human condition and that conformity is aberrant.

As indicated in Chapters 1 and 7, sources of social control that induce conformity to social norms are at the individual, the primary group, the community, and the institutional levels (Reiss, 1951). Deviance from social norms occurs when such sources of control are not strong enough to induce conformity (Reiss, 1951). The strength of such sources of control is indexed in the clarity and magnitude of normative expectations communicated by these sources.

For academic professionals, personal sources of control are indexed in the extent to which the normative expectations of teaching are internalized by the individual academic professional. Primary group controls for academics emanate from their academic departments, community controls stem from the academic discipline (Braxton, 1990), and institutional controls spring from the college or university of appointment. Because the strength or clarity of norms is indexed in the overt behaviors of individuals (Sarbin and Allen, 1968), pressure for individual faculty compliance varies with the degree of conformity to normative expectations for teaching role performance exhibited by academic colleagues at the level of the department, the academic discipline, and the institution. Individual faculty conformity to teaching norms also varies according to the degree of individual norm internalization.

However, Braxton (1990) found that the influence of the academic discipline on deviance from the Mertonian norms of science is more powerful than individual norm internalization. Therefore, social rather than personal controls exert the greatest degree of influence. By extension, the academic department, the academic discipline, and the institution of employment wield more influence on individual faculty compliance with normative expectations of teaching than individual norm internalization. Consequently, teaching misconduct obtains when pressure for normative conformity is weak at the level of the academic department, the academic discipline, and the college or university of employment. Teaching misconduct also occurs when individual internalization of normative expectations is weak.

Based on these formulations and the pattern of findings described in Chapters 5, 6, and 7, we advance the following six hypotheses:

- With the exception of teaching misbehavior taking the form of moral turpitude and authoritarian classroom, malfeasance in the form of the six remaining inviolable and the eight remaining admonitory norms occurs less frequently in the discipline of biology than in history, mathematics, and psychology.
- Incidents of teaching misconduct in the remaining six inviolable and eight admonitory norms occur more frequently in research-oriented universities than in comprehensive universities and colleges II, liberal arts colleges I and II, and two-year colleges.
- Women faculty are less likely to engage in the improprieties of condescending negativism, personal disregard, and inadequate communication than are male faculty members.
- Faculty members with administrative experience are less likely to exhibit behaviors reflective of personal disregard than are faculty without administrative experience.
- Academics with high intrainstitutional status are less likely to exhibit inconvenience avoidance than academics with lower intrainstitutional status.
- Faculty members holding tenure are less likely to engage in behaviors indicative of inadequate course design than untenured faculty.

In addition to understanding why teaching misconduct occurs, a comprehension of mechanisms of deterrence, detection, and sanctioning of misconduct is also necessary to assure that the academic profession meets its obligation to the lay public to regulate itself. Deterrence, detection, and sanctioning are important mechanisms of social control of prohibited behaviors (Zuckerman, 1977, 1988). Consequently, this chapter also advances some theoretical formulations concerning these mechanisms of social control of teaching misconduct.

Detection and Deterrence of Teaching Misconduct

The graduate school socialization process, the public nature of college teaching, and student course ratings are among the social processes that may deter teaching misconduct. Each of these processes also functions as a mechanism of detection.

Graduate School Socialization

The graduate school socialization process is regarded as a fundamental mechanism of deterrence of professional wrongdoing (Goode, 1957; Zuckerman, 1977, 1978; Anderson, Louis, and Earle, 1994). Through this process, graduate students acquire the attitudes, values, knowledge, and skills necessary for professional role performance (Merton, Reader, and Kendall, 1957). This socialization process entails several key dimensions. Formal gate-keeping mechanisms such as course requirements, qualifying examinations, and the dissertation constitute one dimension. Role-taking activities such as research and teaching assistantships represent another socialization dimension (Bucher and Stelling, 1977). Such activities shape professional commitment and identity (Bucher and Stelling, 1977). Informal and formal relationships between faculty and students, including mentoring relationships, also play a key role in the graduate school socialization process (Cole and Cole, 1973). A final dimension of graduate socialization is the structure and climate of the graduate department, as these forces influence professional norms (Anderson and Louis, 1994).

Through these key dimensions of socialization, the seven inviolable normative and the nine admonitory normative orientations may be internalized to varying degrees. The influence of these dimensions may, however, be latent given that preparation for teaching role performance is given little or no attention during graduate study in most graduate departments (Jencks and Reisman, 1969; Bess, 1977). Moreover, uniform internalization of normative preferences is also unlikely since beginning teaching assistants appear to anticipate some of the normative preferences of faculty members (Braxton, Lambert, and Clark, 1995). Thus, the nature of norm internalization may be individual and take various forms such as accentuation, maintenance, or conversion.[1] Some individuals may experience an accentuation or a strengthening of their normative preferences, whereas other individuals maintain their level of norm espousal prior to entering graduate school. Other individuals may experience a conversion of their views on teaching improprieties. In other words, such individuals who once viewed a pattern of behaviors as appropriate may come to regard them as inappropriate, or vice versa.

Informal and formal relationships between faculty and students, mentor-mentee relationships, role-taking activities, and departmental cli-

---

1. Accentuation, conversion, and maintenance are forms of impact that an emphasis on group means obscures (Feldman and Newcomb, 1969). We apply their terms to the internalization of norms through graduate school socialization.

mate and structure may serve such a latent socializing function for the internalization—accentuation, maintenance, or conversion—of undergraduate college teaching normative preferences. Moreover, these mechanisms also play an important role in the detection of teaching wrongdoing. For an individual to label faculty behavior as teaching misconduct, an individual must hold strongly crystallized views on proscribed and prescribed normative orientations for undergraduate college teaching. If ambiguity surrounds the definition of teaching misconduct, then the detection of it becomes problematic.[2] As a consequence, the detection of teaching misconduct is facilitated by strong internalization of the proscriptive inviolable and admonitory normative patterns. Thus, an understanding of the possible role of each of these mechanisms in the internalization of teaching norms is important.

Informal and formal faculty relationships. Graduate students frequently serve as teaching assistants for departmental faculty members. Through such experiences, graduate teaching assistants may observe a range of teaching behaviors exhibited by their faculty supervisor-mentor. These observations may evoke personal rebuke if the behaviors are inappropriate. Personal approval may also be experienced if the behaviors are appropriate. Teaching assistants may also observe the reactions of students to the supervising professor's behaviors. Such student reactions may signal indignation or approval. Such observations may shape the graduate student's views on which teaching behaviors are appropriate or inappropriate. Conversations about course-related matters between the teaching assistant and the supervising faculty member may also lead to the internalization of undergraduate college teaching norms. Such conversations focus on planning for the course, problems with students, and successes with the course.

Role-taking activities. A graduate teaching assistantship provides individuals with role-taking activities important to the internalization of undergraduate college teaching norms. The range of responsibilities for teaching a course assumed by a teaching assistant affects the internalization of the seven inviolable and the nine admonitory norms. The more responsibilities a teaching assistant assumes, the more likely the full range of norms are internalized to varying degrees by such individuals.

---

2. Fox and Braxton (1994) make a similar point about the role ambiguity of definitions plays in the detection of scientific wrongdoing.

Experience with a range of teaching activities helps an individual crystallize their beliefs about appropriate and inappropriate teaching behaviors. Through trial and error, a teaching assistant learns the normative preferences of the supervising professor and students. These preferences are learned through faculty and student reactions of either approval or dislike of the teaching behaviors of the teaching assistant.

Structure and climate. Structure refers to the informal and formal rules and activities of a department (Anderson and Louis, 1994). Structure affects the attitudes and behaviors of individuals (Daft and Becker, 1979).

Van Maanen and Schein (1979) identify six dimensions of organizational socialization that Anderson and Louis (1994) and Anderson, Louis, and Earle (1994) contend may also depict structural dimensions of graduate school socialization processes that influence the internalization of research-oriented norms. These structural dimensions may also influence the internalization of the seven inviolable and the nine admonitory norms. These dimensions are arrayed on a continuum of polar opposites.

The first dimension is termed collective versus individual. The collective-individual dimension pertains to whether new graduate students have a common base of experience or proceed through their studies in an individualized and isolated way. The second dimension is called formal versus informal. This dimension relates to whether the graduate socialization process consists of organized activities that separate new students from others or little or no structure where students learn things like norms through trial and error. Sequential versus variable constitutes the third dimension. If students have clear, discrete steps to achieve their degrees, then such an experience is sequential. If the steps toward receiving the degree are ambiguous, then the socialization process is termed variable. The fourth dimension is labeled serial versus disjunctive. A serial socialization experience would be one where the student has a faculty member who mentors or trains graduate students, whereas a disjunctive experience is marked by an absence of such a designated faculty member. The fifth dimension is termed fixed versus variable. This dimension pertains to whether the time table for movement through various stages of the doctoral socialization process are clearly delineated (fixed) or are unclear or variable. The sixth dimension is called investiture versus divestiture. Investiture refers to socialization that affirms an individual's values, beliefs, and attitudes. In contrast, divestiture is a socialization process that requires graduate students to change those attitudes, values, and beliefs that are incongruent with those instilled by the socialization experience.

Based on these formulations, we advance the following hypothesis: *a graduate school socialization process that is collective, formal, sequential, fixed, serial, and divestitive has the greatest impact on the internalization of undergraduate teaching norms.* This particular configuration of dimensions would likely convert an individual's normative preferences to match the normative orientations toward teaching that prevail in the department. Accentuation of an individual's normative orientations would, however, be influenced by a socialization experience characterized as collective, formal, sequential, fixed, serial, and investitive.

The prestige or reputational standing of a graduate department represents another structural element that may affect the internalization of the seven inviolable and the nine admonitory norms. Like those of individual faculty members of high professional status, the actions of high-ranking academic departments are highly visible and carry much symbolic significance (Carlin, 1966). Thus, the actions of high status departments must be exemplary and beyond reproach (Carlin, 1966). Accordingly, graduate departments possessing high status are more likely to stress the importance of avoiding or denouncing transgressions of the proscribed normative orientations of undergraduate college teaching. As a consequence, we offer the following hypothesis: *the higher the ranking of a graduate department, the stronger the degree of internalization of the seven inviolable and nine admonitory norms.*

Like the structural dimensions of a department's socialization experience, the ethical climate of a department may also shape espousal of undergraduate teaching normative preferences. Ashworth (1985) defines climate as perceptions of a work environment that are psychologically important to an organization's members. Victor and Cullen (1988) contend that the climate of an organization also has ethical dimensions that affect the ethical behavior of its members. Victor and Cullen (1988) describe five such ethical dimensions of organizational climate.

Caring is the first dimension, a dimension that reflects an abiding concern for the good of all members. The second dimension is called the law and code dimension, as it pertains to an assessment of decisions according to whether they violate laws and, also, whether laws and professional standards are followed by members. Rules, the label given to the third dimension, reflect the extent to which members comply with organizational policies and procedures. The fourth dimension is termed instrumental, as individual self-interests transcend the interests of the organization. The fifth dimension is termed independence. Such an organizational climate is marked by individuals who follow their own ethical or moral convictions.

Anderson and Louis (1994) and Anderson, Louis, and Earle (1994) extended these dimensions to the graduate school socialization process and found aspects of them influential in shaping research norm espousal. Thus, such ethical dimensions of departmental climate may also affect the internalization of the seven inviolable and the nine admonitory norms comprising the normative structure of undergraduate college teaching.

These formulations suggest the following hypothesis: *the greater the emphasis on caring, law and code, and rules exhibited by a graduate department, the stronger the internalization of inviolable and admonitory undergraduate college teaching norms.* In contrast, we hypothesize: *the more a graduate department exhibits ethical climates characterized as instrumental and independent the weaker the internalization of these normative orientations.*

Other Mechanisms of Deterrence

The public nature of college teaching and student course ratings are other social processes that may function as deterrents to teaching misconduct. These possible deterrents are discussed below.

Public nature of college teaching. College and university faculty enjoy considerable autonomy in defining and conducting their undergraduate college courses. Moreover, colleagues seldom observe, except for occasional assessments for tenure and promotion purposes, the classroom decorum of other faculty members. Nevertheless, college teaching is a highly public activity as students witness first-hand the teaching behaviors of academic professionals. Because teaching behaviors are highly visible to students, faculty may be reluctant to engage in proscribed behaviors. Moreover, the detection of teaching wrongdoing is aided by the high visibility of faculty teaching behaviors to students. Highly visible teaching improprieties include condescending negativism, inattentive planning, personal disregard, and uncommunicated course details. With the exception of advisement negligence, all of the admonitory normative clusters pertinent to students can be observed by students in any given class. But moral turpitude, particularistic grading, and advisement negligence are more likely to be noted by those students personally affected by such proscribed behaviors than by all members of a class.

Accordingly, the typical class size in an academic department plays a role in both the deterrence and the detection of transgressions of those inviolable and admonitory normative configurations observable at the class level. Because the observability of misconduct is inversely related to group size (Horowitz, 1990), we contend that faculty avoidance of such inviolable and admonitory normative orientations is more likely in small classes. We also posit that the detection of teaching misconduct reflective of these inviolable and admonitory norms is also more probable in small classes.

Departmental meetings, face-to-face informal interactions among colleagues, and other departmental activities such as committee work focusing on teaching and the curriculum render such proscribed behavioral patterns as uncooperative cynicism, teaching secrecy, and undermining colleagues observable by faculty colleagues. As a consequence, faculty may be deterred from behaviors indicative of these inappropriate patterns of behavior. Moreover, departmental meetings and face-to-face informal interactions among colleagues may also facilitate the detection of teaching wrongdoing. Both the deterrence and detection of these proscribed behaviors directed toward colleagues is also influenced by the number of faculty members in an academic department and by the frequency of departmental activities, meetings, periodic performance reviews, and face-to-face interactions. Based on these formulations, we hypothesize that as faculty size increases, the faculty avoidance of these three normative orientations decreases. The ability to detect such improprieties toward colleagues also decreases with increases in the number of faculty in a department. But increases in day-to-day, face-to-face interactions among colleagues facilitate both deterrence and detection of teaching secrecy, undermining colleagues, and uncooperative cynicism.

Student course ratings. In many colleges and universities, students assess their courses using instruments designed for this purpose (see Chapter 9). Centra (1980, 1993) delineates a set of dimensions common to these course rating instruments. Several of these dimensions tap behaviors related to some of the inviolable and admonitory normative clusters comprising the normative structure of undergraduate college teaching. These pertinent dimensions are organization, planning and structure, teacher-student interactions or rapport, grading and examinations, and assignments.

Faculty behaviors indicative of uncommunicated course details, inadequate communication, inadequate course design, and insufficient syllabus may be directly or indirectly noted through course rating items indicative of the organization, planning, and structure dimensions. Course rating items assessing teacher-student interactions and rapport may observe faculty conduct suggestive of condescending negativism and personal disregard. Course rating items addressing grading and examinations may also identify particularistic grading behaviors of faculty. Course rating instruments also contain items asking students to rate the instructor and the course (Centra, 1980, 1993). Such general or global items may also reflect student distress regarding faculty teaching improprieties.

Because some proscribed teaching behaviors may be noted through course ratings, faculty may be deterred from engaging in such behaviors. Thus, course ratings may function as a mechanism of deterrence of teaching misconduct. Moreover, some proscribed teaching behaviors may be detected directly through course ratings by students.

Sanctioning of Teaching Misconduct

Both Black (1976) and Zuckerman (1977, 1988) describe the sanctioning of research misconduct as informal and decentralized. However, no such assessment of the sanctioning of teaching misconduct has been made. It is unknown.

Given the unknown properties of this important mechanism of social control of teaching wrongdoing, the postulation of competing theoretical perspectives on this sanctioning process seems warranted. The description and prediction of unknown properties requires consideration of not a single framework, but rather competing theoretical perspectives. A single framework may lead to a misspecification and incomplete understanding of the nature of sanctions for teaching wrongdoing. The functionalist and power theories, which were described in Chapter 1, constitute the two competing perspectives on the sanctioning of teaching misconduct. The functionalist perspective predicts more formal sanctioning action, whereas power theory anticipates less formal sanctioning action for teaching wrongdoing.

Although official sanctioning agents play an important role in this facet of social control of teaching misconduct, the allocation of sanctions ultimately relies on individuals who personally experience misconduct to report incidents affecting them. Individuals who receive reports of misconduct but do not personally experience it may be inclined to take appropriate action, such as talking to or professionally boycotting the offending individual. Reporting the incident to an appropriate institutional officer or committee constitutes more formal action (Braxton and Bayer, 1996).

Official sanctioning agents have a range of actions of varying degrees of formality to apply to cases of teaching misconduct. The least formal of these actions is a response just short of inaction. Others range from warning the individual to terminating their academic employment.

The hypotheses derived from both the functionalist and power theory perspectives predict the actions of both official sanctioning agents and individuals who either personally experience or receive reports of alleged incidents of teaching wrongdoing.

The Functionalist Perspective

Goode (1969) contends that professions are obligated to make professional choices based on the needs and welfare of their clients. As indicated in Chapter 1, Goode terms this obligation the ideal of service. Because this service ideal makes a profession necessary to society (Abbott, 1983), high social status also accrues to professions.

Given that norms provide informal codes of conduct for professional behavior consistent with the ideal of service (Goode, 1957; Greenwood, 1957; Bucher and Strauss, 1961), the community of the profession allocates the highest rewards of prestige to those individuals who conform to the prescriptions of the normative structure and sanctions those individuals who deviate from them. The sanctioning of offenders is necessary to preserve the prestige, reputation, and autonomy of the community of the profession (Goode, 1957).

The failure to sanction offenders violates the lay public's trust in the community of the profession to safeguard the ideal of service to clients. Failure to sanction offenders also erodes the lay public's belief in the social necessity of the profession. As a consequence, the social status and reputation of the community of the profession is lowered, and professional autonomy is limited. These formulations suggest that the greater the harm done to the welfare of a client by an incident of professional malfeasance, the greater the formality of the actions taken by sanctioning agents of a profession. This hypothesis and its antecedent formulations can be extended to the community of the academic profession in general and to the sanctioning of teaching misconduct in particular.

Because students as individuals (Blau, 1973) or as groups of individuals (Schein, 1972) are the primary clients of teaching role performance, we posit that incidents of teaching misconduct pertinent to the welfare of students as clients will receive the most formal sanctions. Thus, sanctioning agents will mete out formal sanctions for teaching improprieties reflective of such inviolable norms as condescending negativism, inattentive planning, moral turpitude, particularistic grading, personal disregard, and uncommunicated course details. In contrast, those admonitory norms applicable to students as clients are likely to receive either no sanctions or sanctions of a highly informal nature because faculty voice less offense for such proscribed behavioral patterns than for inviolable norms. But the formality of sanctions taken for both inviolable and admonitory norms may be moderated by institutional type and academic discipline. To be specific, we hypothesize that less formal action is likely in research universities and more formal action is probable in the discipline of biology (and, by extension, other hard/life disciplines).

Moreover, such faculty misbehavior as the shunning of departmental responsibility and the role of college teaching may also evoke formal sanctions. Such incidents of uncooperative cynicism are likely to elicit formal sanctions if the prestige or reputation of the academic department or college or university is greatly harmed by such proscribed behaviors. Accordingly, we contend that such sanctions may be minimal in research-oriented universities and more severe in departments of hard/life disciplines. Teaching secrecy and undermining colleagues, two admonitory norms pertinent to relationships with colleagues, are likely to evoke little or no sanctioning action, with the possible exception of hard/life departments, where such action may be more formal.

Power Theory

Professions espouse codes of conduct for professional behavior to persuade the lay public that they are worthy of self-regulation and autonomy (Freidson, 1970a). Put differently, the ideal of service is used by professions to legitimize their demands for autonomy.

When faced with incidents of professional wrongdoing, rules of professional etiquette loom more important than formal or informal codes of conduct or normative prescriptions (Freidson, 1975). The rules of professional etiquette govern the relationships among colleagues. These rules ordain that colleagues should not be criticized in public or in private by another colleague and that the reputations and careers of colleagues should not be damaged (Freidson, 1975). Because professionals view themselves as members of a special and privileged occupational category, professions demand that colleagues be treated with respect, trust, and protection from lay interference (Dibble, 1973; Freidson, 1975).

Thus, most professional improprieties will evoke inaction or highly informal action by individuals who have personally experienced some wrongdoing and by official sanctioning agents. By extension, we hypothesize that faculty behaviors reflective of the admonitory normative configurations of advisement negligence, authoritarian classroom, inadequate communication, inconvenience avoidance, inadequate course design, instructional narrowness, and insufficient syllabus will elicit little or no action by sanctioning agents and individual faculty who have personally experienced or learned of such misbehavior by faculty colleagues. In contrast, we contend that such misbehavior as undermining colleagues will evoke more formal action given that this particular admonitory normative cluster parallels the rules of professional etiquette. To the extent that teaching secrecy exhibits a lack of respect for colleagues, behaviors reflective of this normative pattern will also elicit more formal action.

We also postulate that institutional type and academic discipline affect actions taken. We offer the following five hypotheses based on these formulations and the pattern of findings described in Chapters 5, 6, and 7:

- In contrast to other institutional settings, we hypothesize that inaction is more likely in research universities.
- With the exception of authoritarian classroom, some action of an informal nature is likely in biology and other hard/life fields. In contrast, in other academic disciplines, inaction is more probable.
- Academics with high intrainstitutional status are more disposed toward more formal action for inconvenience avoidance than academics with lower levels of intrainstitutional status.
- Faculty holding tenure are more inclined toward more formal action for inadequate course design than are untenured faculty.
- Women academic professionals take more formal action for inadequate communication than male academic professionals.

Blatant or severe occurrences of wrongdoing are, however, subjected to criteria professions use to mete out sanctions. These criteria fit two categories: functional and symbolic (Freidson, 1975). Functional criteria pertain to an evaluation of whether a sanctioning action will prevent future occurrences of misconduct, whereas symbolic criteria entail whether a sanctioning action will be embarrassing to the offending individual. The application of functional and symbolic criteria will lead to highly informal sanctions by professional sanctioning agents.

As indicated by the pattern of findings reported in Chapters 5 and 6, inviolable proscribed behaviors rouse strong disapproval from faculty. As a consequence, we posit that official sanctioning agents and individual faculty who personally know of these incidents will apply functional and symbolic criteria to decide the actions they will take. Consequently, we hypothesize that sanctions meted out for such faculty teaching misconduct as condescending negativism, inattentive planning, moral turpitude, particularistic grading, personal disregard, and uncommunicated course details will be highly informal. We also postulate that highly informal actions will occur in those situations where uncooperative cynicism is viewed as disrespectful of faculty colleagues.

We also contend that academic discipline, institutional type, and personal sources of control moderate the types of action taken. As a consequence, we offer the following four hypotheses:

- Sanctions taken will be more formal in biology and other hard/life fields than in the other three discipline categories represented in this study for all pertinent inviolable norms except inattentive planning and moral turpitude.
- With the exception of moral turpitude and particularistic grading, sanctions taken for the other five inviolable norms will be less formal in research-oriented universities than in the other four types of colleges and universities represented in this study.
- All else being equal (e.g., similar rank and tenure status, similar administrative experience and time in career, an absence of gender differences in proclivities for confrontational encounters), women academics will be prone toward more formal action for the improprieties associated with condescending negativism, personal disregard, and inadequate communication than male academics.
- Faculty with administrative experience will be more inclined toward more formal sanctions for misconduct involving personal disregard than faculty without administrative experience.

Concluding Thoughts

This chapter advances theoretical perspectives on the social control of teaching misconduct. Control theory was advanced as a possible explanation for why teaching misconduct occurs. Theoretical formulations and hypotheses requiring empirical treatment were also offered pertaining to the mechanisms of deterrence, detection, and sanctioning of teaching misconduct.

The normative structures for undergraduate college teaching described in Chapters 3 and 4 identify informal mechanisms of social control for teaching role performance. Abbott (1983) asserts, however, that most professions have formal codes of conduct. In the next chapter, we review various documents to determine whether more formalized statements of teaching proscriptions and prescriptions exist. We also seek to determine whether the seven inviolable and nine admonitory norms find expression in any of these existing formalized teaching prescriptions and proscriptions.

NINE

Prior Formalized Teaching
Prescriptions and Proscriptions

When we first embarked on developing the CTBI in the late 1980s, as noted in Chapter 2, there was a paucity of materials explicating specific expected teaching behaviors for college and university faculty. With the exception of specific ethical (and legal) treatment of sexual harassment there were virtually no codifications of teaching norms or delineations of expected teaching behaviors.

In the ensuing years, there has been a groundswell of attention to the quality of teaching in postsecondary institutions. One might assume, therefore, that there also may have been greater articulation and codification of normative standards for teaching, such as those identified in the preceding chapters. Hence, as we approach the end of the century—indeed, the end of the millennium—we turn again to searching for evidence for the more formal expression of the types of inviolable and admonitory norms and specific proscribed behaviors that we have found in our research.

For this purpose, we focus on a variety of materials, some very general, some specific to disciplines, some aimed at the individual institutional (or system) level, and some generated at the unit level within higher education institutions:

1. A selection of volumes that, from their titles, might be assumed to address ethical standards and appropriate behaviors of the teaching professoriate, beyond those volumes exclusively focusing on misconduct in the research enterprise.

2. A systematic content search of various policy documents and reports by the American Association of University Professors, the premier association in representing faculty members in both public and private institutions, two-year and senior institutions, both unionized and non-union.

3. A collection of codes of conduct of professional associations, some of which are for disciplines with the majority of their members employed in academia while others, although having members among

the professoriate, have members largely employed in the service sector, and still other associations which have a large proportion of their membership employed in industry and in research and development outside of academia.

4. A broad sampling of collective bargaining contracts for two-year institutions as well as for four-year institutions and for systems.

Finally, there are numerous documents for individual institutions and internal departments that address standards of teaching performance and behavior. These standards might, for example, be applied annually in the salary or performance review process; for decisions regarding promotions in academic rank; and, where tenure systems exist, for awarding tenure. Recently, many institutions have developed standards and procedures for post-tenure review, and these documents might also contain specific teaching-related expectations. Two different sets of such relevant documents are reviewed here:

5. A collection of various forms used for student evaluations of individual classes and instructors from a variety of colleges and universities.
6. A complete collection of documents, written at the departmental and college levels, for one large eastern public university that was mandated by its state legislature in 1997 to develop post-tenure review criteria and procedures.

Books on the Professoriate, Teaching, and Professional Ethics

The volumes that make up the "classics" of the early sociological study of the professoriate gave scant attention to the teaching role and virtually no attention to proper decorum in performing the duties of teaching. Logan Wilson's *The Academic Man* (1942) was the first major sociological work devoted exclusively to higher education faculty as a profession. As a forerunner of a huge outpouring of volumes on the professoriate in the ensuing decades, it would appear to set a standard to address the academic profession in broad fashion while focusing little on the primary role of teaching that is ascribed to the vast majority of those in the profession. Even in Wilson's sequel, *American Academics Then and Now* (1979), written at the end of his career, the focus is on the origins, scholarship, status, and prestige of academics. He only briefly considers professional ethics, largely by quoting passages (pp. 150–55) from statements issued by the Association of American Universities and the American Association of University Professors, little of which addresses the professor-student relationship. Indeed, Wilson continues by noting the work of other scholars and claiming that it is "unfavorable to discuss moral questions" and that "there is nowhere a definitive statement of the standards to be observed and enforced in the academic profession" (p. 155).[1]

In the intervening years between Wilson's two books, other volumes written by sociologists and destined to be classics on the academy and the professoriate appeared. These include Jencks and Riesman's *The Academic Revolution* (1969) and Blau's *The Organization of Academic Work* (1973). But, like Wilson's work, virtually nothing is said about the roles and responsibilities of college and university faculty members vis-à-vis their students. Indeed, in the concluding pages of the work of Jencks and Riesman, there is a suggestion of why this oversight tends to pervade the work of this period: "there is no guild within which successful teaching leads to greater prestige and influence than mediocre teaching, nor any professional training program that develops pedagogic skills in a systematic way" (p. 531).

Recent General Works

If we turn from these older classics to more recent general works on the professoriate, do we find that there has been any substantial shift in focus and concomitant increase in addressing teaching ethics and classroom decorum by faculty? The answer is a qualified "no." Fairweather's (1996) volume on faculty work, focusing on teaching and service, totally avoids the question of good pedagogy and inappropriate professional behavior. In their volume titled *Faculty at Work*, Blackburn and Lawrence (1995) devote but a single chapter to teaching behavior. In part, this may be because their research shows that only those faculty members in community colleges regularly read books and articles about teaching (p. 185) and, in general, "faculty cannot obtain consensus on what constitutes high quality teaching" (p. 177). Nevertheless, they are among the first to introduce the notion of a prevailing normative structure among the professoriate: they claim that their volume's theoretical framework "includes faculty members' understanding of how others expect them to behave (subjective norms) and their beliefs about others in the environment, individuals with whom they interact and on whom they may depend" (p. 17).

With this minor and undeveloped exception, the lack of explicit attention to norms in postsecondary teaching in general volumes on the professoriate may be explained in part by the recent conclusions posed by

---

1. In an endnote to these passages, Wilson (p. 292) notes that this does not, however, apply to addressing proper and improper behavior in the conduct of scientific research.

Lionel Lewis (1996). He contends that there is a continuous glut in the academic labor market of those who can teach. Thus the rewards for teaching are minimal, and there is little impetus to scrutinize teaching behavior because of the limitless supply of college and university teachers and the prevailing attitude that virtually all are considered adequate, and most are characterized as above average (the Lake Woebegone effect).

Another possible explanation for this oversight is that academics tend to view most classroom improprieties and misconduct as emanating from their students rather than themselves and their colleagues. Indeed, only recently has the prevalence of faculty misconduct been empirically documented. This is now illustrated by the recent work of Boice (1996), who reports on his research on classroom incivilities in postsecondary institutions. He notes that virtually all studies of incivility have focused on students' actions and assume that teachers are not guilty of incivility although his research clearly demonstrates that faculty members are the most crucial initiators.

While general volumes on the professoriate—both classic and contemporary—provide meager attention to appropriate teaching behavior, there is a second body of literature that comes closer to doing so. These are the large number of contemporary reports and commission studies addressing the issue of improving undergraduate education. In fact, many of these publications come to a remarkable consensus concerning the initiatives that might be implemented to enhance the undergraduate student's academic experience. For example, it is not difficult to find recommendations that have encouraged more interaction between students and faculty both in and out of class, called for faculty members to provide students with more feedback on assignments, or urged faculty to employ multiple modes of evaluating student performance. Other reports have suggested that undergraduates deserve systematic advising, that faculty members need to cultivate more learning experiences outside the classroom, and that, in general, administrators and faculty members should continually strive to improve undergraduate education within their institutions.

We have reviewed these many reports elsewhere (Braxton, Eimers, and Bayer, 1996), but we have found that few of even these general recommendations enjoy consensus by faculty. Normative support for broad general statements of teaching improvements as advocated by national consortiums, commissions, panels, and individual scholars is weak among the professoriate.

In an effort to uncover more specific prescriptive (or proscriptive) statements of proper teaching decorum, we now turn to two other bodies of literature. The first focuses on contemporary volumes whose titles expressly suggest a focus on the *ethics* in teaching for the professoriate. A second set of volumes are explored that may be characterized as how-to-do-it *handbooks* for college and university teachers.

Books on Ethics in College Teaching

The neglect of strong statements on proper decorum by college and university faculty in their teaching role stands in sharp contrast to the clear behavioral guidelines applicable to elementary and secondary teachers. For example, Strike and Soltis, in *The Ethics of Teaching* (1992), address a series of "shall . . ." and "shall not . . ." statements promulgated by the National Education Association for school teachers. No comparable clear statements of prescriptive and proscriptive faculty behavior in relation to students exists for postsecondary educators.

The paucity of attention to teaching malfeasance at the postsecondary level is also particularly notable in light of the widespread attention over the past decade to research misconduct in academe, for example, the literature review, analysis, and discussion on research misconduct in the special issue of the *Journal of Higher Education* (Braxton, 1994). This is not to say, however, that ethics beyond conduct in the research role has been totally neglected. Indeed, another, earlier, special issue of the *Journal of Higher Education,* titled "Ethics and the Academic Profession" appeared in the early 1980s (Dill, 1982). But no empirical studies are presented and almost all of the articles in this special issue address the teaching of ethics or debate the desirability and feasibility of a code of ethics for academics. The exception is an essay by Scriven (1982), which, although not research-based, addresses in particular ethical malfeasance concerning testing and the evaluation of college student performance.

Other works of this period, particularly that of Rich (1984) and Shils (1984), mark a beginning of a spate of volumes addressing ethics in academia, including ethics in the teaching role. This section briefly overviews a cross-section of these books, approaching them in approximate chronological order.

Beginning in 1984, the volumes at this time can be characterized as taking a cautious approach and selective delineation of faculty behaviors that could be viewed as inappropriate. Few of the inviolable and admonitory normative behaviors that are identified in the preceding chapters are mentioned. Indeed, Shil's *The Academic Ethic* (1984) is careful to take delicate stances on the infrequent occasions when teaching-related improprieties are addressed. For example, unfairness and arbitrariness in the assessment of students' academic performance is characterized as "carelessness," and teachers are advised to *attempt* to avoid discrimination in favor or against some students (pp. 48–49). Only in regard to sexual relationships between teachers and students is avoidance strongly advocated; and in part this stricter stance is rationalized because of its potential harm to the reputation of the educational institution where it happens.

Likewise, Rich's *Professional Ethics in Education* (1984) deals little with ethics in college teaching, instead focusing on academic freedom, professional association codes of conduct, and the ethics of research. One exception is again with regard to testing and evaluating students, and again a "soft" stance is articulated: "failure to develop a system of evaluation reflects more upon competence than ethics" (p. 67). While a few other grievous acts related to the teaching role are summarily listed—including sexual advances toward students, using vulgar and obscene language with students, and excessive drinking—Rich strains to avoid outright condemnation and in fact concludes that while such acts may set a bad example for students they do not likely impair teaching effectiveness (p. 124).

A decade later (1994), books on professional ethics in the teaching role of academics address a wider range of improprieties and advocate stronger statements regarding their severity (Cahn 1994; Markie, 1994; Whicker and Kronenfeld, 1994). While again, these works are not predicated on empirical research, they are closer than their predecessor volumes from a decade earlier in advocating clear prescriptive and proscriptive behaviors appropriate to the professoriate.

Of these three volumes on professional ethics, all published in the same year, only Whicker and Kronenfeld (1994) are tentative and cautious on many matters of improprieties by college and university faculty members. They take a firm proscriptive stance in regard to normative violations in the research domain and on sexual harassment. But other ethical concerns, including student-related issues, are classified as "fuzzy" ethical norms of behavior (Chapter 6). Other than sexual harassment, clear teaching-related improprieties—incompetence, neglect of duty, and insubordination—are addressed in a mere five pages of the book (Whicker and Kronenfeld, 1994, pp. 115–19). The authors provide discussion of guidelines and pitfalls for the academic administrator who must deal with ethical breaches. No doubt, such administrative dilemmas are far more prevalent in dealing with the teaching role than with the research role, yet little in this volume assists the administrator in addressing improprieties in teaching.

In contrast, Cahn (1994) condemns a broad range of behaviors covered in the CTBI—not preparing a syllabus or planning for the first day of class, habitually arriving late to class, missing class, being unavailable outside of class, returning exams and papers in untimely manner, grading on non-universalistic standards, demonstrating ideological zeal, developing close friendships or romantic relationships with students. Moreover, his condemnation is couched in terms firmer than those in discussions a decade earlier. He labels these varieties of acts as "despicable," "egregious," "inexcusable," and "entirely inappropriate," and he clearly prescribes behaviors with "ought" and "should" statements.

Similarly, Markie, in *Professor's Duties: Ethical Issues in College Teaching* (1994), sets out to "provide an initial map of the content and source of some of our obligations in teaching." In page after page he uses the term "obligation" in discussing behaviors of faculty. He is definitive in his judgment, labeling acts unequivocally as "violations of duty," "unethical," or "clearly wrong."

Finally, Fisch (1996) brings us an additional step closer to the objectives we seek in this present work. In David Smith's contribution (Chapter 1) to this edited work, he explicates four *norms* in the college teacher-student relationship: honesty, promise-keeping, respect for other persons, and fairness. Subsequently, three other contributors address principles and responsibilities of the professoriate. Clark Kerr (Chapter 7) lists fifteen components of "academic ethics" that pertain to teaching. Harry Murray and his associates (Chapter 8) offer nine "ethical principles" for college and university teaching. Finally, Charles Reynolds (Chapter 9) posits twenty-seven "academic principles of responsibility."

While our research design and data collection for our present endeavor predates this volume by Fisch and contributors, they perfectly set the stage for our work. They squarely frame their work as an exercise in delineating the *normative system* in academic teaching and in enumerating its components. In that sense, Fisch's (1996) edited work may be viewed as a quasi-precursor to our analysis and codification, now predicated on quantitative research and analysis.

Handbooks on College Teaching

When one turns to guidebooks and handbooks that address the craft of college teaching, the content closely parallels the volumes on ethics in collegiate teaching. There is little discussion of behavioral improprieties and less condemnation of any actions.

Books of this genre, from the mid-1980s into the 1990s, focus largely on classroom mechanics and pedagogical technique (Gullette, 1984; Deneef, Goodwin, and McCrate, 1988; Eble, 1988; Brookfield, 1991; Prichard and Sawyer, 1994). They deal primarily with such matters as teaching techniques and methods; improving lecture approaches; tips on improving student writing assignments and skills; methods to cultivate critical thinking by students; how to design tests and grade papers; and discussion of how to handle troublesome students and the problems of cheating and plagiarism.

This is not to say that some of the items of behavior we have delineated as part of the clusters of derived norms are totally absent; a few are mentioned. Gullette's volume (1984) mentions the need to provide a syllabus on the opening day of class (pp. 10–11) and that "a teacher must avoid even the appearance of having favorites, flirtations, or special access" (p. 81). Deneef, Goodwin, and McCrate (1988) stress that students should be informed of grading standards at the outset of the course (p. 137). Eble (1988) emphasizes keeping regular office hours and always giving prompt feedback on tests, *if possible* (our emphasis; p. 151).

As remarkable as the sparseness of comments on faculty personal behavior is the rarity of any strong evaluative statements regarding improper behavior by the professoriate. Deneef, Goodwin, and McCrate's volume (1988) notes only that there may be one "unforgivable sin"—the lack of organization of one's lectures. But even this evaluative comment is disassociated from colleague opinion and assigned to the student: "if there is an unforgivable sin in the eyes of students, it is the lack of organization" (p. 133). Indeed, within this entire set of volumes, we found only a single behavioral instance by faculty members that was expressly labeled as "unethical," and it is in reference to faculty members selling their free desk copies of textbooks to used book dealers (Eble, 1988, p. 131).

As a final approach to tracing the evolution of focus on faculty misconduct in books on college teaching, we select two sets of multiple-edition handbooks on college teaching. It is presumed that these handbooks, by virtue of their being reissued a number of times, are among the most widely adopted and used books on pedagogical advice for postsecondary teachers. We briefly analyze the content of these editions with particular focus on determining an evolving emphasis over time on normative proscriptions and prescriptions.

The first of these sets is *A Handbook for Teachers in Universities and Colleges,* by David Newble and Robert Cannon, with a first edition in 1989 and the most recent, third edition, appearing in 1995. A most remarkable aspect of these volumes is the virtual lack of any change in substantive content. Indeed, the table of contents and subheads—and even pagination—is virtually identical between the first and the third edition. Prescriptive comments are infrequent and general, and evaluations of poor actions are "soft" (and identical in each edition). Readers are advised, for example, to be constructive and helpful in criticism of students (1995, p. 2), to have a positive attitude and be friendly and available to students (1995, p. 58), and the instructor "*should consider*" (our emphasis) selecting course content that at least acknowledges women's contributions and avoids sexist language (1995, pp. 74–75).

The other multiple edition popular reader is Wilbert McKeachie's *Teaching Tips: A Guidebook for the Beginning College Teacher,* now in its ninth edition. Content analysis shows more significant revision over time and at least marginal improvement in introducing behavior norms related to the college teaching role. Indeed, the seventh edition (1978) included no discussion of teaching ethics. The eighth edition (1986) for the first time introduces a chapter titled "Ethical Standards in Teaching," a mere two and one-half pages of five paragraphs quoting sections of the code of ethics of the American Psychological Association and one paragraph defining sexual harassment.

Finally, in the ninth edition (1994), there is a nine-page chapter titled "Ethics in College Teaching," which begins to address a broader range of unethical teaching behaviors and provides guidelines for evaluating the ethicality of one's actions in regard to the teaching role. This chapter notes "that the ethical decisions in teaching are difficult to learn because they are not generally in the public view" (p. 270). Numerous examples of "violations of standards" are then provided:

- failing adequate class preparation;
- insisting on students adopting the instructor's values and philosophies, that is, indoctrination;
- ridiculing a student;
- disclosing confidential information regarding a student;
- failing to adopt a fair system of evaluating students;
- exploiting, harassing, or discriminating against particular students;
- adopting an inadequate textbook because of publishers' "incentives";
- ignoring the inadequate teaching of colleagues

While this list of examples is relatively short and incomplete, McKeachie's ninth edition (1994) of *Teaching Tips* clearly comes closer than the other volumes we reviewed to addressing the variety of component behaviors making up the inviolable and admonitory norms for teaching that we have previously introduced.

Pertinent Documents of the American Association of University Professors

The American Association of University Professors (AAUP) is the nation's most prominent umbrella organization for the professoriate. Its mission is as follows:

> The basic purposes of the American Association of University Professors are to protect academic freedom, to establish and strengthen institutions of faculty governance, to provide fair procedures for resolving grievances, to promote the economic well-being of faculty and other academic professionals, and to advance the interests of higher education. (AAUP, 1990, p. 145)

This mission statement does not explicitly claim that the AAUP exists in part to assure or foster high standards of behavior and performance by faculty members in their teaching role. But it is implicit and, indeed, the association has addressed some teaching norms, or standards of behavior by faculty members, over the years.

Nevertheless, the so-called AAUP Red Book (AAUP, 1990), containing policy documents and the major reports endorsed by the association, discloses relatively scant attention to teaching roles and responsibilities. Rather, the published endorsed statements and policies focus most on protection of faculty rights and academic freedom—an historical mission of AAUP even before it also assumed the role of a collective bargaining agent at various educational institutions and systems. Thus, the AAUP policy and position statements catalogued in the Red Book address such matters as protocol for faculty dismissal proceedings, standards for non-renewal of appointments, arbitration for grievances, tenure procedures, faculty workload policy, fringe benefit policies, affirmative action recommendations, and issues in the role of faculty in governance at American colleges and universities.

There are three documents, however, that expressly specify the role and responsibilities of teaching faculty vis-à-vis their undergraduate students. One of these is the brief two-page AAUP "Statement of Professional Ethics," one paragraph of which addresses responsible behavior in the teaching domain. The full passage follows:

> As teachers, professors encourage the free pursuit of learning in their students. They hold before them the best scholarly and ethical standards of their discipline. Professors demonstrate respect for students as individuals and adhere to their proper roles as intellectual guides and counselors. Professors make every reasonable effort to foster honest academic conduct and to ensure that their

evaluations of students reflect each student's true merit. They respect the confidential nature of the relationship between professor and student. They avoid any exploitation, harassment, or discriminatory treatment of students. They acknowledge significant academic or scholarly assistance from them. They protect their academic freedom. (AAUP, 1990, p. 76)

An additional document, "Sexual Harassment: Suggested Policy and Procedures for Handling Complaints," further clarifies the harassment prohibition in the preceding statement. It says:

> The Association reiterates the ethical responsibility of faculty members to avoid "any exploitation of students for . . . private advantage." The applicability of this general norm to a faculty member's use of institutional position to seek unwanted sexual relations with students (or anyone else vulnerable to the faculty member's authority) is clear. (AAUP, 1990, p. 113)

Among all of these documents and statements of principles, the only other definitive statement pertaining to proscriptive and prescriptive behaviors of faculty members in reference to their students is in the Association's "Statement on Freedom and Responsibility." This document advises:

> Students are entitled to an atmosphere conducive to learning and to even-handed treatment in all aspects of the teacher-student relationship. Faculty members may not refuse to enroll or teach students on the grounds of their beliefs or the possible uses to which they may put the knowledge to be gained in a course. Students should not be forced by the authority inherent in the instructional role to make particular personal choices as to political action or their own part in society. Evaluation of students and the award of credit must be based on academic performance professionally judged and not on matters irrelevant to that performance, whether personality, race, religion, degree of political activism, or personal beliefs.
>
> It is the mastery teachers have of their subjects and their own scholarship that entitles them to their classrooms and to freedom in the presentation of their subjects. Thus, it is improper for an instructor persistently to intrude material that has no relation to the subject, or to fail to present the subject matter of the course as announced to the students and as approved by the faculty in their collective responsibility for the curriculum. (AAUP, 1990, pp. 77–78)

In conclusion, the nationally prominent American Association of University Professors addresses some key professorial behaviors as regards students, but in contrast to our research findings of a broad range of abhorrent behaviors in the teaching role, the AAUP addresses a relatively narrow spectrum of behaviors. In the next section, we analyze a range of other association "codes of conduct" to determine if those organizations further expand on the types of teaching-related behaviors considered by the AAUP.

Disciplinary Associations' Codes of Conduct

Many disciplinary associations—but by no means all—have promulgated professional codes of conduct. Indeed, one might expect codes of conduct to be fairly common among professional associations, inasmuch as "one of the distinguishing marks of a profession is a code of ethics that is defensible and properly enforced" (Rich, 1984, p. 3) although they might not usually be expected to provide an explication and detail of proper decorum. As Wagner (1996) notes:

> Professional codes of ethics do not provide a set of "do's and don'ts" for every possible situation. The point of a code of ethics is not to tell the professional what to do in each and every instance, but to draw his or her attention generally to the most important moral considerations. (P. 10)

Additionally, many associations, while having members from academe, have a preponderance of their members from other sectors. To the degree that large proportions of members are not engaged in teaching roles, it is not entirely surprising that some codes of conduct, if they exist at all, are silent as regards appropriate performance and behavior in one's role as a collegiate teacher.

Indeed, professional association codes of conduct likely developed early for those fields and disciplines that were more engaged in the human services professions; e.g., counseling psychology, child and family therapy, and social work. More recently, formulation of codes of conduct by disciplinary associations was given impetus by the burgeoning publicity over misconduct in research and scholarship, both outside and within academe.

Hence, we may expect *relatively* scant attention to the teaching role in existing codes of conduct. In this section, we survey a broad representation of codes of conduct to ascertain the degree to which teaching is addressed, and the types of behaviors covered when it is addressed.

For this analysis, we draw upon the set of professional association documents gathered by Stephanie Bird and her associates for the Council of Scientific Society Presidents Ethics in Science Committee (Jorgensen, 1995). In that study, information was received from 62 organizations, of which 36 had written ethics policies. These documents provide the sources for the information reported here.[2]

Remarkably few of these codes of ethics/codes of conduct (or documents with similar titles) contain any policy statements whatsoever as regards improprieties in teaching. In contrast, more than one-half of the ethics policies address matters of authorship, conflict of interest, and responsibilities to society (Jorgensen, 1995). Indeed, the topic of humane treatment of animals was addressed more frequently (26 percent of documents) than is the treatment of one's students!

Physical and Biological Sciences

Among those professional organizations in the agricultural, mathematical, engineering, physical, and biological sciences that have codes of conduct, one distinguishing characteristic is their brevity. Most are simply one-page documents. A second distinguishing characteristic is that few even mention students, and if they do it is only in a single broad statement (except the National Association of Biology Teachers—see discussion later in this section). These are:

- "Members . . . have responsibilities to promote high standards in the education and training of students and post-doctoral associates" (American Society of Limnology and Oceanography).
- "As a chemist, I have a responsibility to my students and associates to be a fellow learner with them, to strive for clarity and directness of approach, to exhibit patience and encouragement, and to lose no opportunity for stimulating them to carry on the great tradition" ("The Chemist's Creed," American Chemical Society).
- "Members . . . will be honest and impartial in their interactions with the public, their employers, their clients, patients in whose diagnosis and treatment they are involved, their colleagues, their students, and their employees" (American Society for Microbiology).

Two other professional associations in agriculture mention students (American Society of Agronomy, Crop Science Society of America). Both are identical single-page "Statement of Ethics" and refer to students only as regards conveying their code: "As mentors of the next generation of scientific and professional leaders, [members shall] strive to instill these ethical standards in students at all educational levels."

2. We are indebted to Stephanie Bird, past president of the Association for Women in Science, for providing us with this set of collected documents.

As we note in Chapter 6, our research results show that academic biologists generally tend to show stronger sentiment regarding the normative patterns we derive than do those in the other disciplines we studied. Hence we devote some particular attention to the numerous biological science associations included in Stephanie Bird's survey to determine if this difference among academic disciplines is reflected in the content of codes of conduct. Professional associations in the biological sciences appear no more likely to have such codes, or to address faculty-student relations if there are codes, than do associations in other physical and mathematical sciences. Indeed, the primary umbrella organization, the American Institute of Biological Sciences does not have a statement of ethical guidelines or codes. On the other hand, the National Association of Biology Teachers stands out as having one of the most extensive statements regarding students among all codes of ethics. The "student-directed" section of that code follows:

1. In providing services, members shall avoid action that will injure or violate the rights of students.

2. Members should not discriminate against students on the basis of race, color, religion, age, sex, physical disability or national ancestry.

3. Members shall protect students from the misuse of information collected about them.

4. Members shall respect the privacy of their students.

5. Members shall provide clear and precise statements of performance expectations in catalogs, course syllabi and graduation requirements.

6. As teachers, members should sensitize students to the rights of research subjects.

7. Members should present information fully, accurately and objectively.

8. Members should provide timely and accurate evaluations of a student's performance.

9. Members shall encourage students to attain their highest performance and ambitions through appropriate counseling about career and educational opportunities.

10. Exploitation of students is unacceptable under any circumstances.

11. Members should encourage and assist students in the free pursuit of learning.

Behavioral and Social Sciences

In sharp contrast to the conciseness of most of the ethical codes described above, representative professional associations in the behavioral and social sciences have adopted much longer and more detailed codes of conduct. They also address the responsibilities of collegiate teachers in greater degree.

Illustrative is the 28-page American Psychological Associations's document titled "Ethical Principles of Psychologists and Code of Conduct." Excerpts of statements pertaining to the teaching role follow:

- Psychologists who are responsible for education and training programs seek to ensure that the programs are competently designed, provide the proper experiences, and meet the requirements for licensure, certification or other goals for which claims are made by the program.
- Psychologists responsible for education and training programs seek to ensure that there is a current and accurate description of the program content, training goals and objectives, and requirements that must be met for satisfactory completion of the program. This information must be made readily available to all interested parties.
- Psychologists seek to ensure that statements concerning their course outlines are accurate and not misleading, particularly regarding the subject matter to be covered, bases for the evaluating process, and the nature of course experiences.
- When engaged in teaching or training, psychologists present psychological information accurately and with a reasonable degree of objectivity.
- When engaged in teaching or training, psychologists recognize the power they hold over students or supervisees and therefore make reasonable efforts to avoid engaging in conduct that is personally demeaning to students or supervisees.
- In academic and supervisory relationships, psychologists establish an appropriate process for providing feedback to students and supervisees.
- Psychologists evaluate students and supervisees on the basis of their actual performance on relevant and established program requirements.
- Psychologists do not exploit persons over whom they have supervisory, evaluative, or other authority such as students. . . .
- Psychologists do not engage in sexual relationships with students or supervisees in training over whom the psychologist has evaluative or direct authority, because such relationships are so likely to impair judgment or be exploitative.
- Psychologists provide services, teach, and conduct research only within the boundaries of their competence, based on their education, training, supervised experience, or appropriate professional experience.
- Psychologists provide services, teach, and conduct research in new areas or involving new techniques only after first undertaking appropriate study, training, supervision, and/or consultation from persons who are competent in those areas or techniques.

- Psychologists do not knowingly engage in behavior that is harassing or demeaning to persons with whom they interact in their work based on factors such as those persons' age, gender, race, ethnicity, national origin, religion, sexual orientation, disability, language, or socioeconomic status.
- Psychologists recognize that their personal problems and conflicts may interfere with their effectiveness. Accordingly, they refrain from undertaking an activity when they know or should know that their personal problems are likely to lead to harm to a patient, client, colleague, student, research participant, or other person to whom they may owe a professional or scientific obligation.

The American Sociological Association's "Code of Ethics" expressly adopts some of the content of the American Psychological Association code. Primary pertinent statements as regards the teaching role in the document follow:

- Sociologists conscientiously perform their teaching responsibilities. They have appropriate skills and knowledge or are receiving the appropriate training.
- Sociologists provide accurate information at the outset about their courses, particularly regarding the subject matter to be covered, bases for evaluation, and the nature of course experiences.
- Sociologists make decisions concerning textbooks, course content, course requirements, and grading solely on the basis of educational criteria without regard for financial or other incentives.
- Sociologists provide proper training and supervision to their teaching assistants and other teaching trainees and take reasonable steps to see that such persons perform these teaching responsibilities responsibly, competently, and ethically.
- Sociologists do not permit personal animosities or intellectual differences with colleagues to foreclose students' or supervisees' access to these colleagues or to interfere with student or supervisee learning, academic progress, or professional development.
- Sociologists respect the rights, dignity, and worth of all people. They strive to eliminate bias in their professional activities, and they do not tolerate any forms of discrimination based on age; gender; race; ethnicity; national origin; religion; sexual orientation; disability; health conditions; or marital, domestic, or parental status.
- Sociologists, to the extent possible, protect the confidentiality of student records, performance data, and personal information, whether verbal or written, given in the context of academic consultation, supervision, or advising.
- When undertaking research at their own institutions with human subjects who are students or subordinates, sociologists take special care to protect the

prospective subjects from adverse consequences of declining or withdrawing from participation.

▪ Sociologists do not seek or coerce personal, economic, or professional advantages from persons over whom they have supervisory, evaluative, or other authority such as students, supervisees, employees, or human subjects.

▪ Sociologists do not engage in sexual relationships with persons over whom they have supervisory, evaluative, or other authority such as students, supervisees, employees, or human subjects.

▪ Sociologists do not engage in sexual harassment of any person, including students, supervisees, employees, or human subjects.

An Independent Assessment of Association Codes of Conduct

Rupert and Holmes (1997) sought to analyze professional associations' codes of conduct to ascertain the degree to which they address the in-class and outside of classroom "dual relationship," that is, the interaction between the professor and the student. They contacted 59 professional associations, and of these, 23 (39 percent) indicated that they did not have written guidelines regarding faculty roles.

Of the 36 organizations providing documents, only 20 (56 percent) addressed teaching responsibilities in any manner, and only 7 (19 percent) contained statements expressly related to the faculty-student relationship. Among these, the focus was generally confined to either sexual or financial exploitation in the faculty-student relationship. Moreover, most of those organizations that had at least addressed these issues were human services and mental health associations. Consistent with the preceding findings based on the compilation of similar documents collected by Stephanie Bird, professional associations in the physical, mathematical, and biological sciences almost uniformly fail to address and proscribe conduct in the teaching role, and few other professional associations in other fields and disciplines do so either. The prospect for change in this regard in the future appears dim: Stanley Katz, president of the American Council of Learned Societies, which is composed of 58 professional societies and organizations, stated in his keynote address to the Association for the Study of Higher Education (1995):

The learned societies have heretofore exercised almost no influence over the course of education policy, and the prospects for an increase in their influence are poor. The reasons for this situation have to do both with, on the one hand, the lack of concern the societies have shown in educational policy and, on the other, the inability of scholars as faculty to exercise influence even on their own campuses, much less nationally.

Collective Bargaining Contracts

We next turn to a content analysis of selected current higher education collective bargaining contracts. For this analysis we started with the full-text contract database compiled by the National Education Association as the Higher Education Contract Analysis System (HECAS).[3]

This database includes 503 higher education collective bargaining contracts, of which 356 are faculty collective bargaining contracts (National Education Association, 1996). From these, we selected those contracts for perusal that most frequently contained keywords pertaining to teaching and teachers or to class and classrooms or to students, using standard Boolean electronic search logic. An additional selection criterion was whether the contract was for (1) faculty in a community college or community college district, or (2) faculty in a four-year college or university, or state system. From each of these two groups, we selected the 25 contracts that most frequently contained the keywords in our document search (more than 450 "hits" per document and as many as 1,735). The results of searching for prescriptive and proscriptive statements regarding the faculty teaching role in the 50 documents is described below.

The vast majority of these collective bargaining contracts contain general articles of almost routine content: classifications of faculty (often involving librarians) and collective bargaining unit membership inclusions and exclusions; workload statements; promotion, tenure, and retirement procedures; sabbatical and leave policies; grievance and disciplinary proceedings; fringe benefit and compensation procedures; permissible contents in faculty personnel files; and guidelines for layoffs and reductions in staff. Many also contain articles addressing union dues provisions, sexual harassment, and summer appointments.

Also frequently included is a statement on academic freedom and, occasionally, reference to a professional code of ethics. If these codes of ethics define a source, it is typically the AAUP (which, as stated above, is

---

3. We are indebted to Gary D. Rhoades, University of Arizona, for informing us of the availability and utility of this database; and to Christine Maitland, National Education Association, for arranging the release of the Higher Education Contract Analysis System (HECAS) database to us. Rhoades (1998) has employed the HECAS database for intensive analyses of collective bargaining contracts. But his detailed study did not include analysis on the contract components on teaching that we address here.

quite brief and limited as regards specific teaching-related conduct). Illustrative examples are:

- "The faculty adopts the statement on Ethics from the American Association of University Professors ... and shall encourage all faculty to adhere to the statements contained therein" (Article 17, Oakland Community College, Michigan).
- "The college subscribes to the 1940 'Statement on Academic Freedom and Tenure' issued by the American Association of University Professors and the Association of American Colleges as endorsed by the American Association of Colleges for Teacher Education, the Association for Higher Education, the National Education Association, and other professional groups" (Article 6, Clark College, Washington).
- "Although no set of rules or professional code can either guarantee or take the place of a scholar's personal integrity, Regis University believes that the 'Statement of Professional Ethics' promulgated by the American Association of University Professors may serve as a reminder of the variety of obligations assumed by all members of the academic profession" (Article 12, Regis University, Colorado).

Beyond these allusions to a document that in part addresses responsibilities of faculty members in the teaching role, a remarkable number of these collective bargaining contracts also address other aspects of teaching, although these are quite circumscribed. Indeed, they are largely devoted to:

1. Required administration of forms for student evaluation of teaching (together with a consistent caveat that they should not be the sole source of evaluating teaching performance and often prescribing administrator and peer evaluation as well). Some examples are:

   ▪ "The evaluation will be structured ... to ... include evaluations by the immediate supervisor, the faculty member's students and any other sources agreed upon by the faculty and immediate supervisor" (Article 26, Cuyahoga Community College District, Ohio).
   ▪ "Members of the bargaining unit shall be evaluated by students every winter quarter in all classes they teach" (Article 11, Youngstown State University, Ohio).
   ▪ "Student evaluations ... shall be conducted in each class taught by a unit faculty member in at least one semester of each academic year" (Article 18, Western Michigan University).

- "The Department Chair shall annually obtain student evaluations of the classroom effectiveness and of the courses taught by each member of the faculty" (Article 8, Massachusetts Higher Education Coordinating Council).
- "Mandatory student evaluations, using the official student evaluation instruments and procedures, delineated herein, will be completed by two classes each year for tenured faculty, and by two classes each semester by probationary faculty. . . . Student evaluations also never may be used as the sole justification for a decision in summative evaluation" (Article 15, San Diego Community College District, California).

2. A required course syllabus, generally including some specification of its contents and its timely availability. Some examples are:

- "A syllabus will be developed for each course taught at the College. The division chairperson will take the responsibility to see this task is completed. . . . The course syllabus must be prepared and filed with the Vice President for Instruction two weeks prior to the starting date of the course. . . . Each course syllabus shall include: (a) the learning objectives for the course . . ., (b) the instructional procedure, including the types of assignments to be made, (c) the types of evaluation and the marking system the instructor plans to use for that course" (Article 4, Green River Community College, Washington).
- "Faculty shall provide a syllabus to students and to the administration . . . by the end of the first week of class" (Article 4, Dowling College, New York).
- "Each faculty member shall develop a syllabus and distribute it to students. . . . The syllabus shall include the following: course title, course prefix, credit hours, instructor name, instructor office hours and location, telephone number, course meeting time, course description, textbook requirements, grading/examination system, attendance policy, instructional methodologies" (Article 8, Hillsborough Community College District, Florida).

3. Required office hours and availability for advising. Illustrative are:

- "Each faculty member teaching a full load shall schedule and keep a minimum of 6 scheduled office hours each week" (Article 8, Lincoln Land Community College District, Illinois).
- "Each faculty member shall post and maintain five office hours per week which must be a minimum of thirty consecutive minutes in du-

ration over a period of not less than four days" (Article 8, Hillsborough Community College District, Florida).

- "A faculty member is expected to be available on a regular basis to advise students who have been assigned to him [sic] as advisee or who seek him out for academic counseling" (Article 4, Dowling College, New York).

Other matters relating to teaching behavior and practices are rarely addressed in collective bargaining documents. However, a few speak to deviating sharply from specific course content:

- "The teacher is entitled to freedom in the classroom in discussing the subject, but he/she should be careful not to introduce into his/her teaching controversial matter which has no relation to his/her subject" (Chapter I, Eastern Washington University).
- "The faculty member may not . . . claim as his/her right the privilege of persistently discussing in the classroom any matter which has no relation to the course subject" (Article 20, Minnesota State Colleges and Universities).

A few expressly prohibit selling materials to students:

- "The private sale of instructional materials by faculty members is not permitted" (Article 12, Regis University, Colorado).
- "A faculty member creates a potential conflict of interest when he or she profits financially from a course requirement that students buy either materials or a book he or she has written, assembled, or edited" (Article 12, Montana University System).

Of the documents examined, only a few extend the prescription of teaching performance and responsibility beyond those domains described above. Two that provide some extension are quoted below:

- "The performance of instructional responsibilities extends beyond duties in the classroom and includes such activities as: preparation for class, evaluation of student performance, syllabus preparation and revision, and review of current literature and research in the subject area, including instructional methodology" (Article 20, California State University System).
- "Obligations to classes and students:
  1. To meet and teach classes at the time and dates as published in the official schedule. (Proposed changes from the schedule, other than al-

ternate on-campus locations, must be approved in advance by the division chair.)

2. To meet classes during the scheduled final examination periods for final examinations or other legitimate instructional purposes.

3. To be available for meeting with students or staff without appointments for a minimum of one posted office hour each class day with some variance of hours during the week for the convenience of students, and at other times by appointment to accommodate community members and faculty and staff whose schedules preclude meeting during scheduled office hours. An additional five hours each week will be used at the discretion of the individual faculty for professional activities.

4. To provide students with clearly stated course expectations and grading practices.

5. To assign, evaluate, and, within a reasonable length of time, return to students appropriate assignments.

6. To advise students in planning their educational programs and in selecting courses. Faculty may be assigned to advising days consistent with the faculty work calendar and their individual college assignments" (Section 304, Highline Community College, Washington).

In sum, collective bargaining agreements reflect some of the teaching proscriptions and prescriptions we derive from our survey research with the professoriate. Yet only a few aspects are frequently entertained in collective bargaining agreements. Indeed, it can be said that while collective bargaining agreements are frequently prefaced by discussion of academic freedom, the purpose of such agreements contain little that explicitly serves students' interests for receiving fair and ethical treatment in the learning process.

We now turn from more general types of higher education documents and how they reflect, or fail to reflect, our research findings to more institution-specific documents. Two sets of such documents that may more specifically address teaching malpractice concerns at the campus level are reviewed below.

Student Feedback Assessment of Instruction

In the preceding section, we note that one of the most frequent teaching-related mandates in our selected sample of 50 faculty collective bargaining agreements regards the requirement that faculty members routinely administer student instructional assessment forms. For this section, we collected teaching assessment instruments used at 22 different colleges and universities across the United States. While this is a convenience sample rather than a scientific sample of such documents, they can be assumed to be reasonably representative of most such instruments administered in colleges and universities today.

In general, these instructional rating forms include little of the content of our CTBI items or those items that were derived as components of our sets of inviolable norms and admonitory norms. Put another way, the rating forms generally focus more on classroom learning climate and course organization than on specific behaviors of the instructor. Nevertheless, a number of these instruments contained a few items that make up some of the components of a few of the inviolable and admonitory norm sets we derive. Some illustrations follow:[4]

Condescending Negativism (inviolable):

- "The instructor did NOT insult students" (North Carolina State University).
- "I was treated with respect in this class" (Iowa State University).
- "Concern and respect for students as individuals [was excellent . . . poor]" (Virginia Tech).

Particularistic Grading (inviolable):

- "Were the criteria for successful performance clear, and the grading practices fair?" (UCLA).
- "The instructor graded students without showing favoritism" (Roanoke College).
- "The grading procedures for the course were [very fair . . . very unfair]" (University of North Carolina, Greensboro).

Inattentive Planning (inviolable) or Insufficient Syllabus (admonitory):

- "The direction of the course was adequately outlined" (SIRS).

Inadequate Communication (admonitory):

- "Course work was conducted and returned within a reasonable amount of time" (North Carolina State University).

---

4. Three of the institutions represented in this assessment—Florida State University, University of Memphis, Michigan State University—employ the same form: Student-Instructional Rating System (SIRS). An excerpt from this standard form is noted as "SIRS" rather than by institutional identification.

- "Did the instructor make clear what were the objectives of the course?" (University of Wisconsin, Parkside).

Advisement Negligence (admonitory):

- "Availability of extra help when needed [was easily available . . . generally not available]" (University of Missouri, Columbia).
- "The instructor was willing to provide assistance outside of class" (Roanoke College).

Instructional Narrowness (admonitory) or Authoritarian Classroom (admonitory):

- "The instructor encourages student involvement and allows students freedom to ask questions and express ideas in this course" (University of Texas, Arlington).
- "The instructor encouraged students to express opinions" (SIRS).
- "The instructor appeared receptive to new ideas and others' viewpoints" (SIRS).
- "The instructor encouraged students to think for themselves" (Ohio State University).
- "Did the instructor encourage thoughtful and critical responses to the course materials?" (UCLA).

In contrast to all other rating forms reviewed here, the University of Michigan requires only four questions, of broad-based overall generalizations, together with a shopping list of more than 180 optional questions from which individual instructors may choose up to 26 additional items. Some of these optional items address components of the same normative clusters as listed above, but it is not apparent how frequently these may be employed.

In conclusion, students' instructional rating forms for their individual classes and instructors frequently tap *some* aspects of *some* of the normative clusters derived from our research. Inasmuch as these forms are highly variable across the national community of colleges and universities—yet frequently mandated through collective bargaining agreements or administrative policy—they are often readily subject to modification and revision. Such changes may be informed by some of the items in the CTBI and, particularly, those items that contribute to the inviolable and admonitory norms derived here.

Post-Tenure Review Policies

Finally, we turn to one set of institutional policy documents regarding faculty review that might be expected to address teaching performance and specify evaluation criteria. Most individual institutions would have many such sources that might be analyzed: faculty handbooks, stated criteria for evaluating faculty for promotion or tenure, documents stating performance measures used in annual review and for salary raise recommendations. For the present analysis, we select a set of documents that are relatively new to many postsecondary institutions, but have been recently mandated by a number of state legislatures, system central offices, or institutional governing boards. These are documents describing procedures and criteria for periodic post-tenure review and retention of faculty members.

For this analysis, we collected all post-tenure review documents for one large eastern public university. For this institution, the legislature mandated that these documents be written for the first time and approved in 1997. Each unit of the university—departments and colleges—prepared its own post-tenure review document. We consider this set of documents with regard to content pertaining to individuals' teaching performance.

There is considerable uniformity among the 45 academic department and three collegewide (in lieu of individual departmental documents) post-tenure review statements that we examined. This in part reflects the recommended prescribed content and document review and approval process being coordinated through the chief academic officer's division. Nevertheless, there is some variation. Indeed, some units label the teaching section of their post-tenure review document "minimum standards," while others label it "instructional assignments," "standards in instructional activities," "reasonable expectations related to teaching," "review criteria for teaching," "faculty obligations and standards," or "teaching expectations."

Regardless of the document section heading, however, the great majority focus on only a few components of teaching behavior. The typical areas that are generally addressed, and an illustrative statement, are delineated below:

1. Regularly meet classes.
    "Faculty are expected to meet all scheduled classes except for university-wide cancellations, absences sanctioned by the department and/or university, or absences related to illness or emergencies. When faculty cannot meet a class, it is their responsibility to follow depart-

mental procedures so that appropriate measures can be taken to deal with the situation."

2. Provide informative syllabus.

"Faculty are expected to provide students in each course with a course syllabus. . . . In particular, students are to be informed of the expected performance for which grades will be assigned, the instructor's attendance policy (if any), how the Honor System is to be applied, and the prerequisites for the course. The syllabus should also include information about the instructor's office hours and how he or she can be reached."

3. Maintain office hours.

"Faculty are expected to provide regularly scheduled office hours each week and be available during those times for consultation with students. With reasonable effort a student should be able to confer with the teacher in a timely manner, either at scheduled office hours or by other arrangement. (In applying this standard it must be recognized that other professional duties, emergencies, travel, etc. will sometimes conflict with scheduled office hours. In such events, alternate arrangements should be made.)"

4. Provide informative and prompt feedback.

"Tenured faculty are expected to make a thorough and useful criticism of student work and return written work and examinations on a timely basis."

5. Be inclusive and recognize diversity.

"Faculty are expected to maintain a good learning environment in the classroom, an environment that is inclusive and accepting of students without regard to race, color, sex, sexual orientation, disability, age, veteran status, national origin, religion, or political affiliation and an environment that promotes mutual respect, honesty, and integrity."

6. Keep up-to-date and well-prepared.

"Faculty are expected to be keeping course materials and classroom presentations up to date, and delivering lectures and laboratories or presenting material in a well-prepared, professional, and competent manner."

Apart from these six common elements, only a few units address other behavioral expectations, and these are limited. Two departments, for example, include "providing services to student clubs," and two others specify expectations for faculty members to attend teaching workshops or other "educational training opportunities" on a periodic basis.

In summary, from the possible range of behaviors relating to teaching that might be addressed, only a few are regularly delineated by the academic units' post-tenure review documents examined here. Moreover, in many cases the items addressed are stated in broad general terms and open to somewhat diverse interpretations.

Concluding Comments

As with the institutional unit documents that we reviewed, all of the materials discussed in this chapter are limited in scope in terms of prescriptive and proscriptive statements pertaining to behaviors in the teaching role. Indeed many aspects of the inviolable and admonitory norms addressed in earlier chapters are not mentioned at all.

Moreover, those areas that are addressed are typically expressed in broad terms rather than through enumeration in detailed manner. While such vagueness lends itself to interpretative disagreement, and is less enforceable cause for formal intervention and remedial action, too great specificity—such as many of the individual items in the CTBI—would be both inappropriate for a profession and impossible to accomplish in an exhaustive manner. One can reasonably assume that there will always be some unanticipated transgression of severe consequence to the teaching role that would not be explicit in a code of ethics, a faculty handbook, or other appropriate document applying to the professoriate. Indeed, even in our own attempt, in developing the CTBI, to be relatively exhaustive by employing a wide range of resources for listing possible grave improprieties in the teaching role, we soon identified some oversights (see Chapter 2).

In conclusion, the review in this chapter of the contents of a wide variety of documents is not merely to illustrate how little specificity there is to guide the professoriate in their professional roles as teachers. Rather, the point is that there are entire domains or clusters of behaviors (i.e., some of the domains derived from our factor analyses) that are neglected in virtually all policy-related documents—from books on academic ethics, to professional codes of conduct, to documents such as collective bargaining agreements and institutional policy statements developed largely through faculty input. Whether for self-regulation as a profession, or for strengthened guidelines for appropriate administrative intervention, the gaps that are obvious through this review require both formal and informal consideration.

TEN

Conclusions and Implications for Theory, Research, Policy, and Practice

This concluding chapter summarizes the findings of this research project, posits conclusions from these findings, offers a set of implications for theory and research, and concludes with recommendations for policy and practice. Before summarizing the findings of this inquiry, several limitations to this research need discussion. These limitations are as follows:

1. The College Teaching Behaviors Inventory (CTBI) was not derived from an extensive base of literature. Rather, it was largely developed from suggestions and perceptions of individual academics. Thus, the 126 behaviors included in the CTBI are not exhaustive of the universe of behaviors subject to normative criteria.

2. This research is also limited to selected fields from those academic disciplines described by Biglan (1973a, 1973b) as pure life and nonlife academic subject matter areas exhibiting high and low degrees of paradigmatic development. Consequently, the normative preferences of faculty in applied disciplines are not registered in this study.

3. Although most categories of the Carnegie *Classification of Institutions of Higher Education* (1987) are included in this study, research universities II, doctorate-granting universities I and II, and comprehensive universities and colleges I are not represented.

4. The inviolable and admonitory normative patterns identified in this research pertain to lower-division courses in classes of 40 enrolled students. Thus, the normative structure delineated in this research may not apply to lower-division courses enrolling more than 40 students, upper-division courses of various numbers of students enrolled, or to graduate-level instruction.

5. Although there is probably some diversity among the faculty members who comprise the aggregate sample used in this research, our questionnaire did not ask respondents to indicate their ethnic or racial identity. Moreover, the sampling design common to all three

studies described in Chapter 2 used two strata: institutional type by academic discipline. It was not stratified by gender or by race or ethnicity. As a consequence, the normative preferences of particular faculty groups are not reflected in this research.

6. The normative structure consisting of the inviolable and admonitory proscriptive orientations that we have identified are based on faculty perceptions of normative standards for various teaching behaviors. Thus, actual experiences of faculty are not ascertained. Actual encounters with deviance are not necessary, however, for faculty to register their normative preferences. Moreover, the extent to which faculty avoid these proscribed behaviors in their day-to-day teaching role performance and in their relationships with colleagues is also not recorded in the current study.

7. This research is based solely on faculty perceptions of levels of appropriate and inappropriate teaching behavior. Studies of other groups, particularly students and academic administrators, with regard to both their experiences and normative expectations for teaching might further inform our results.

The summary of findings, the conclusions derived, the implications for theory and research, and the proposals for policy and practice suggested by the pattern of findings of this research project are presented within the context of these limitations.

Summary of Findings

The summary of findings is organized around the five research questions described in Chapter 1 of this book.

1. What inviolable patterns of behavior comprise the normative structure of undergraduate college teaching?

Chapter 3 describes a set of seven empirically derived proscriptive behavioral orientations meeting inviolable normative criteria. Put differently, a set of behaviors assessed as requiring severe sanctions for their occurrence were discerned. These inviolable normative patterns are: condescending negativism, inattentive planning, moral turpitude, particularistic grading, personal disregard, uncommunicated course details, and uncooperative cynicism. With the exception of uncooperative cynicism, these inviolable normative clusters pertain to the treatment of students as clients of teaching role performance. Uncooperative cynicism, however, proscribes the failure of faculty to meet their institutional obligations in the larger realm of university administration. All seven of these proscribed, inviolable normative arrays also provide empirical grounding for various ethical principles promulgated for college teaching.

2. What admonitory patterns of behavior comprise the normative structure of undergraduate college teaching?

Admonitory normative orientations are inappropriate behaviors that elicit a less severe reaction than inviolable norms. Chapter 4 describes a set of nine empirically derived admonitory normative patterns: advisement negligence, authoritarian classroom, inadequate communication, inadequate course design, inconvenience avoidance, instructional narrowness, insufficient syllabus, teaching secrecy, and undermining colleagues. Teaching secrecy and undermining colleagues delineate inappropriate relationships with faculty colleagues within the teaching arena. Although authoritarian classroom and instructional narrowness affect student learning, it is the knowledge base of an academic discipline that is most adversely affected. Hence, these two admonitory norms serve the knowledge base of an academic discipline as client of teaching role performance. In contrast, the five other admonitory normative clusters define improper faculty treatment of students as clients of undergraduate college teaching. With the exception of inadequate communication, these admonitory normative configurations also offer empirical support for various ethical principles of teaching infrequently found in the literature.

3. Are any of the inviolable norms or admonitory patterns similar across all types of educational institutions? Are there core inviolable or admonitory patterns for all types of colleges and universities? Are there inviolable or admonitory normative arrays that vary in their level of disapproval among faculty by institutional type?

The configuration of findings reported in Chapter 5 show that particularistic grading and moral turpitude are two core, inviolable proscribed behavioral patterns identified for research universities I, comprehensive universities and colleges II, liberal arts colleges I, liberal arts colleges II, and two-year colleges. Moreover, three admonitory normative behavioral configurations were also identified as core, admonitory norms for all five types of colleges and universities: authoritarian classroom, inadequate course design, and teaching secrecy.

But the inviolable proscribed behavioral patterns of condescending negativism, inattentive planning, personal disregard, uncommunicated course details, and uncooperative cynicism as well as the admonitory normative behavioral clusters of advisement negligence, inadequate communication, inconvenience avoidance, instructional narrowness, insufficient syllabus, and undermining colleagues are differentiated by institutional type: they are less severely denounced by faculty in research universities I.

4. Are there core inviolable or admonitory norms for all four academic disciplines? Are there inviolable or admonitory normative arrays that vary according to academic discipline in their level of faculty disapproval?

The pattern of findings described in Chapter 6 indicate that two inviolable and one admonitory proscribed behavioral patterns constitute core norms for the four academic disciplines of biology, mathematics, history, and psychology. Inattentive planning and moral turpitude are the core, inviolable norms for the four academic disciplines, whereas authoritarian classroom constitutes the sole core admonitory norm for the four academic disciplines. Moreover, faculty in the discipline of biology express more disapproval than their colleagues in the other academic fields of the inviolable normative behavioral orientations of condescending negativism, particularistic grading, personal disregard, uncommunicated course details, and uncooperative cynicism, as well as the admonitory normative arrays of advisement negligence, inadequate communication, inconvenience avoidance, inadequate course design, instructional narrowness, insufficient syllabus, teaching secrecy, and undermining colleagues.

The findings of Chapters 5 and 6 taken together indicate that the inviolable proscribed norm of moral turpitude and the admonitory norm of authoritarian classroom form a set of core norms that are invariant across institutional type *and* academic discipline.

5. Do individual faculty characteristics, including administrative experience, gender, professional status, research activity, and tenure status, affect espousal of inviolable or admonitory normative patterns above and beyond the effects of institutional type and academic discipline?

The findings of Chapter 7 demonstrate that none of these five individual faculty characteristics wields an influence on the espousal of the core inviolable norm regarding behaviors involving moral turpitude. In contrast, the core admonitory norm proscribing authoritarian classroom is affected by gender, as women faculty tend to accord greater contempt for this inappropriate behavioral pattern than do male academics.

The five faculty characteristics also exert little or no influence on the level of disapproval expressed for the inviolable normative arrays prohibitive of inattentive planning, uncooperative cynicism, and uncommunicated course details as well as the admonitory normative clusters prohibitive of advisement negligence, instructional narrowness, insufficient syllabus, and teaching secrecy.

Nevertheless, some individual faculty characteristics exert an influence on six normative patterns above and beyond the influence of institutional type and academic discipline. More specifically, women faculty voice greater support for the inviolable norms prohibiting condescending negativism, and personal disregard, as well as the admonitory normative arrays proscribing inadequate communication and undermining colleagues. Also, faculty with administrative experience voice more disapproval of personal disregard; faculty possessing high intraprofessional status express greater contempt for inconvenience avoidance; and faculty holding tenure more strongly denounce inadequate course design. Of the five individual faculty characteristics only research activity fails to exercise an influence on any of the seven inviolable and the nine admonitory normative patterns. The absence of any influence of research activity on faculty teaching norm espousal corroborates similar findings obtained by Sullivan (1996).

In addition, the academic discipline and institutional type—two structural dimensions of the academic profession—affect faculty espousal of both inviolable and admonitory normative arrays to a greater extent than individual faculty characteristics. Thus, social sources wield a greater influence than personal sources of control, but vast proportions of variability in these proscribed norms are unexplained.

Conclusions Derived from Findings

Seven conclusions are derived from the pattern of findings described in this book:

1. The proscribed normative patterns identified by this research project establish moral boundaries for the teaching role performance of college and university faculty members. Faculty hold a great deal of autonomy in their performance of the role of undergraduate college teaching. Ben-Yehuda (1985) contends that deviance, or the violation of social norms, sets moral boundaries for a society. By extension, the proscribed normative patterns identified by this research project establish moral boundaries for the teaching role performance of college and university faculty members. Thus, the seven inviolable and nine admonitory norms described in Chapters 3 and 4 provide moral boundaries to faculty teaching autonomy. These normative orientations circumscribe faculty autonomy in advising students (advisement negligence), course planning and course design (inattentive planning, inadequate course design, and insufficient syllabus), communication with a class (uncommunicated course details, inadequate communication), grading of student assignments and

examinations (particularistic grading), treatment of course content (authoritarian classroom, instructional narrowness), treatment of students in class (inconvenience avoidance, condescending negativism, personal disregard, and moral turpitude), relationships with colleagues (teaching secrecy, undermining colleagues), and the discharge of institutional obligations regarding teaching (uncooperative cynicism).

With the exception of the core proscriptive norms involving authoritarian classroom and moral turpitude, however, the strength of the moral boundaries for faculty autonomy set by these normative orientations varies across different types of colleges and universities and academic disciplines. These boundaries are strongest in the discipline of biology in comparison with the disciplines of mathematics, history, and psychology. These boundaries are also the weakest in research universities I in comparison with comprehensive universities and colleges II, liberal arts colleges I and II, and two-year colleges.

2. Some of the inviolable and admonitory proscribed normative patterns identified by this research protect the welfare of clients of undergraduate college teaching role performance: students and the knowledge base of academic disciplines. Professions display an asymmetry of expertise in relationship to their clients (Parsons, 1951; Abbott, 1983). College and university faculty members possess an asymmetry of expertise in relationship to students. Academics also have an asymmetrical power relationship with students because of their power to award grades (Wilson, 1982). Given such asymmetries of expertise and power, faculty must maintain an ideal of service toward students as clients and toward the knowledge base of an academic discipline because faculty teaching performance affects the manner in which knowledge is transmitted (Braxton, Bayer, and Finkelstein, 1992). The ideal of service is the obligation of professionals to base their professional choices on the needs and welfare of their clients (Goode, 1969). The ideal of service also constitutes a fiduciary relationship between the client and the professional, a relationship based on the client's trust of the professional (Sokolowski, 1991).

Accordingly, norms that proscribe behaviors that are harmful to the welfare of both students and the disciplinary knowledge base as clients of teaching role performance are imperative. Some of the inviolable and admonitory proscribed normative patterns identified by this research protect the welfare of both of these clients of undergraduate college teaching role performance. To elaborate, course planning, course design, and communication with a class are teaching activities that require attention to the welfare of students as clients. Poor course planning, course design, and communication with a class can result in students getting behind in their readings and having trouble completing graded assignments (Braxton, Bayer, and Finkelstein, 1992). Moreover, poor course planning by faculty also negatively affects the development of students' cognitive skills (Pascarella, Edison, Nora, Hagedorn, and Braxton, 1996; Edison, Doyle, and Pascarella, 1998). Thus, the proscribed normative arrays of inattentive planning, inadequate course design, insufficient syllabus, uncommunicated course details, and inadequate communication safeguard the welfare of students as clients of teaching.

A classroom social context marked by interpersonal strain and disharmony can detrimentally affect student learning (Braxton, Bayer, and Finkelstein, 1992). Strain and disharmony in a classroom can result if a faculty member treats students in a condescending and demeaning manner, displays a disrespect for the needs and sensitivities of students, or commits such unprincipled acts as coming to class intoxicated. Such proscribed normative orientations as condescending negativism, personal disregard, and moral turpitude insure the welfare of students as clients by assuring a favorable classroom social context.

Grading of examinations and other assignments affects both the learning and future careers of students. Grading based on merit assures that unbiased estimates of student learning are made (Braxton, Bayer, and Finkelstein, 1992). Grades based on merit communicate accurate information about the achievement of students. Such unbiased estimates of student course learning help students in future course performance and in their future careers. Consequently, the proscribed normative pattern of particularistic grading vouchsafes that merit provides the basis for the awarding of grades. Thus, the welfare of students as clients of teaching is guarded by prohibitions to particularistic grading.

Teaching of course content that is biased toward a particular perspective as well as the use of a narrow range of teaching and assessment methods negatively affect the transmission of knowledge of an academic discipline to students (Braxton, Bayer, and Finkelstein, 1992). Authoritarian classroom and instructional narrowness prohibit such behaviors that are injurious to the knowledge base of an academic discipline as a client of teaching role performance.

Nevertheless, institutional type and academic discipline attenuate faculty commitment to the ideal of service. With the exception of the core norms proscribing authoritarian classroom and moral turpitude, attenuation of such norms is greatest in research universities I in contrast to the other four types of colleges and universities represented in this inquiry.

Moreover, attenuation of such norms is the least in the discipline of biology in comparison to the other three academic disciplines included in this study.

3. Although proscribed normative configurations protective of the welfare of both students and disciplinary knowledge as clients of teaching exist to guide faculty teaching role performance, harm to the welfare of the knowledge base of an academic discipline evokes less reproach from faculty than harm to the welfare of students as clients. More specifically, both authoritarian classroom and instructional narrowness are admonitory proscriptive norms, norms that elicit less condemnation from faculty than inviolable norms. In contrast, faculty behaviors injurious to the welfare of students as clients evoke a greater degree of disapproval. Of the nine normative orientations protective of students as clients, six of them are inviolable proscriptive norms: condescending negativism, inattentive planning, moral turpitude, particularistic grading, personal disregard, and uncommunicated course details.

4. Because college teaching exhibits one marker of professionalization, some claims of professional status for undergraduate college teaching are warranted. Much debate centers on the locus of professionalism for the academic profession: teaching activity, research activity, or both (Braxton, 1989).[1] Ascertaining the locus of professionalism involves the drawing of parameters of membership in the academic profession. Activities performed by faculty have been the primary basis for the setting of such parameters of membership in the academic profession (Light, 1974; Parsons and Platt, 1973; and Blau, 1973).

Light (1974) asserts that the academic profession is a subset of the scholarly profession. The advancement of knowledge is the core activity of the scholarly profession. Hence, research activity is the key criterion for membership in the academic profession. Consequently, he suggests that college and university faculty members who teach and do not publish research are not members of the academic profession. In contrast, Blau (1973) asserts that faculty claims to professional status emanate from service to clients through the act of teaching. Middle ground is occupied by Parsons and Platt (1973), as they contend that both teaching and research comprise an integrated core of professional activities.

One marker of professionalism is the existence of a code of conduct (Carr-Saunders and Wilson, 1933; Barber, 1963; Millerson, 1964; Green-

1. Public service is also often a component of activities for academics, but it is not the principle activity for the population we are studying.

wood, 1957; Harries-Jenkins, 1970; Moore, 1970; Abbott, 1983). Norms serve as informal codes of conduct (Abbott, 1983; Bayer and Braxton, 1998). Because this study identified a normative structure for undergraduate college teaching, college teaching exhibits one marker of professionalization. Consequently, some claims of professional status for undergraduate college teaching are warranted.

Moreover, the ideal of service to clients is a core generating trait of professionalism (Goode, 1969). As a consequence, additional claims of professional status for undergraduate college teaching stem from the existence of normative behavioral arrays that safeguard the ideal of service to clients of teaching role performance.

5. Four previously unrecognized value patterns of the academic profession are indexed in inviolable normative patterns. Norms delineate acceptable means for the achievement of group goals (Merton, 1968). Moreover, norms depict the "collective conscience" of a social group (Durkheim, 1982 [1894]). Accordingly, deep-seated values and moral precepts surrounding teaching role performance held by the academic profession are indexed in the inviolable normative patterns identified in this research. Because inviolable norms reflect a harsher degree of condemnation than admonitory norms, they index deep-seated values of the academic profession.

Four value patterns emerge from the inviolable normative arrays identified in this study: respect for students as individuals, equal consideration for all students, the professional obligation to prepare for courses, and the obligation to participate in the teaching-related governance and operation of one's college or university. These deep-seated values flow from espoused ethical principles for college teaching that are empirically grounded in one or more of the seven inviolable normative configurations. Since condescending negativism, moral turpitude, and personal disregard constitute violations of the principle of "respect for persons" (Smith, 1996) and its corollary "respect for students as individuals" (Reynolds, 1996; Svinicki, 1994), such respect emerges as a deep-seated value of the academic profession.

The principle of equal consideration of students in advisement, teaching, and grading (Cahn, 1986; Markie, 1994) also emerges as a salient value pattern of the academic profession. This principle is analogous to the research norm of universalism that ordains that research findings be assessed on the basis of merit and not social or personal characteristics (Merton, 1942, 1973). This principle finds empirical support from the proscribed normative orientations of moral turpitude and particularistic grading.

The professional obligation to plan courses promulgated by Cahn (1986) constitutes another value pattern of the academic profession. This value pattern manifests itself in condemnation of inattentive planning and uncommunicated course details.

The obligation that faculty shoulder responsibility for the operation and governance of their colleges and universities of appointment is the fourth value pattern. This pattern reveals itself in uncooperative cynicism.

These four value patterns join the ranks of other value patterns held by the academic profession: cognitive rationality (Parsons and Platt, 1968, 1973), professional autonomy, academic freedom, and the principle of merit (Finkelstein, 1984).

Moreover, the existence of respect for students as individuals as a deep-seated value pattern stands in contrast to the prevailing value patterns of the academic profession, values that emphasize the primacy of cognitive matters. The primacy of cognitive matters strongly suggests that college and university faculty members are relatively unconcerned about the affective needs of students (Bess, 1978, 1982). The primacy of cognitive concerns is manifested in the goals faculty espouse for undergraduate education (Platt, Parsons, and Kirshstein, 1976), the preferred tasks of faculty (Bess, 1978, 1982), as well as the value patterns of cognitive rationality, professional autonomy, academic freedom, and universalism. Yet respect for students as individuals reflects a concern as well for affective needs of students.

6. The seven inviolable and nine admonitory proscribed normative orientations provide parameters for changes in faculty teaching role performance. Normative structures impede or facilitate the enactment of change in faculty teaching role performance (Braxton, Eimers, and Bayer, 1996). Without supportive norms in place, the reliability of the enactment of policies and activities designed to alter faculty teaching role performance is uncertain. Otherwise faculty are free to carry out a policy or activity according to their own preferences if supportive norms do not exist. This contention emanates from Durkheim's postulation that nonconformity is the natural human condition.

The seven inviolable and nine admonitory proscribed normative orientations set parameters for changes in faculty teaching role performance. Supportive norms appear in place for changes in policies and activities concerning student advisement (advisement negligence), course planning and course design (inattentive planning, inadequate course design, and insufficient syllabus), faculty communication with a class (uncommunicated course details, inadequate communication), grading criteria for student assignments and examinations (particularistic grading), treatment of course content (authoritarian classroom, instructional narrowness), relationships with students in class (inconvenience avoidance, condescending negativism, personal disregard, and moral turpitude), relationships with colleagues (teaching secrecy, undermining colleagues), and the fulfillment of institutional obligations (uncooperative cynicism).

7. Undergraduate college teaching norms function as a source of further differentiation in the structure of the academic profession. Powerful forces of differentiation fragment the structure of the academic profession. Institutional type and academic discipline constitute two key differentiating forces (Ruscio, 1987). Such differentiation occurs around the emphasis placed on teaching and research, attitudes, values, beliefs, work styles, reference groups, and professorial roles (Blackburn and Lawrence, 1995; Braxton and Hargens, 1996; Ruscio, 1987; Fulton and Trow, 1974). With the exception of the core norms of authoritarian classroom and moral turpitude, the remaining six inviolable and remaining eight admonitory proscribed normative clusters identified also function as further forces of fragmentation along either institutional or disciplinary lines. Yet the two core norms function as compensatory integrating mechanisms against fragmentation in structure of the academic profession.

Implications for Theory

Three configurations of findings invite possible explanations. These explanations offer theoretical leads for a better understanding of faculty espousal of both inviolable and admonitory normative orientations. Scholars are invited to address empirically the following explanations for these three patterns of findings.

Institutional and Disciplinary Differences

With the exception of core norms, faculty espousal of inviolable and admonitory normative proscriptions vary in statistically significant ways across different types of colleges and universities and among academic disciplines. More specifically, faculty in research universities I exhibit a systematic tendency to espouse less disdain for the following proscriptive normative orientations than their counterparts in other types of colleges and universities: condescending negativism, inattentive planning, personal disregard, uncommunicated course details, uncooperative cynicism, ad-

visement negligence, inadequate communication, inconvenience avoidance, instructional narrowness, insufficient syllabus, and undermining
colleagues.

One explanation for such a uniform pattern of differences is that faculty in research-oriented universities attach less social significance to behavioral transgressions in teaching than their colleagues in other types of
colleges and universities because they attach less value to the role of college teaching (Braxton, Bayer, and Finkelstein, 1992). This study's findings
also demonstrate, however, a uniform pattern of differences between academic biology, a discipline of high paradigmatic development, and the
other three academic disciplines. Specifically, with the exception of core
norms, academic biologists tend to voice greater condemnation for the
following inviolable and admonitory norms than their counterparts in
mathematics, history, and psychology: condescending negativism, personal disregard, uncommunicated course details, uncooperative cynicism,
advisement negligence, inadequate communication, inconvenience avoidance, inadequate course design, instructional narrowness, insufficient
syllabus, teaching secrecy, and undermining colleagues. This pattern of
disciplinary differences is surprising given that faculty in academic disciplines with high levels of paradigmatic development tend to be more oriented toward research than their academic counterparts in disciplines of
low paradigmatic development (Braxton and Hargens, 1996). Obversely,
faculty in disciplines exhibiting low paradigmatic development tend to be
more oriented toward teaching (Braxton and Hargens, 1996) and display
an affinity toward practices designed to improve undergraduate education
(Braxton, 1995; Braxton, Olsen, and Simmons, 1998).

As a consequence, a high value placed on research does not appear to
influence faculty to attach less social significance to prohibited teaching
behaviors. This contention is reinforced by the failure of individual faculty
research activity to exert an independent influence on faculty espousal of
any of the inviolable and admonitory normative arrays, a finding similar
to that of Sullivan (1996).

One possible explanation for both institutional and disciplinary differences focuses on the value placed on faculty autonomy. Faculty autonomy constitutes one of the defining value patterns of the academic profession (Finkelstein, 1984). It seems reasonable to hypothesize that faculty
in types of institutions and academic disciplines where individual faculty
autonomy is high strive to preserve their autonomy. As a consequence,
such faculty believe that colleague or administrative interventions should
be avoided in matters of teaching impropriety. Hence, such academics are

less likely to endorse harsh sanctions for inviolable and admonitory proscribed behaviors.

Autonomy tends to be highest in research universities (Birnbaum, 1988; Baldridge, Curtis, Ecker, and Riley, 1978), whereas faculty in fields having high levels of paradigmatic development tend to have less autonomy in such matters as personal workloads, faculty appointments, and promotions (Lodahl and Gordon, 1972). Hence, with the exception of the core norms of moral turpitude and authoritarian classroom, proscribed inviolable and admonitory normative patterns evoke a less severe reaction from academics in research universities I than their faculty colleagues in other types of colleges and universities. In contrast, faculty in the discipline of biology express a greater degree of contempt for violations of the proscribed inviolable and admonitory normative arrays.

These formulations strongly suggest that the value placed on the importance of teaching by different types of colleges and universities and different academic disciplines may exert less of an effect on the espousal of normative standards for teaching than might be expected. Instead, the value placed on faculty autonomy in different types of colleges and universities and different academic disciplines may exert a much greater degree of influence on faculty espousal of normative standards for teaching. These formulations await an empirical treatment.

Unexplained Variance in Norm Espousal

Institutional type, academic discipline, and individual faculty characteristics explain a small percentage of the variability in faculty espousal of inviolable and admonitory normative arrays. These sources of explained variance represent three levels of the academic profession: the level of institutional type, the level of the academic discipline, and the level of the individual faculty member. Primary groups constitute a neglected level of the academic profession in the structure of this research project. The academic department and informal colleague groups are primary groups that exert social control (Reiss, 1951).

Academic departments may vary in the extent to which normative teaching preferences are valued. Teaching norms may develop in departments where teaching conduct is viewed as important by most members of the department (Hackman, 1976). In such departments, teaching propriety is a defining characteristic of the group's professional identity (Feldman, 1984). Teaching propriety looms more important than a general orientation to teaching in such departments. Such departments value not only good pedagogical practice but also teaching that exhibits an abiding concern for the welfare of the clients of teaching role performance. Accordingly, proscribed teaching behaviors hold considerable social significance for such academic departments. Consequently, faculty in such academic departments ascribe a greater degree of condemnation to inviolable and admonitory proscribed behavioral patterns than their counterparts in academic departments where teaching propriety is of less social significance to departmental members. Future studies should focus on the academic department and its influence on teaching norm espousal.

Informal colleague groups may also wield an influence on faculty espousal of proscribed teaching norms. Such groups of faculty may form in part because they share a common interest in both pedagogical excellence and teaching propriety. Conversations about teaching abound in such informal faculty groups. Such conversations focus not only on effective and ineffective instructional approaches, but also on inappropriate teaching behaviors of colleagues. From such conversations or face-to-face interactions among colleagues about teaching, a teaching culture emerges in such groups (LaCelle-Peterson and Finkelstein, 1993). From such interactions, informal colleague groups of this type develop strong consensus on appropriate and inappropriate teaching behaviors. As a consequence, faculty holding membership in such informal colleague groups voice more condemnation of inviolable and admonitory proscribed normative patterns than faculty who do not affiliate with such informal colleague groups.[2] Future studies should attend to the possible effect of informal colleague groups on faculty normative standards for their teaching roles.

Disciplinary Knowledge as Client

As indicated in the third conclusion, the proscribed behaviors—authoritarian classroom and instructional narrowness—that harm the knowledge base of an academic discipline elicit less condemnation from faculty than prohibited behaviors that harm students as clients of teaching role performance. Such marked differences may stem from differences in the social control of technical and moral performance (Bosk, 1979). When technical performance is characterized by uncertainty, minimal social control obtains when errors in technical performance occur. In contrast, moral transgressions result in greater social control (Bosk, 1979).

---

2. These formulations extend Blau's (1973) postulation that informal colleague groups vary by institutional type. He asserts that in research-oriented universities such groups form and are organized around research. Members discuss their research experiences, give advice, and offer research leads to group members (Blau, 1973).

Both authoritarian classroom and instructional narrowness entail behaviors that are akin to technical performance as these proscribed normative behavioral orientations involve faculty choices of course perspectives, teaching methods, and assessment methods. In other words, these normative orientations proscribe pedagogical choice by faculty. Faculty experience much uncertainty over such choices. This uncertainty principally stems from the graduate school socialization process. To elaborate, individuals acquire the knowledge, skills, and competencies necessary for research role performance during graduate study (Merton, Reader, and Kendall, 1957). This socialization process also instills in individuals a commitment to a particular methodological and theoretical perspective. Hence, faculty experience much uncertainty over the incorporation of perspectives on course content different from their own. Thus, faculty view behaviors reflective of an authoritarian classroom less harshly than proscribed behaviors pertinent to students as clients.

Most college and university faculty also receive little or no training in pedagogy during their graduate studies (Jencks and Reisman, 1969; Liebert and Bayer, 1975; Bess, 1977). As a consequence, most faculty are unfamiliar with a wide range of teaching and assessment methods except with what they may have experienced first hand when they were students in classrooms. Thus, faculty feel diffident about their choice of teaching and assessment methods. Consequently, faculty are more tolerant about teaching improprieties reflective of the proscribed normative pattern of instructional narrowness. Future research should focus on the role of faculty uncertainty over pedagogical choices in influencing teaching normative preferences.

Toward a More General Theory of Norm Espousal

Several constructs emerge from these sets of possible explanations, constructs that may lead to the formulation of a theory of norm espousal. These constructs are the value pattern of faculty autonomy, teaching propriety as an organizing value pattern for academic departments and informal faculty groups, and uncertainty in making instructional choices. It might be hypothesized that both high levels of faculty autonomy and high levels of uncertainty serve to lessen the severity of faculty reactions to proscribed normative patterns. Conversely, a high value placed on teaching propriety leads to greater levels of faculty condemnation of proscribed normative arrays. These hypotheses may account for variations in faculty espousal of each of the seven inviolable and nine admonitory normative orientations. These hypotheses await further conceptual development.

Recommendations for Further Research

In addition to research pursuing the above theoretical formulations, five sets of recommendations for future research are advanced. These sets of recommendations are described below.

1. Limitations of the current study should be addressed in future research on the normative structure of undergraduate college teaching. Such suggested future inquiries are:

   A. The current research should be extended to applied academic disciplines such as engineering, accounting, finance, social work, economics, education, law, and medicine. Because such fields are concerned with the application of their knowledge to practice (Biglan, 1973a, 1973b; Stark, 1998), faculty in these fields may espouse different levels of disdain for the inviolable and admonitory normative orientations identified in this research. Those normative orientations that serve the knowledge base as client—authoritarian classroom and instructional narrowness—may evoke particularly high levels of disdain from faculty in applied academic disciplines. Because professional practice depends on the transmission of a field's knowledge base, reactions to these two admonitory norms might be particularly strong given the adverse effect these proscribed behaviors can have on the knowledge base of an academic discipline.

   B. The research described in this book should be extended to types of colleges and universities not represented in the current study. Such categories of the Carnegie Classification of Institutions include research universities II, doctorate-granting universities I and II, and comprehensive universities and colleges I. The primary purpose of such research would be to determine if varying degrees of institutional research emphasis affect the espousal of the inviolable and admonitory normative clusters identified in this research, an effect that is not fully substantiated in the current research. The above types of colleges and universities are arrayed in descending order of their research emphasis (Blackburn and Lawrence, 1995; Finkelstein, 1984). With a measure of the value faculty place on professional autonomy included, both the influence of institutional research emphasis and the faculty autonomy hypothesis described above could be empirically assessed through the extension of the current research to these additional four types of colleges and universities.

C. A different pattern of proscribed inviolable and admonitory normative arrays might emerge if the context for faculty reactions to the 126 behaviors of the CTBI was different from the lower-division classes with 40 or fewer students used in this study. To elaborate, larger, lower-division classes might serve to alter the views faculty hold regarding the treatment of students as clients. It can be posited that large classes increase the social distance between professors and students in class. Thus, class-based interactions between students and faculty would be minimal. Consequently, such inviolable norms as condescending negativism and personal disregard might attain admonitory normative status. In contrast, such admonitory normative behavioral patterns as inadequate communication, inadequate course design, and insufficient syllabus might acquire inviolable normative status. Large classes require thorough preparation and attention to details by their instructors. Consequently, faculty reactions to such patterns of behavior might be harsh enough to reach inviolable normative stature.

A different pattern of inviolable and admonitory normative orientations might also emerge if the context for faculty reactions to the 126 behaviors of the CTBI was graduate level instruction. The current inventory of 126 behaviors of the CTBI might be used in such research. A different approach, however, would be to design and construct an instrument similar to the CTBI, but one that contained behaviors more relevant to graduate level instruction. For example, such behaviors might pertain to faculty-student relationships inherent in their research apprenticeship experiences and dissertation supervision.

D. This research should be extended to include additional individual faculty characteristics. The faculty member's ethnicity is one important characteristic not represented in the current study. Faculty of color might register normative preferences that differ from those of faculty represented in the current study. Such differences might stem from variations in reference group orientations and profound subcultural differences in U.S. society generally to the unique difficulties faculty of color may experience in adjusting to the professorial role. In addition to the diverse cultural backgrounds many faculty of color represent, these difficulties include different graduate school socialization, weak mentoring, fewer networking opportunities, and divergent priorities (Tierney and Rhoads, 1993). These difficulties strongly suggest that faculty of color may hold different normative standards for teaching role performance.

A significant proportion of the American professoriate is drawn from an international pool, many from societies with cultural norms and traditions, including educational environments with norms and status ascriptions to professors, quite different from American standards. The influence that these cultural variations may play in teaching behaviors merits inquiry.

In addition to ethnicity and national origin, professional age constitutes another individual faculty characteristic that might exert an influence on faculty espousal of the seven inviolable and nine admonitory normative clusters. Professional age not only reflects generational differences in faculty socialization but also a greater opportunity for older individual academics to witness various proscribed teaching behaviors (Braxton and Bayer, 1996). As a consequence, professional age may exert an influence on the level of faculty disdain for the various inviolable and admonitory norms.

The goals faculty hold for their undergraduate teaching represent another personal source of control that might affect normative standards for teaching role performance. Liebert and Bayer (1975) make a critical distinction between profession-centered and client-centered teaching goals that future research should incorporate. Both profession-centered and client-centered teaching goals may exert differential effects on the seven inviolable and nine admonitory normative arrays.

2. Merton (1976), Gibbs (1981), and Zuckerman (1988) point out that there is a disjuncture between the normative orientations individuals hold and their actual behavior. Thus, future research should focus on the extent to which individual faculty members avoid the proscriptive inviolable and admonitory patterns identified in the current study. Put differently, faculty conformity to prescriptive forms of the normative patterns identified in this research should be assessed. As suggested in Chapter 8, control theory could serve as a theoretical framework for accounting for faculty avoidance or enactment of these proscribed behavioral patterns. Such social sources of control as institutional type and academic discipline should be included in such research. In addition to norm espousal, other sources of personal control such as gender, administrative experience, research activity, professional status, tenure status, cultural background, professional age, and teaching goals should also be included.

Two approaches to measuring faculty avoidance of these proscribed behavioral orientations could be used. One approach is to ask
individual academics to indicate the extent to which they engage in
the various behaviors reflective of the nine admonitory and seven inviolable normative clusters included in the CTBI. The design of such
studies should include faculty employed at different types of colleges
and universities and of different academic disciplines. Although
Zuckerman (1977) notes that self-reports of normative conformity or
deviance are not without shortcomings, it is also true that self-reports
typically demonstrate higher rates of deviance than official statistics
(Reiss, 1973).

The other approach to measuring faculty avoidance of the seven
inviolable and nine admonitory proscribed orientations is to ask students to indicate the extent to which they observe faculty engaging in
those behaviors. Undergraduate college students enrolled in various
types of colleges and universities and majoring in different academic
disciplines should be built into the research designs of such studies.
In addition to surveying students, the normative evaluations of the
behaviors listed in the CTBI by academic administrators should also
be assessed. Such research would allow a comparison of the degree of
disjunction in the perceptions of the different members of the academic community.

3. The social mechanisms of inviolable and admonitory norm internalization are not known. The graduate school socialization process is regarded as a rudimentary mechanism for the internalization of normative standards (Goode, 1957; Zuckerman, 1977, 1988; Anderson,
Louis, and Earle, 1994). Graduate students acquire the attitudes, values, norms, knowledge, and skills essential to professional role performance through the graduate school socialization process (Merton,
Reader, and Kendall, 1957; Cole and Cole, 1973). Given such antici-
pated effects, graduate school socialization can serve as a fundamental mechanism of deterrence for teaching misconduct. As a consequence, research should focus on the extent to which the seven
inviolable and the nine admonitory normative orientations are internalized during the graduate school socialization process. Such research should also concentrate on the influence of various dimensions of graduate school socialization on the internalization of
normative orientations. These dimensions include role-taking activities, informal relationships between students and faculty, mentoring

arrangements, and the structure and climate of the graduate department. The theoretical formulations regarding the influence of these various dimensions on the internalization of undergraduate college teaching normative preferences are described in Chapter 8. These theoretical formulations should undergird research on the effects of the graduate school socialization process on the internalization of normative standards for undergraduate college teaching.

Such research should also attend to the possibility that norm internalization may vary from individual to individual. Because beginning teaching assistants anticipate some of the normative behavioral proscriptions of faculty (Braxton, Lambert, and Clark, 1995), uniform internalization of teaching normative orientations is unlikely. Hence, research on the graduate school socialization process should also seek to determine the extent to which graduate students experience norm accentuation, maintenance, or conversion. These forms of norm internalization are described in Chapter 8.

4. Future research should also consider the mechanisms through which faculty behaviors reflective of the admonitory and inviolable proscribed normative configurations are observed by students and faculty colleagues. In Chapter 8, the public nature of college teaching and student course ratings are posited as possible mechanisms of observation of misconduct affecting students as clients. Future research should concentrate on the extent to which teaching improprieties in the form of the inviolable and admonitory normative arrays are observed through these mechanisms. Such research should also focus on the effects of class size on the observability of such teaching misbehavior. Additional research questions recommended for study include: How often do students who are victims of teaching improprieties discuss such incidents with faculty members or academic administrators? Do students who witness incidents of teaching wrongdoing discuss such occurrences with faculty? Do faculty hearing such reports from students give them serious consideration? What are the consequences for whistle blowers when they attempt corrective action?

In addition, future research should also consider the role of departmental meetings, face-to-face interactions, and committee work in observing colleague misbehavior in the form of uncooperative cynicism, teaching secrecy, and undermining colleagues. Such research should also consider the following questions: Do faculty members who either witness or are victims of such improprieties discuss such incidents with their faculty colleagues? Are such complaints taken seriously by colleagues or administrators?

5. In addition to deterrence and detection, the social control of teaching misconduct also requires the sanctioning of such wrongdoing. The characteristics of this sanctioning process are not known, however, and require an empirical treatment. Some fundamental questions requiring attention are: What types of actions do individual faculty members who personally experience or receive reports of behaviors reflective of the inviolable and admonitory normative patterns take? Do they elect to do nothing, talk to the offending colleague, professionally boycott the offending colleague, or report the incident to their department chairperson, academic dean, or institutional professional ethics committee? What types of sanctions do official sanctioning agents apportion for teaching misconduct?

Moreover, Chapter 8 postulates two competing theoretical perspectives on the sanctioning process: functionalism and power theory. Both of these perspectives focus on the actions of both official sanctioning agents and individual faculty members who either personally experience or receive reports of occurrences of teaching malfeasance in the form of the seven inviolable and nine admonitory proscribed normative orientations. Scholars should test both of these theoretical formulations.

Implications for Policy and Practice

Nine sets of recommendations for policy are offered. Presidents, chief academic officers, department chairpersons, and individual faculty members should give serious consideration to the implementation of these recommendations at their colleges and universities.[3] These sets of recommendations are described below.

1. *Systematic records of incidents of teaching misconduct should be kept by colleges and universities.* As indicated in Chapter 8, the rate of teaching misconduct in higher education is not known. Despite an unknown rate,

---

3. We acknowledge the members of the graduate level course titled the "American Academic Profession" offered in Spring 1997 at Peabody College of Vanderbilt University for their insights that contribute to our formulation of these nine recommendations for policy and practice. The members of this course were: Francis Alexander, Mia Alexander-Snow, Susanna Baxter, Robert Buckla, Juanita Buford, James Coaxum, Rodney Cohen, Marietta Del Favero, Karen Elsey, Darlene Franklin, Scott Gilmer, Patricia Helland, Barbara Johnson, Anthony Jones, Laurel Raimondo, Monique Robinson-Wright, Ross Scott, and Evans Whitaker.

it is fatuous to believe that teaching misbehavior does not exist since disjunctures between normative preferences and actual behavior naturally occur (Merton, 1976; Gibbs, 1981; Zuckerman, 1988). Indeed, anecdotal accounts of misconduct in teaching abound in academia (Lewis, 1997). Consequently, systematic record-keeping of incidents of faculty behaviors reflective of inviolable and admonitory proscribed normative patterns is greatly needed. Such record-keeping should entail the compilation of data on how many formal charges of teaching misconduct are made in a given time period, how many formal charges resulted in an investigation, and how many formal charges result in sanctions.

Without such systematic record-keeping, teaching wrongdoing is viewed as a rare event, an event not important enough to exercise social control. The social control of teaching wrongdoing is necessary to assure the lay public that the teaching role performance of college and university faculty members attends to the welfare of students as clients. Such record-keeping should be done at the level of the individual department or college.

2. *A formal code of teaching conduct should be developed.* As evidenced in Chapter 9, scant attention has focused on the development of a formal code of conduct for teaching role performance by professional associations and individual colleges and universities. Such a code of conduct would serve to identify the responsibilities of the academic profession to the clients of teaching role performance (Schurr, 1982). Both the inviolable and admonitory global normative clusters identified in the preceding chapters could serve as a foundation for the development of such general codes that address the teaching role (for further discussion see recommendation eight below).

3. *Colleges and universities, and academic departments within them, should conduct audits of the prevailing normative proscriptions at their institutions and within their individual departments.* Such audits are warranted given the degree of unexplained variance in faculty espousal of inviolable and admonitory normative configurations and variations by institutional type, academic discipline, and faculty characteristics as shown in Chapters 5, 6, and 7. The delineation of behaviors constituting teaching misconduct at individual institutions and departments could be derived from the findings of such audits of normative orientations. Results might augment those norms identified in Chapters 3 and 4, thereby reflecting the possible uniqueness of individual settings and traditions.

4. *Individual colleges and universities should establish a formal committee that considers reported incidents of teaching misconduct.* In universities,

such committees might be created for each college, whereas in liberal arts colleges and two-year colleges a single committee would suffice. Such a teaching integrity committee would have responsibilities similar to those of research integrity committees now common at many universities. Steneck (1994) offers some guidelines for research integrity committees that apply equally to our proposed teaching integrity committees. These guidelines suggest that such committees institute the following process. The committee must first consider whether an allegation does constitute a form of teaching misconduct. If an allegation meets the defining parameters of teaching misconduct, then the committee must conduct an investigation. If the accused individual is found guilty, then sanctions are recommended by the committee. Such a committee must assure that the accused individual knows and has an opportunity to confront the evidence. Moreover, the committee must assure that individuals making the accusation of teaching misconduct are protected from retaliation. If the accuser is a student enrolled in the accused faculty member's class, then the confidentiality of the accuser should be strictly maintained.

5. *Sanctions for teaching misconduct should be formulated.* To assure the effectiveness of teaching integrity committees, individual colleges and universities need to develop a range of suitable sanctions for various forms of teaching impropriety. Sanctions are important because they provide evidence of professional self-regulation of teaching role performance to the lay public. Sanctions also serve as deterrents to misconduct in teaching if they are known and communicated (Ben-Yehuda, 1985; Tittle, 1980).

The severity of faculty response to each of the seven inviolable and nine admonitory proscribed normative arrays offers a starting point for the delineation of sanctions. In addition, such sanctions should also reflect the degree of harm done to students as clients, to the careers and reputations of colleagues, and to the department and institution of academic appointment.

A clear demarcation between inviolable and admonitory norms is necessary, however. Although faculty regard the nine admonitory normative behavioral clusters as inappropriate behaviors, their reactions to them indicate a disinclination to sanction colleagues for engaging in these behaviors. Nevertheless, sanctions might be warranted in cases where an individual faculty member has committed such offenses so frequently that action is necessary. Also, sanctions might be justified in cases in which extreme harm has come to a student because of engagement in admonitory normative behaviors.

6. *Colleges and universities offering graduate level degrees should attend to the role of the graduate school socialization process in inculcating prescribed and proscribed forms of the teaching normative patterns identified in this book.* Certainly, training programs for teaching assistants should include a discussion of proscribed teaching behaviors. Moreover, a growing number of universities are developing programs and offering experiences to prepare students for college teaching (Gaff and Lambert, 1996). Such efforts should also concentrate some attention on prescribed and proscribed teaching behaviors. In both types of training programs for college teaching, normative patterns for teaching could be discussed in courses offered on college teaching.

In addition, faculty who supervise teaching assistants and other graduate students who aspire to the professoriate should steadfastly model the prescriptive forms of undergraduate college teaching normative standards (Braxton, Lambert, and Clark, 1995). Faculty supervisors should also discuss teaching improprieties with teaching assistants when such improprieties occur (Braxton, Lambert, and Clark, 1995).

7. *Colleges and universities should reward faculty for their teaching integrity.* In addition to sanctions, effective social control of teaching role performance requires a system of rewards for faculty avoidance of proscribed normative patterns. Put differently, colleges and universities should reward faculty not only for their teaching effectiveness, but also for their teaching propriety. Accordingly, student course rating instruments should include items of the CTBI that are reflective of the proscribed behaviors of such inviolable norms as condescending negativism, inattentive planning, moral turpitude, particularistic grading, personal disregard, and uncommunicated course details. Items indicative of the proscribed behaviors of such admonitory norms as authoritarian classroom, inadequate communication, inconvenience avoidance, inadequate course design, instructional narrowness, and insufficient syllabus should also be included on course rating instruments.

By including such items on student course rating instruments, teaching propriety could be used as a criterion for such faculty personnel decisions as increments in salary, reappointment of untenured faculty, the awarding of tenure, and promotion in rank.[4] In addition, the deterrence

---

4. This recommendation is advanced with full knowledge of research that strongly indicates that teaching is not fully rewarded by colleges and universities (Tuckman, Gapinski, and Hagemann, 1977; Tuckman and Hageman, 1976; Lewis, 1996). This recommendation is advanced with the hope that teaching will become more equally rewarded along side research.

and detection of teaching misconduct would be assisted. The inclusion of proscribed teaching behaviors on student course rating instruments would also provide colleges and universities with an estimate of the frequency of teaching misconduct at their institutions.

8. *Normative expectations for teaching should be codified in collective bargaining agreements.* Postsecondary faculty collective bargaining agreements contain a primary focus on conditions of employment, including evaluation procedures and criteria for layoffs and dismissal. Yet, as noted in Chapter 9, little in collective bargaining contracts address broad areas of teaching performance and teacher decorum. In those institutions and systems under collective bargaining agreements, it would be advisable that faculty negotiators consider codification of the inviolable and admonitory norms in such agreements. Without such content, institutional administrators may treat cases of teaching impropriety in individual instances on an ad hoc basis and make decisions that might be ambiguous as regards the collective bargaining agreement. In such events, faculty are essentially abrogating their authority as professionals in negotiating the definition of proper teaching behavior and associated appropriate procedures for sanctions.

9. *Formal institutional policies should be expanded to encompass more expressly a wider variety of general prescribed and proscribed teaching behaviors.* Many institutional-level documents (handbooks; statements on evaluation criteria for salary increases, promotion, tenure, and annual review; and post-tenure review policies) could be enhanced in the amount of attention given to the role of teaching.

This is not to say, however, that institutional documents should (or could) attempt to list all improprieties on all items of proper decorum for which faculty can reach some level of consensus. Indeed, academic freedom, pedagogical "style," individual preferences, special circumstances, and discipline differences must be accommodated. Moreover, an almost infinite variety of possibilities exists; thus, exhaustive inclusion of detailed behavioral incidents would almost certainly get quickly mired in debate on definition and inclusiveness of such statements. Rather, general categories of behavior ought to be specified—parallel to the broadly defined areas of scientific misconduct (e.g., fraud and fabrication, "cooking" or "trimming" data)—such as the general factor clusters of teaching improprieties we identify in Chapters 3 and 4.

Conclusion

For college and university faculty members, professional roles, and hence the possibilities of job-related improprieties, rest in four domains (see Table 10.1):

1. Employee misconduct such as embezzlement of institutional funds, falsification of payroll records or travel reimbursement forms, introducing a computer virus.
2. Scholarly or scientific misconduct such as plagiarism, intentional misallocation of authorship credit, fabrication of laboratory data and results.
3. Teaching misconduct such as habitual failure to meet class, variable or biased grading of individual students' classwork and examinations, public ridicule of students' class performance.
4. Professional service misconduct such as failure to attend a professional meeting session after having agreed to be a presenter or discussant, not writing a promised letter of recommendation for an associate, failure to attend or fulfill role responsibilities on departmental or college committee assignments.

Some improprieties transcend two or more of these domains. For example, serving on a review panel for confidential assessment of a funding proposal and using that opportunity to appropriate ideas for one's own research, would violate both scientific and professional service norms. Sexual harassment and fabrication of credentials transcend all four domains.

The degree of formalization and codification of institutional or colleague response to deviance from professional norms varies among each of these domains. The most formal policies, often embedded in the legal code, regards grievous employee misconduct. More recently, as noted earlier, broad formalization and definition of scientific misconduct has been promulgated by both professional associations and individual educational institutions, as well as by the federal government. Procedural guidelines and appropriate sanctioning actions are often specified, and even separate federal agencies, professional society boards, and institutional committees have been established solely to deal with scientific misconduct.

In contrast, virtually no formal written norms exist for professional service misconduct. And only recently have some aspects of teaching misconduct been addressed by professional associations, collective bargaining agreements, or institutional documents and student instructional rating forms.

TABLE 10.1. Domains of Misconduct by the Professoriate

Domain	Illustrative Transgressions	Controlling or Sanctioning Agents
Employee Misconduct	Embezzlement of institutional funds	High-level academic administration
	Falsification of payroll records or travel reimbursement forms	Courts, legal system
	Introducing a computer virus	
Scholarly Misconduct	Plagiarism	Federal agencies
	Fabrication of data or laboratory results	Professional association codes of ethics
	Misallocation of authorship credit	Institutional panels
		Colleagues
Teaching Misconduct	Nonuniform or biased grading of individual student's classwork and exams	Middle management academic administration
	Habitual failure to meet class	Colleagues
	Public ridicule of a student's performance	Students (?)
Service Misconduct	Failure to fulfill role responsibilities for departmental or college committee assignments	(No formal or informal sanctions, generally ignored)
	Not writing promised letter of recommendation for an associate	
	Failure to attend professional meeting session after agreeing to participate	

Note: Transgressions may transcend domains; for example, appropriating ideas from serving on a federal proposal review panel violates both scholarship and service norms; sexual harassment or fabrication of academic degree credentials transcends all four domains.

But how important is it that normative standards be written for each of these four domains? Does the profession of postsecondary faculty teachers provide adequate self-regulation, as some other professions do? Or are the impressions among some policymakers and, through the press, among much of the general public that there is rampant malfeasance by the professoriate supported by any evidence?

While the evidence of the pervasiveness of misconduct in the various role domains of the professoriate is substantially incomplete, there is some evidence that general perceptions are at least partially based on reality. It is likely that only the most grievous incidents or those which are perpetrated by the most visible college officials are reported. Nevertheless, reports of such misconduct are regularly found in *The Chronicle of Higher Education* and local newspapers that serve college and university communities. Still, it is generally considered in the best interest of the academic institution to minimize the publicity of such incidents—or indeed prohibit disclosure of personnel actions against a faculty member for employee misconduct, except in those cases where legal charges have been filed.

The extent of scientific misconduct is somewhat better documented although still largely incomplete. Nevertheless, analyses that have looked at the prevalence of scientific misconduct suggest that such incidents are not especially unusual or rare (Office of Inspector General, 1990; Swazey, Anderson, and Louis, 1993; National Academy of Sciences, 1995; Braxton and Bayer, 1996).

Least explored is the incidence of misconduct in the service role. In part, this is because these violations are often within the local institutional context and are hence often handled by means of informal social controls. At the more visible extrainstitutional level, only journal policies on how to deal with confidential manuscripts and federal policies precluding the appropriation of materials evaluated on proposal review panels are explicit. Otherwise, most such incidents of violation of service role ethics and norms appear to be tolerated and carry meager sanctions. Indeed, it is exceptional to have misconduct in this domain addressed in the professional literature—one rare example where this has been addressed in published professional association outlets is the observation of frequent dereliction of accepted roles on professional meeting programs (Bayer and Clair, 1984).

Finally, we return to the question of the prevalence of faculty misconduct in the teaching role in academe. As we note earlier in this chapter, the prevalence of teaching misconduct is not known and wrongdoing is generally viewed by the professoriate as a rare event. But one piece of recent research, addressing one aspect of teaching impropriety, demonstrates that teaching misconduct is by no means an extraordinary event in American colleges and universities. According to the qualitative and empirically based research by Boice (1996), faculty-initiated classroom incivility and teaching improprieties are "more common than uncommon" (p. 479), and traditionally there is "too large a role [attributed] to students, too small a part to teachers" (p. 484).

Hence, the evidence of frequent misconduct in the teaching role, together with the research results reported here, which show strong consensus among the professoriate on several proscriptive domains of inviolable and admonitory norms in teaching, suggest that greater attention to and formalization of teaching norms is sorely needed. Our review of documents at the associational, system, and institutional levels shows that insufficient attention is at present given to the appropriate behavior of the professoriate in relation to their teaching role.

Increased formalization and articulation of the norms of teaching in conjunction with the codified norms and associated sanctions already in place with regard to some of the other role domains of college and university faculties, can curtail the erosion of public trust and esteem of the professoriate. Such measures will also strengthen rather than undermine the professionalism of the professoriate. By faculty members themselves taking a more proactive role in identifying misconduct and prescribing sanctioning actions, they can retain the level of autonomy normally accorded to those in the professions.

American college students deserve to be assured that teaching misconduct is viewed as a severe transgression by the professoriate and by their employing institutions. So, too, do the many of the more than 900,000 instructional faculty at more than 3,000 institutions of higher education in the United States (National Center for Education Statistics, 1997, 1998) who continually play a conscientious and dedicated role in exercising high standards for teaching and teaching decorum deserve to know that their adherence to normative standards in teaching are recognized, reinforced, and rewarded.

College Teaching Behaviors Inventory©

COLLEGE TEACHING BEHAVIORS INVENTORY ©

Teaching is a complex activity composed of many behaviors and expectations. Listed below are some behaviors related to college teaching. These may appear to be inappropriate to some faculty members but not to others. Using the response codes listed below, please indicate your opinion on each of the listed behaviors as you think they might best ideally apply to a faculty member teaching a *lower division college course in your field of about 40 enrolled students, whether or not you teach such a course yourself.* The response categories are as follows:

1 = Appropriate behavior, should be encouraged

2 = Discretionary behavior, neither particularly appropriate nor inappropriate

3 = Mildly inappropriate behavior, generally to be ignored

4 = Inappropriate behavior, to be handled informally by colleagues or administrators suggesting change or improvement

5 = Very inappropriate behavior, requiring formal administrative intervention

A. PRE-PLANNING FOR THE COURSE

		Appropriate/encourage	Discretionary	Mildly inappropriate/ignore	Inappropriate/handle informally	Very inappropriate/requires intervention
A1.	Required texts and other reading materials are not routinely ordered by the instructor in time to be available for the first class session.	1	2	3	4	5
A2.	A course outline or syllabus is not prepared for a course.	1	2	3	4	5
A3.	Prior to the first meeting of a class, the instructor does not visit the assigned classroom and assess its facilities.	1	2	3	4	5
A4.	A course outline or syllabus does not contain dates for assignments and/or examinations.	1	2	3	4	5
A5.	Objectives for the course are not specified by the instructor.	1	2	3	4	5
A6.	Changes in a course are made without seeking information from students who have previously taken the course.	1	2	3	4	5
A7.	The instructor does not read reviews of appropriate textbooks.	1	2	3	4	5
A8.	The course is designed without taking into account the needs or abilities of students enrolling in the course.	1	2	3	4	5
A9.	Colleagues teaching the same or similar courses are not consulted on ways to teach the particular course.	1	2	3	4	5
A10.	Required course materials are not kept within reasonable cost limits as perceived by students.	1	2	3	4	5
A11.	New lectures or revised lectures which reflect advancements in the field are not prepared.	1	2	3	4	5
A12.	In-class activities are not prepared and anticipated in advance, but are developed while the class is in session.	1	2	3	4	5
A13.	The instructor does not request necessary audio-visual materials in time to be available for class.	1	2	3	4	5
A14.	Assigned books and articles are not put on library reserve by the instructor on a timely basis for student use.	1	2	3	4	5

<table>
<tr><th></th><th>Appropriate/encourage</th><th>Discretionary</th><th>Mildly inappropriate/ignore</th><th>Inappropriate/handle informally</th><th>Very inappropriate/require intervention</th></tr>
</table>

B. FIRST DAY OF CLASS

	Appropriate/encourage	Discretionary	Mildly inappropriate/ignore	Inappropriate/handle informally	Very inappropriate/require intervention
B1. Class roll is not taken.	1	2	3	4	5
B2. The instructor does not introduce her/himself to the class.	1	2	3	4	5
B3. Office hours are not communicated to the students.	1	2	3	4	5
B4. The instructor changes classroom location to another building without informing students in advance.	1	2	3	4	5
B5. The instructor changes class meeting time without consulting students.	1	2	3	4	5
B6. Students are not informed of the instructor's policy on missed or make-up examinations.	1	2	3	4	5
B7. Students are not informed of extra credit opportunities which are available in the course during the term.	1	2	3	4	5
B8. Students are not asked to record their background, experiences and interests for reference by the instructor.	1	2	3	4	5
B9. An overview of the course is not presented to students on the first day.	1	2	3	4	5
B10. An introduction to the first course topic is not begun on the first day.	1	2	3	4	5
B11. The first class meeting is dismissed early.	1	2	3	4	5
B12. The first reading assignment is not communicated to the class.	1	2	3	4	5
B13. A course outline or syllabus is not prepared and passed out to students.	1	2	3	4	5
B14. The instructor does not ask students if they have questions regarding the course.	1	2	3	4	5

C. IN-CLASS BEHAVIORS

	Appropriate/encourage	Discretionary	Mildly inappropriate/ignore	Inappropriate/handle informally	Very inappropriate/require intervention
C1. Class sessions are begun without an opportunity for students to ask questions.	1	2	3	4	5
C2. The topics or objectives to be covered for the day are not announced at the beginning of the class.	1	2	3	4	5
C3. Joke-telling and humor unrelated to course content occurs routinely in class.	1	2	3	4	5
C4. The instructor frequently uses profanity in class.	1	2	3	4	5
C5. Class is usually dismissed early.	1	2	3	4	5
C6. The instructor meets the class without having reviewed pertinent materials for the day.	1	2	3	4	5
C7. The instructor routinely allows one or a few students to dominate class discussion.	1	2	3	4	5
C8. Instructions and requirements for course assignments are not clearly described to students.	1	2	3	4	5
C9. Class does not begin with a review of the last class session.	1	2	3	4	5
C10. Joke-telling and humor related to course content occurs frequently in class.	1	2	3	4	5

	Appropriate/encourage	Discretionary	Mildly inappropriate/ignore	Inappropriate/handle informally	Very inappropriate/requires intervention
C11. The instructor does not end the class session by summarizing material covered during the class.	1	2	3	4	5
C12. The instructor is routinely late for class meetings.	1	2	3	4	5
C13. The instructor routinely holds the class beyond its scheduled ending time.	1	2	3	4	5
C14. The instructor does not take class attendance every class meeting.	1	2	3	4	5
C15. The instructor does not introduce new teaching methods or procedures.	1	2	3	4	5
C16. The instructor does not provide in-class opportunities for students to voice their opinion about the course.	1	2	3	4	5
C17. The instructor calls on students to answer questions in class on a non-voluntary basis.	1	2	3	4	5
C18. The instructor does not follow the course outline or syllabus for most of the course.	1	2	3	4	5
C19. The instructor practices poor personal hygiene and regularly has offensive body odor.	1	2	3	4	5
C20. The instructor routinely wears a sloppy sweatshirt and rumpled blue jeans to class.	1	2	3	4	5
C21. While able to conduct class, the instructor frequently attends class while obviously intoxicated.	1	2	3	4	5

D. TREATING COURSE CONTENT

D1. The instructor does not have students evaluate the course at the end of the term.	1	2	3	4	5
D2. The instructor insists that students take one particular perspective on course content.	1	2	3	4	5
D3. The instructor's professional biases or assumptions are not explicitly made known to students.	1	2	3	4	5
D4. The instructor frequently introduces opinion on religious, political or social issues clearly outside the realm of the course topics.	1	2	3	4	5
D5. The instructor does not include pertinent scholarly contributions of women and minorities in the content of the course.	1	2	3	4	5
D6. Memorization of course content is stressed at the expense of analysis and critical thinking.	1	2	3	4	5
D7. Connections between the course and other courses are not made clear by the instructor.	1	2	3	4	5
D8. The relationship of the course content to the overall departmental curriculum is not indicated.	1	2	3	4	5
D9. A cynical attitude toward the subject matter is expressed by the instructor.	1	2	3	4	5

E. EXAMINATION AND GRADING PRACTICES

E1. The instructor does not give assignments or examinations requiring student writing skills.	1	2	3	4	5

		Appropriate/encourage	Discretionary	Mildly inappropriate/ignore	Inappropriate/handle informally	Very inappropriate/require intervention
E2.	When examinations or papers are returned, student questions are not answered during class time.	1	2	3	4	5
E3.	Graded tests and papers are not promptly returned to students by the instructor.	1	2	3	4	5
E4.	Individual student course evaluations, where students can be identified, are read prior to the determination of final course grades.	1	2	3	4	5
E5.	Examination questions do not represent a range of difficulty.	1	2	3	4	5
E6.	Grades are distributed on a "curve."	1	2	3	4	5
E7.	An instructor lowers course standards in order to be popular with students.	1	2	3	4	5
E8.	The standards for a course are set so high that most of the class receives failing grades for the course.	1	2	3	4	5
E9.	Individual students are offered extra-credit work in order to improve their final course grade *after* the term is completed.	1	2	3	4	5
E10.	Explanation of the basis for grades given for essay questions or papers is not provided to students.	1	2	3	4	5
E11.	Written comments on tests and papers are consistently not made by the instructor.	1	2	3	4	5
E12.	The instructor allows personal friendships with a student to intrude on the objective grading of their work.	1	2	3	4	5
E13.	Student papers or essay examination questions are not read at least twice before a grade is given.	1	2	3	4	5
E14.	Social, personal or other non-academic characteristics of students are taken into account in the awarding of student grades.	1	2	3	4	5
E15.	Final examinations are administered during a regular class period rather than at the official examination period.	1	2	3	4	5
E16.	Student class participation is considered in awarding the final course grade.	1	2	3	4	5
E17.	Student attendance in class is weighed in determining the final course grade.	1	2	3	4	5
E18.	Student opinions about the method of grading are not sought.	1	2	3	4	5
E19.	Students' work is not graded anonymously.	1	2	3	4	5
E20.	The final course grade is based on a single course assignment or a single examination.	1	2	3	4	5
E21.	Examination questions do not tap a variety of educational objectives ranging from the retention of facts to critical thinking.	1	2	3	4	5
E22.	Sexist or racist comments in students' written work are not discouraged.	1	2	3	4	5
E23.	An instructor does not hold review sessions before examinations.	1	2	3	4	5
E24.	All student grades are publicly posted with social security numbers and without names.	1	2	3	4	5
E25.	Graded papers and examinations are left in an accessible location where students can search through to get back their own.	1	2	3	4	5

F. FACULTY-STUDENT IN-CLASS INTERACTIONS

		Appropriate/encourage	Discretionary	Mildly inappropriate/ignore	Inappropriate/handle informally	Very inappropriate/requires intervention
F1.	Stated policies about late work and incompletes are not universally applied to all students.	1	2	3	4	5
F2.	Students are not permitted to express viewpoints different from those of the instructor.	1	2	3	4	5
F3.	The instructor expresses impatience with a slow learner in class.	1	2	3	4	5
F4.	The instructor does not encourage student questions during class time.	1	2	3	4	5
F5.	An instructor makes condescending remarks to a student in class.	1	2	3	4	5
F6.	The instructor does not learn the names of all students in the class.	1	2	3	4	5
F7.	A clear lack of class members' understanding about course content is ignored by the instructor.	1	2	3	4	5
F8.	Shy students are not encouraged to speak in class.	1	2	3	4	5
F9.	The instructor does not allow students to direct their comments to other members of the class.	1	2	3	4	5

G. RELATIONSHIPS WITH COLLEAGUES

G1.	A faculty member refuses to share academic information about mutual students with colleagues.	1	2	3	4	5
G2.	A faculty member does not tell an administrator or appropriate faculty committee that there are very low grading standards in a colleague's course.	1	2	3	4	5
G3.	A faculty member does not tell an administrator or appropriate faculty committee that a colleague's course content largely includes obsolete material.	1	2	3	4	5
G4.	A faculty member refuses to share course syllabi with colleagues.	1	2	3	4	5
G5.	A faculty member avoids sharing ideas about teaching methods with colleagues.	1	2	3	4	5
G6.	A faculty member refuses to allow colleagues to observe his/her classroom teaching.	1	2	3	4	5
G7.	A faculty member assumes new teaching responsibilities in the specialty of a colleague without discussing appropriate course content with that colleague.	1	2	3	4	5
G8.	A faculty member makes negative comments in a faculty meeting about the courses offered by a colleague.	1	2	3	4	5
G9.	A faculty member makes negative comments about a colleague in public before students.	1	2	3	4	5
G10.	A faculty member aggressively promotes enrollment in his/her courses at the expense of the courses of departmental colleagues.	1	2	3	4	5
G11.	The requirements in a course are so great that they prevent enrolled students from giving adequate attention to their other courses.	1	2	3	4	5
G12.	A faculty member refuses to team teach a course.	1	2	3	4	5
G13.	A faculty member avoids talking about his/her academic specialty with departmental colleagues.	1	2	3	4	5

		Appropriate/encourage	Discretionary	Mildly inappropriate/ignore	Inappropriate/handle informally	Very inappropriate/require intervention
G14.	A faculty member gives unsolicited advice on the content of a colleague's course.	1	2	3	4	5
G15.	A faculty member gives unsolicited advice to a colleague about teaching methods.	1	2	3	4	5
G16.	A faculty member refuses to participate in departmental curricular planning.	1	2	3	4	5

H. OUT-OF-CLASS PRACTICES

		Appropriate/encourage	Discretionary	Mildly inappropriate/ignore	Inappropriate/handle informally	Very inappropriate/require intervention
H1.	Office hours scheduled for student appointments are frequently not kept.	1	2	3	4	5
H2.	Individual counseling on matters unrelated to course content is not provided to students enrolled in one's courses.	1	2	3	4	5
H3.	A faculty member criticizes the academic performance of a student in front of other students.	1	2	3	4	5
H4.	A faculty member avoids spending time with students outside of class time and/or regular office hours.	1	2	3	4	5
H5.	A faculty member insists that they never be phoned at home by students, regardless of circumstances.	1	2	3	4	5
H6.	A faculty member makes suggestive sexual comments to a student enrolled in the course.	1	2	3	4	5
H7.	A faculty member has a sexual relationship with a student enrolled in the course.	1	2	3	4	5
H8.	A faculty member does not refer a student with a special problem to the appropriate campus service.	1	2	3	4	5
H9.	An advisee is treated in a condescending manner.	1	2	3	4	5
H10.	A faculty member avoids giving career or job advice when asked by students.	1	2	3	4	5
H11.	A faculty member refuses to write letters of reference for any student.	1	2	3	4	5
H12.	A faculty member neglects to send a letter of recommendation that they had agreed to write.	1	2	3	4	5
H13.	A faculty member refuses to advise departmental majors.	1	2	3	4	5
H14.	A cynical attitude toward the role of teaching is expressed by an instructor.	1	2	3	4	5
H15.	A faculty member's involvement in scholarship is so great that he/she fails to adequately prepare for class.	1	2	3	4	5
H16.	Scholarly literature is not read for the purpose of integrating new information into one's courses.	1	2	3	4	5
H17.	A faculty member avoids reading literature on teaching techniques or methods.	1	2	3	4	5
H18.	A faculty member avoids professional development opportunities that would enhance their teaching.	1	2	3	4	5

1. How important is *each* of the following as: (a) your personal goal or aim in your teaching of undergraduate students, and (b) your institution's goal in undergraduate education?

	(a) My teaching goals. (circle one)	(b) Overall Institutional goals. (circle one)
1 = Essential		
2 = Very important		
3 = Somewhat important		
4 = Not important, or irrelevant		

	My teaching goals	Overall Institutional goals
To master knowledge in a discipline	1 2 3 4	1 2 3 4
To convey a basic appreciation of the liberal arts	1 2 3 4	1 2 3 4
To increase the desire and ability to undertake self-directed learning	1 2 3 4	1 2 3 4
To develop the ability to think clearly	1 2 3 4	1 2 3 4
To develop creative capacities	1 2 3 4	1 2 3 4
To develop the ability to pursue research	1 2 3 4	1 2 3 4
To prepare students for employment after college	1 2 3 4	1 2 3 4
To prepare students for graduate or advanced education	1 2 3 4	1 2 3 4
To develop moral character	1 2 3 4	1 2 3 4
To develop religious beliefs or convictions	1 2 3 4	1 2 3 4
To provide for students' emotional development	1 2 3 4	1 2 3 4
To achieve deeper levels of students' self-understanding	1 2 3 4	1 2 3 4
To develop responsible citizens	1 2 3 4	1 2 3 4
To provide the local community with skilled human resources	1 2 3 4	1 2 3 4
To provide tools for the critical evaluation of contemporary society	1 2 3 4	1 2 3 4
To prepare students for family living	1 2 3 4	1 2 3 4

A FEW QUESTIONS ABOUT YOU AND YOUR INSTITUTION

1. Are you considered a full-time faculty member by your institution for the current academic year? (check one)
    _____ Yes, full-time
    _____ No, part-time, but more than half-time
    _____ No, half-time
    _____ No, less than half-time

2. Your academic rank: (check one)
    _____ Professor
    _____ Associate Professor
    _____ Assistant Professor
    _____ Instructor
    _____ Lecturer
    _____ Other(specify:_____)

3. Your tenure status: (check one)
    _____ Tenured   _____ Untenured, but on tenure track   _____ Untenured, and not on tenured track

4. Are you, or have you ever been, a Department Head/Chair or a Dean? (check one)
    _____ No   _____ Yes, but not now   _____ Yes, and am currently

5. Your gender:
    _____ Female   _____ Male

6. Name of your present employing institution:_____

7. What kind of academic year calendar is there at your institution? (check one)
   _____ Semester calendar   _____ Quarter system   _____ Other (specify: _____)

8. Year you were first employed at present institution:_____

9. Discipline of your present academic department:_____

10. Which one statement do you think best reflects the attitude of the principle administrator for your department or program?   (check one):
   _____ Consistently strong advocate of quality undergraduate teaching
   _____ Intermittently advocates maintaining or improving teaching quality
   _____ Laissez-faire on teaching; generally neither emphasizes nor deprecates teaching
   _____ Stresses other professional roles (e.g. research and writing) over teaching

11. Information concerning your highest earned degree:

   Highest earned degree:_____

   Year highest degree received:_____

   Name of degree-granting institution:_____

   Discipline/field of highest degree:_____

12. During the past three years, how many of each of the following have you published:

   Journal articles (circle one):   None   1-2   3-4   5-10   11 or more

   Books and monographs (circle one):   None   1   2   3 or more

13. How many classes did you teach during the past full academic year? _____

14. How many *different course preparations* did you have during the past full academic year? _____

15. During the past full academic year, have you taught any lower division (freshman or sophomore) courses? (check one)   _____ yes   _____ no

16. During the past full academic year, what is the approximate total number of *undergraduate* students enrolled in all the classes you taught: (check one)
   _____ none   _____ 100 or fewer   _____ 101 to 200   _____ 201 to 500   _____ over 500

17. Do your interests lie primarily in teaching or in research?
   _____ heavily in research
   _____ in both, but leaning toward research
   _____ in both, but leaning toward teaching
   _____ heavily in teaching

On a separate sheet, please note any comments or clarifications of your answers which you would like to provide; and insert it inside this booklet.

THANK YOU FOR YOUR HELP AND YOUR RESPONSES.

Please return this completed form to: National College Teaching Project Survey
                                           Center for Survey Research
                                           Virginia Polytechnic Institute and State University
                                           207 West Roanoke Street
                                           Blacksburg, VA 24061-0543

APPENDIX B

Response Bias Analysis

Mail survey response rates by college and university faculty are known generally to fall below return rates for similar studies of the general population. This is also the case for our three surveys. Therefore, it is important to ascertain whether substantial bias may be introduced through nonresponse.

For this purpose, we use a method delineated a number of years ago by Goode and Hatt (1952) and by Leslie (1972) that is routinely used to analyze response bias in mail surveys. This procedure assumes that late responders to mail surveys are more like nonresponders, and thus a comparison of early responders to late responders can be used to uncover similarities or significant differences between the two groups. Such differences can then be assumed to extend to the nonrespondents to ascertain whether major response biases may be present in the data. This procedure typically compares responses from the respondents to the first mailing of the survey to the respondents to subsequent waves of mailings. This approach to assessing the representativeness of the three studies was used in this research. Both t-tests and chi-square tests of independence were used to make these comparisons between respondents to the first mailing of the survey to respondents to the second mailing. T-tests were used to compare initial and later survey respondents on their factor scores for inviolable and admonitory norms, as well as for publication productivity. Chi-square tests of independence were used to compare initial and later survey respondents on administrative experience, gender, intraprofessional status, and tenure status. The 0.05 level of statistical significance was applied in making these comparisons.

For the present project, we conducted this test for respondent bias separately for each of the three surveys. In each analysis, we compare the two respondent groups on the average factor score for each of the inviolable norms (see Chapter 3), the admonitory norms (see Chapter 4), and on selected demographic and career characteristics—administrative experience, gender, intrainstitutional professional status, research activity, and tenure status. These demographic and career characteristics were selected because they are the focus of research questions posed by this project (see

TABLE B.1-A. Respondent Bias Assessment for Study One:
t-Test Comparisons between Initial and Subsequent Survey Mailings

Variables	Mean Initial Mailing	Mean Subsequent Mailing	*t*-statistic
INVIOLABLE NORMS			
Condescending negativism	4.11	4.08	0.22
Inattentive planning	4.12	4.04	0.42
Moral turpitude	4.86	4.75	1.56
Particularistic grading	4.33	4.24	0.89
Personal disregard	4.15	4.01	1.16
Uncommunicated course details	4.29	4.31	−0.12
Uncooperative cynicism	4.13	4.31	−2.08[a]
ADMONITORY NORMS			
Advisement negligence	3.63	3.85	−1.58
Authoritarian classroom	3.72	3.62	0.74
Inadequate communication	3.59	3.61	−0.12
Inconvenience avoidance	3.75	3.69	0.39
Inadequate course design	3.64	3.71	−0.49
Instructional narrowness	3.29	3.29	−0.04
Insufficient syllabus	3.45	3.34	0.66
Teaching secrecy	3.29	3.33	−0.19
Undermining colleagues	3.55	3.64	−0.66
FACULTY CAREER CHARACTERISTIC			
Research Activity	3.45	3.71	−0.75

[a] $p < .05$.

TABLE B.1-B. Respondent Bias Assessment for Study One:
Chi-Square Tests of Independence between Initial and Subsequent
Survey Mailings

Variables	Initial Mailing	Subsequent Mailing	Chi-Square Statistic
FACULTY CAREER CHARACTERISTICS			
Administrative experience			
Yes	43.9%	32.0%	
No	56.1%	68.0%	1.34
Gender			
Male	77.1%	64.0%	
Female	22.9%	36.0%	2.19
Professional status			
Higher	50.3%	32.0%	
Lower	49.7%	68.0%	3.11
Tenure status			
Tenured	80.2%	80.0%	
Untenured	19.8%	20.0%	0.01

Chapter 7). Tables B.1, B.2, and B.3 display the results of these comparisons. The results are reported below.

Survey I. The sample obtained from Survey I exhibits little or no bias on any of the five faculty demographic and career characteristics. The sample also displays little or no bias on any of the nine admonitory normative patterns. Although little or no bias is indicated on six of the inviolable normative clusters, some bias was detected for the proscriptive norm of uncooperative cynicism. Later respondents (mean = 4.31) voice a somewhat greater degree of disapproval, which is statistically reliable, for this pattern of behaviors than do initial survey respondents (mean = 4.13). But the extent of this bias is minimal given that both initial and later respondents accord inviolable normative status to this cluster of proscribed behaviors. Table B.1-A exhibits the results of the *t*-tests conducted, and Table B.1-B exhibits the results of the chi-square tests executed.

Survey II. The sample obtained from Survey II demonstrates little or no bias on the nine admonitory normative behavioral patterns. Moreover, little or no bias is suggested on any of the five faculty demographic and career characteristics. In addition, little or no bias exists on five of the seven inviolable normative clusters. But some bias exists on the proscriptive norm of moral turpitude, as initial survey respondents accord a statistically significant greater degree of disapproval (mean = 4.92) than do later survey respondents (mean = 4.84). Moroever, some bias also exits on the proscriptive norm of particularistic grading since initial survey respondents ascribe a statistically significant greater disapproval (mean = 4.38) than do subsequent respondents to the survey (mean = 4.25). Such bias is, however, minimal given that both initial and later respondents ascribe inviolable normative status to both of these particular normative patterns. Table B.2-A displays the results of the *t*-tests performed, whereas Table B.2-B shows the results of the chi-square tests conducted to assess bias.

Survey III. The sample obtained from Survey III exhibits little or no bias on any of the seven inviolable normative behavioral patterns. Some bias exists, however, on one of the five faculty demographic and career characteristics. More specifically, a statistically significant greater proportion of male academics responded to the initial mailing (69.2 percent) than to the second mailing (46.5 percent). Thus, the sample obtained from Survey III appears to be somewhat biased toward male faculty respondents.

TABLE B.2-A. Respondent Bias Assessment for Study Two: *t*-Test Comparisons between Initial and Subsequent Survey Mailings

Variables	Mean Initial Mailing	Mean Subsequent Mailing	*t*-statistic
INVIOLABLE NORMS			
Condescending negativism	4.20	4.12	1.23
Inattentive planning	4.19	4.29	−1.06
Moral turpitude	4.92	4.84	2.11[a]
Particularistic grading	4.38	4.25	2.42[a]
Personal disregard	4.17	4.13	0.52
Uncommunicated course details	4.28	4.29	−0.09
Uncooperative cynicism	4.28	4.22	0.90
ADMONITORY NORMS			
Advisement negligence	3.73	3.65	0.91
Authoritarian classroom	3.76	3.79	−0.45
Inadequate communication	3.66	3.60	0.75
Inconvenience avoidance	3.68	3.68	−0.05
Inadequate course design	3.71	3.75	−0.43
Instructional narrowness	3.34	3.31	0.38
Insufficient syllabus	3.55	3.72	−1.66
Teaching secrecy	3.39	3.27	1.30
Undermining colleagues	3.68	3.61	0.89
FACULTY CAREER CHARACTERISTIC			
Research Activity	1.07	0.87	1.27

[a] p. < .05.

TABLE B.2-B. Respondent Bias Assessment for Study Two: Chi-Square Tests of Independence between Initial and Subsequent Survey Mailings

Variables	Initial Mailing	Subsequent Mailing	Chi-Square Statistic
FACULTY CAREER CHARACTERISTICS			
Administrative experience			
Yes	36.6%	44.2%	
No	63.4%	55.8%	1.03
Gender			
Male	72.8%	75.7%	
Female	27.2%	24.3%	0.25
Professional status			
Higher	46.6%	45.7%	
Lower	53.4%	54.3%	0.02
Tenure status			
Tenured	68.7%	71.4%	
Untenured	31.3%	28.6%	0.20

TABLE B.3-A. Respondent Bias Assessment for Study Three:
t-Test Comparisons between Initial and Subsequent Survey Mailings

Variables	Mean Initial Mailing	Mean Subsequent Mailing	*t*-statistic
INVIOLABLE NORMS			
Condescending negativism	4.23	4.30	−0.84
Inattentive planning	4.30	4.22	0.47
Moral turpitude	4.89	4.91	0.71
Particularistic grading	4.35	4.43	−0.93
Personal disregard	4.26	4.29	−0.38
Uncommunicated course details	4.46	4.49	−0.43
Uncooperative cynicism	4.07	4.14	−0.68
ADMONITORY NORMS			
Advisement negligence	3.46	3.50	−0.34
Authoritarian classroom	3.63	3.75	−1.05
Inadequate communication	3.75	3.68	0.65
Inconvenience avoidance	3.88	3.80	0.78
Inadequate course design	3.74	3.61	1.12
Instructional narrowness	3.50	3.46	0.39
Insufficient syllabus	3.43	3.61	−1.17
Teaching secrecy	3.25	3.46	−1.80
Undermining colleagues	3.56	3.82	−2.45[a]
FACULTY CAREER CHARACTERISTIC			
Research activity	0.50	0.45	0.25

[a] p. < .05.

TABLE B.3-B. Respondent Bias Assessment for Study Three:
Chi-Square Tests of Independence between Initial and Subsequent
Survey Mailings

Variables	Initial Mailing	Subsequent Mailing	Chi-Square statistic
FACULTY CAREER CHARACTERISTICS			
Administrative experience			
Yes	15.7%	18.2%	
No	84.3%	81.8%	0.13
Gender			
Male	69.2%	46.5%	
Female	30.8%	53.5%	8.12[a]
Professional status			
Higher	46.6%	37.9%	
Lower	53.4%	62.1%	0.75
Tenure status			
Tenured	72.1%	72.1%	
Untenured	27.9%	27.9%	0.00

[a] p. < .05.

For eight of the admonitory normative behavioral patterns little or no bias appears to exist. But subsequent survey respondents (mean = 3.82) voiced a statistically significant greater degree of disapproval of under-mining colleagues than do initial survey respondents (mean = 3.56). Such bias is minimal, however, since admonitory normative status is given this normative cluster by both initial and subsequent survey respondents. Table B.3-A shows the results of the *t*-tests conducted, and Table B.3-B displays the results of the chi-square tests executed.

Means and Standard Deviations for Behaviors Included in the College Teaching Behaviors Inventory (CTBI)

Behaviors	Mean	Standard Deviation
A. PREPLANNING FOR THE COURSE		
A1. Required texts and other reading materials are not routinely ordered by the instructor in time to be available for the first class session.	4.27	0.84
A2. A course outline or syllabus is not prepared for a course.	4.12	0.97
A3. Prior to the first meeting of a class, the instructor does not visit the assigned classroom and assess its facilities.	2.76	0.89
A4. A course outline or syllabus does not contain dates for assignments and/or examinations.	3.11	1.11
A5. Objectives for the course are not specified by the instructor.	3.65	0.96
A6. Changes in a course are made without seeking information from students who have previously taken the course.	2.31	0.81
A7. The instructor does not read reviews of appropriate textbooks.	2.74	0.91
A8. The course is designed without taking into account the needs or abilities of students enrolling in the course.	3.87	0.89
A9. Colleagues teaching the same or similar courses are not consulted on ways to teach the particular course.	2.88	0.95
A10. Required course materials are not kept within reasonable cost limits as perceived by students.	3.31	0.92
A11. New lectures or revised lectures that reflect advancements in the field are not prepared.	3.90	0.78
A12. In-class activities are not prepared and anticipated in advance, but are developed while the class is in session.	3.25	1.07
A13. The instructor does not request necessary audiovisual materials in time to be available for class.	3.75	0.80

Note: These data are based on the aggregate responses from all three surveys. The total *n* for these surveys is 949. However, the *n* on which the data are based varies and is slightly less than this total number because of occasional missing responses on individual questions on the CTBI.

Behaviors	Mean	Standard Deviation
A14. Assigned books and articles are not put on library reserve by the instructor on a timely basis for student use.	3.89	0.78
B. First day of class		
B1. Class roll is not taken.	2.86	1.11
B2. The instructor does not introduce her/himself to the class.	3.51	0.91
B3. Office hours are not communicated to the students.	3.93	0.79
B4. The instructor changes classroom location to another building without informing students in advance.	4.30	0.81
B5. The instructor changes class meeting time without consulting students.	4.62	0.65
B6. Students are not informed of the instructor's policy on missed or make-up examinations.	4.08	0.80
B7. Students are not informed of extra credit opportunities which are available in the course during the term.	3.60	0.99
B8. Students are not asked to record their background, experiences, and interests for reference by the instructor.	2.21	0.67
B9. An overview of the course in not presented to students on the first day.	2.81	0.93
B10. An introduction to the first course topic is not begun on the first day.	2.47	0.85
B11. The first class meeting is dismissed early.	2.60	0.93
B12. The first reading assignment is not communicated to the class.	3.47	0.93
B13. A course outline or syllabus is not prepared and passed out to students.	3.88	1.01
B14. The instructor does not ask students if they have questions regarding the course.	3.43	0.91
C. In-class behaviors		
C1. Class sessions are begun without an opportunity for students to ask questions.	2.80	0.97
C2. The topics or objectives to be covered for the day are not announced at the beginning of the class.	2.72	0.89
C3. Joke-telling and humor unrelated to course content occurs routinely in class.	3.04	1.03
C4. The instructor frequently uses profanity in class.	4.23	0.84
C5. Class is usually dismissed early.	4.11	0.84
C6. The instructor meets the class without having reviewed pertinent materials for the day.	4.00	0.84
C7. The instructor routinely allows one or a few students to dominate class discussion.	3.56	0.78
C8. Instructions and requirements for course assignments are not clearly described to students.	4.04	0.68
C9. Class does not begin with a review of the last class session.	2.41	0.76

Behaviors	Mean	Standard Deviation
C10. Joke-telling and humor related to course content occurs frequently in class.	1.91	0.85
C11. The instructor does not end the class session by summarizing material covered during the class.	2.31	0.63
C12. The instructor is routinely late for class meetings.	4.26	0.66
C13. The instructor routinely holds the class beyond its scheduled ending time.	3.96	0.75
C14. The instructor does not take class attendance every class meeting.	2.30	0.89
C15. The instructor does not introduce new teaching methods or procedures.	2.70	0.88
C16. The instructor does not provide in-class opportunities for students to voice their opinion about the course.	2.91	1.01
C17. The instructor calls on students to answer questions in class on a nonvoluntary basis.	2.02	0.66
C18. The instructor does not follow the course outline or syllabus for most of the course.	3.89	0.81
C19. The instructor practices poor personal hygiene and regularly has offensive body odor.	4.15	0.80
C20. The instructor routinely wears a sloppy sweatshirt and rumpled blue jeans.	3.17	1.10
C21. While able to conduct class, the instructor frequently attends class while obviously intoxicated.	4.92	0.34
D. TREATING COURSE CONTENT		
D1. The instructor does not have students evaluate the course at the end of the term.	3.37	1.15
D2. The instructor insists that students take one particular perspective on course content.	3.86	0.92
D3. The instructor's professional biases or assumptions are not explicitly made known to students.	2.96	1.01
D4. The instructor frequently introduces opinion on religious, political, or social issues clearly outside the realm of the course topics.	3.86	0.95
D5. The instructor does not include pertinent scholarly contributions of women and minorities in the content of the course.	3.46	1.01
D6. Memorization of course content is stressed at the expense of analysis and critical thinking.	3.59	0.93
D7. Connections between the course and other courses are not made clear by the instructor.	3.03	0.89
D8. The relationship of the course content to the overall departmental curriculum is not indicated.	2.97	0.88
D9. A cynical attitude toward the subject matter is expressed by the instructor.	3.82	0.94

Behaviors	Mean	Standard Deviation
E. EXAMINATION AND GRADING PRACTICES		
E1. The instructor does not give assignments or examinations requiring student writing skills.	3.21	1.07
E2. When examinations or papers are returned, student questions are not answered during class time.	2.94	1.02
E3. Graded tests and papers are not promptly returned to students by the instructor.	3.66	0.78
E4. Individual student course evaluations, where students can be identified, are read prior to the determination of final course grades.	4.55	0.70
E5. Examination questions do not represent a range of difficulty.	3.36	0.92
E6. Grades are distributed on a "curve."	2.61	1.06
E7. An instructor lowers course standards in order to be popular with students.	4.33	0.70
E8. The standards for a course are set so high that most of the class receives failing grades for the course.	4.32	0.80
E9. Individual students are offered extra-credit work in order to improve their final course grade after the term is completed.	4.40	0.87
E10. Explanation of the basis for grades given for essay questions or papers is not provided to students.	3.90	0.80
E11. Written comments on tests and papers are consistently not made by the instructor.	3.55	0.93
E12. The instructor allows personal friendships with a student to intrude on the objective grading of their work.	4.58	0.58
E13. Student papers or essay examination questions are not read at least twice before a grade is given.	2.55	0.89
E14. Social, personal, or other non-academic characteristics of students are taken into account in the awarding of student grades.	4.44	0.79
E15. Final examinations are administered during a regular class period rather than at the official examination period.	3.79	1.17
E16. Student class participation is considered in awarding the final course grade.	1.81	0.75
E17. Student attendance in class is weighed in determining the final course grade.	2.11	0.83
E18. Student opinions about the method of grading are not sought.	2.34	0.85
E19. Students' work is not graded anonymously.	2.77	1.08
E20. The final course grade is based on a single course assignment or a single examination.	3.84	1.02
E21. Examination questions do not tap a variety of educational objectives ranging from the retention of facts to critical thinking.	3.35	0.95

Behaviors	Mean	Standard Deviation
E22. Sexist or racist comments in students' written work are not discouraged.	3.86	1.00
E23. An instructor does not hold review sessions before examinations.	2.32	0.74
E24. All student grades are publicly posted with social security numbers and without names.	2.60	1.33
E25. Graded papers and examinations are left in an accessible location where students can search through to get back their own.	3.40	1.13
F. FACULTY-STUDENT IN-CLASS INTERACTIONS		
F1. Stated policies about late work and incompletes are not universally applied to all students.	4.09	0.83
F2. Students are not permitted to express viewpoints different from those of the instructor.	4.16	0.84
F3. The instructor expresses impatience with a slow learner in class.	4.01	0.74
F4. The instructor does not encourage student questions during class time.	3.44	0.96
F5. An instructor makes condescending remarks to a student in class.	4.24	0.72
F6. The instructor does not learn the names of all students in the class.	2.87	0.86
F7. A clear lack of class members' understanding about course content is ignored by the instructor.	3.84	0.78
F8. Shy students are not encouraged to speak in class.	2.84	0.90
F9. The instructor does not allow students to direct their comments to other members of the class.	2.80	0.95
G. RELATIONSHIPS WITH COLLEAGUES		
G1. A faculty member refuses to share academic information about mutual students with colleagues.	2.70	1.03
G2. A faculty member does not tell an administrator or appropriate faculty committee that there are very low grading standards in a colleague's course.	2.73	0.97
G3. A faculty member does not tell an administrator or appropriate faculty committee that a colleague's course content largely includes obsolete material.	3.03	1.02
G4. A faculty member refuses to share course syllabi with colleagues.	3.39	1.02
G5. A faculty member avoids sharing ideas about teaching methods with colleagues.	3.24	0.93
G6. A faculty member refuses to allow colleagues to observe his or her classroom teaching.	3.41	1.09

Behaviors	Mean	Standard Deviation
G7. A faculty member assumes new teaching responsibilities in the speciality of a colleague without discussing appropriate course content with that colleague.	3.36	0.92
G8. A faculty member makes negative comments in a faculty meeting about the courses offered by a colleague.	3.72	0.98
G9. A faculty member makes negative comments about a colleague in public before students.	4.41	0.69
G10. A faculty member aggressively promotes enrollment in his/her courses at the expense of the courses of departmental colleagues.	3.89	0.86
G11. The requirements in a course are so great that they prevent enrolled students from giving adequate attention to their other courses.	3.77	0.84
G12. A faculty member refuses to team teach a course.	2.72	1.03
G13. A faculty member avoids talking about his/her academic specialty with departmental colleagues.	3.03	0.91
G14. A faculty member gives unsolicited advice on the content of a colleague's course.	2.85	0.94
G15. A faculty member gives unsolicited advice to a colleague about teaching methods.	2.72	0.92
G16. A faculty member refuses to participate in departmental curricular planning.	4.01	0.86

H. OUT-OF-CLASS PRACTICES

Behaviors	Mean	Standard Deviation
H1. Office hours scheduled for student appointments are frequently not kept.	4.26	0.62
H2. Individual counseling on matters unrelated to course content is not provided to students enrolled in one's course.	2.37	0.96
H3. A faculty member criticizes the academic performance of a student in front of other students.	4.26	0.73
H4. A faculty member avoids spending time with students outside of class time and/or regular office hours.	2.86	1.11
H5. A faculty member insists on never being phoned at home by students, regardless of circumstances.	2.57	1.01
H6. A faculty member makes suggestive sexual comments to a student enrolled in the course.	4.87	0.38
H7. A faculty member has a sexual relationship with a student enrolled in the course.	4.86	0.47
H8. A faculty member does not refer a student with a special problem to appropriate campus service.	3.79	0.81
H9. An advisee is treated in condescending manner.	4.07	0.70
H10. A faculty member avoids giving career or job advice when asked by students.	3.38	0.94
H11. A faculty member refuses to write letters of reference for any student.	3.66	1.11

Behaviors	Mean	Standard Deviation
H12. A faculty member neglects to send a letter of recommendation that they had agreed to write.	4.26	0.66
H13. A faculty member refuses to advise departmental majors.	4.21	0.87
H14. A cynical attitude toward the role of teaching is expressed by an instructor.	4.02	0.88
H15. A faculty member's involvement in scholarship is so great that he/she fails to adequately prepare for class.	4.29	0.66
H16. Scholarly literature is not read for the purpose of integrating new information into one's courses.	3.67	0.87
H17. A faculty member avoids reading literature on teaching techniques or methods.	3.14	0.94
H18. A faculty member avoids professional development opportunities that would enhance their teaching.	3.50	0.92

Zero-Order Intercorrelation Matrix among Independent Variables

Table D. Zero-Order Intercorrelation Matrix among Independent Variables

	1	2	3	4	5	6	7	8	9	10	11	12
1. Biology	1.0											
2. History	-.35	1.0										
3. Psychology	-.35	-.33	1.0									
4. RU	.01	.03	-.02	1.0								
5. CUCII	-.04	.02	.01	-.22	1.0							
6. LAI	.05	-.03	-.01	-.20	-.25	1.0						
7. 2YR	-.02	-.01	.04	-.25	-.31	-.28	1.0					
8. Administrative experience	-.03	.08	.04	-.02	.19	-.03	-.22	1.0				
9. Gender	-.01	.07	-.04	.08	.01	.01	-.09	.13	1.0			
10. Professional status	.02	.07	.00[a]	.07	-.03	.01	-.02	.30	.21	1.0		
11. Tenure status	.01	.06	-.03	.11	.03	-.03	-.03	.28	.16	.46	1.0	
12. Research activity	-.03	.08	.05	.62	.26	-.11	-.42	.08	.12	.06	.08	1.0

[a] r is ± <.009.

REFERENCES

Abbott, A. 1983. Professional ethics. *American Journal of Sociology*, 88: 855–85.

———. 1988. *The system of professions*. Chicago: University of Chicago Press.

Amada, G. 1994. *Coping with the disruptive college student: a practical model*. Asheville, N.C.: College Administration Publications.

American Association of University Professors. 1990. *Policy documents and reports*. 7th ed. Washington, D.C.: American Association of University Professors.

Anderson, M. S., and Louis, K. S. 1994. The graduate student experience and subscription to the norms of science. *Research in Higher Education*, 35: 273–99.

Anderson, M. S., Louis, K. S., and Earle, J. 1994. Disciplinary and departmental effects on observations of faculty and graduate student misconduct. *Journal of Higher Education*, 65: 331–50.

Ashworth, B. 1985. Climate formation: issues and extensions. *Academy of Management Review*, 19: 837–47.

Baldridge, J. V., Curtis, D. V., Ecker, G., and Riley, G. L. 1978. *Policy making and effective leadership*. San Francisco: Jossey-Bass.

Barber, B. 1963. Some problems in the sociology of the professions. *Daedalus*, 92: 669–88.

Barnes, S. B., and Dobly, R. G. 1970. The scientific ethos: A deviant viewpoint. *European Journal of Sociology*, 11: 3–25.

Baumgarten, E. 1982. Ethics in the academic profession: A socratic view. *The Journal of Higher Education*, 53: 282–95.

Bayer, A. E. 1973. *Teaching faculty in academe, 1972-73*. (American Council on Education Research Reports, Vol. 8). Washington, D.C.: American Council on Education.

Bayer, A. E., and Astin, H. S. 1975. Sex differentials in the academic reward system. *Science*, 188 (May 23): 796–802.

Bayer, A. E., and Braxton, J. M. 1998. The normative structure of community college teaching: a marker of professionalism. *Journal of Higher Education*, 69 (March–April): 187–205.

Bayer, A. E., and Clair, J. 1984. On session participants who fail to participate: professional courtesy and obligation by society program participants. *The Southern Sociologist*, 15 (Spring): 6.

Becher, T. 1989. *Academic tribes and territories: intellectual inquiry and the culture of disciplines*. Bristol, Pa.: Open University Press.

Ben-Yehuda, N. 1985. *Deviance and moral boundaries: witchcraft, the occult, science fiction, deviant sciences and scientists*. Chicago: University of Chicago Press.

Berlant, J. L. 1975. *Profession and monopoly.* Berkeley: University of California Press.

Bess, J. L. 1977. The motivation to teach. *Journal of Higher Education,* 48: 243–58.

———. 1978. Anticipatory socialization of graduate students. *Research in Higher Education,* 8, 289–317.

———. 1982. *University organization: a matrix analysis of the academic professions.* New York: Human Sciences Press.

Biglan, A. 1973a. The characteristics of subject matter in different academic areas. *Journal of Applied Psychology,* 57: 195–203.

———. 1973b. Relationships between subject matter area characteristics and output of university departments. *Journal of Applied Psychology,* 57: 204–13.

Birnbaum, R. 1988. *How colleges work: the cybernetics of academic organizations and leadership.* San Francisco: Jossey-Bass.

Black, D. 1976. *The behavior of law.* New York: Academic Press.

Blackburn, R. T., and Lawrence, J. H. 1995. *Faculty at work: motivation, expectation, satisfaction.* Baltimore: Johns Hopkins University Press.

Blau, P. 1973. *Organization of academic work.* New York: Wiley.

Boice, R. 1992. *The new faculty member: supporting and fostering professional development.* San Francisco: Jossey-Bass.

———. 1996. Classroom incivilities. *Research in Higher Education,* 37 (August): 453–85.

Bosk, C. L. 1979. *Forgive and remember: managing medical failure.* Chicago: University of Chicago Press.

Boyer, E. L. 1990. *Scholarship reconsidered: priorities for the professoriate.* Princeton, N.J.: Carnegie Foundation for the Advancement of Teaching.

Braxton, J. M. 1986. The normative structure of science: social control in the academic profession. In J. C. Smart, ed., *Higher education: handbook of theory and research,* 2, 309–57. New York: Agathon Press.

———. 1989. Institutional variation in faculty conformity to the norms of science: a force of fragmentation in the academic profession? *Research in Higher Education,* 30: 419–33.

———. 1990. Deviancy from the norms of science: a test of control theory. *Research in Higher Education,* 31: 461–76.

———, ed. 1994. Perspectives on research misconduct. Special issue of *Journal of Higher Education,* 65 (May–June).

———. 1995. Disciplines with an affinity for the improvement of undergraduate education. In N. Hativa and M. Marincovich, eds., *Disciplinary differences in teaching and learning: implications for practice,* 59–64. San Francisco: Jossey-Bass.

Braxton, J. M., and Bayer, A. E. 1994. Perceptions of research misconduct and an analysis of their correlates. *Journal of Higher Education,* 65: 351–72.

———. 1996. Personal experiences of research misconduct and the response of individual academic scientists. *Science, Technology and Human Values,* 21: 198–213.

Braxton, J. M., Bayer, A. E., and Finkelstein, M. J. 1992. Teaching performance norms in academia. *Research in Higher Education,* 33: 553–69.

Braxton, J. M., Eimers, M. T., and Bayer, A. E. 1996. The implications of teaching norms for the improvement of undergraduate education. *Journal of Higher Education,* 67 (November–December): 603–25.

Braxton, J. M., and Hargens, L. L. 1996. Variations among academic disciplines: analytical frameworks and research. In J. C. Smart, ed., *Higher education: handbook of theory and research,* 11: 1–46. New York: Agathon Press.

Braxton, J. M., Lambert, L. M., and Clark, S. C. 1995. Anticipatory socialization of undergraduate college teaching norms by entering graduate teaching assistants. *Research in Higher Education,* 36: 671–86.

Braxton, J. M., Olsen, D., and Simmons, A. 1998. Affinity disciplines and the use of principles of good practice for undergraduate education. *Research in Higher Education,* 39: 299–318.

Braxton, J. M., and Toombs, W. 1982. Faculty uses of doctoral training: consideration of a technique for the differentiation of scholarly effort from research activity. *Research in Higher Education,* 16: 265–82.

Brookfield, S. D. 1991. *The skillful teacher.* San Francisco: Jossey-Bass.

Brown, R. D., and Krager, L. 1985. Ethical issues in graduate education: faculty and student responsibilities. *Journal of Higher Education,* 56 (July–August): 403–18.

Bucher, R., and Strauss, A. 1961. Professions in Process. *American Journal of Sociology,* 66: 325–34.

Bucher, R., and Stelling, J. G. 1977. *Becoming professional.* Beverly Hills, Calif.: Sage Publications.

Cahn, S. M. 1986. *Saints and scamps: ethics in academia.* 1st ed. Totowa, N.J.: Rowman & Littlefield.

———. 1994. *Saints and scamps: ethics in academia.* Rev. ed. Totowa, N.J.: Rowman & Littlefield.

Callahan, D. 1982. Should there be an academic code of ethics? *Journal of Higher Education,* 53: 335–44.

Carlin, J. 1966. *Lawyers' ethics.* New York: Sage.

Carnegie Foundation for the Advancement of Teaching. 1987. *A classification of institutions of higher education.* Princeton: Princeton University Press.

Carr-Saunders, A. M., and Wilson, P. A. 1933. *The professions.* Oxford: Clarendon Press.

Centra, J. A. 1980. *Determining faculty effectiveness: assessing teaching, research and service for personnel decisions and improvement.* San Francisco: Jossey-Bass.

———. 1993. *Reflective faculty evaluation: enhancing teaching and determining faculty effectiveness.* San Francisco: Jossey-Bass.

Churchill, L. R. 1982. The teaching of ethics and moral values in teaching: some contemporary confusions. *Journal of Higher Education,* 53: 296–306.

Cohee, G. E., Daumer, E., Kemp, T. D., Krebs, P. M., Lafky, S., and Runzo, S., eds. 1998. *The feminist teacher anthology: pedagogies and classroom strategies.* New York: Teachers College Press.

Cole, J. R., and Cole, S. 1973. *Social stratification in science.* Chicago: University of Chicago Press.

Commission on Research Integrity. 1995. *Integrity and misconduct in research: report of the commission on research integrity.* Washington, D.C.: U.S. Department of Health and Human Services, Public Health Service.

Creamer, E. G. 1998. *Assessing faculty publication productivity.* ASHE-ERIC Higher Education Report, vol. 26. Washington, D.C.: George Washington University, Graduate School of Education.

Creswell, J., and Roskens, R. 1981. The Biglan studies of differences among academic areas. *The Review of Higher Education,* 4: 11–16.

Daft, R., and Becker, S. 1979. *The innovative organization.* New York: Elsevier.

Deneef, A. L., Goodwin, C. D., and McCrate, E. S., eds. 1988. *The academic's handbook.* Durham, N.C.: Duke University Press.

Dibble, V. K. 1973. What is and what ought to be: a comparison of certain characteristics of the ideological and legal styles of thought. *American Journal of Sociology,* 79: 511–49.

Dill, D. D., ed. 1982. Ethics and the academic profession. Special issue of *Journal of Higher Education,* 53 (May–June).

Durkheim, E. 1951 (1897). *Suicide: a study in sociology.* Trans. J. A. Spaulding and G. Simpson. Glencoe, Ill.: Free Press.

———. 1982 (1894). *The rules of sociological method.* Trans. W. D. Halls. New York: Free Press.

———. 1995 (1912). *The elementary forms of religious life.* Trans. K. E. Fields. New York: Free Press.

Eble, K. E. 1988. *The craft of teaching: a guide to mastering the professor's art.* 2d ed. San Francisco: Jossey-Bass.

Edison, M., Doyle, S., and Pascarella, E. T. 1998. Dimensions of teaching effectiveness and their impact on student cognitive development. Paper presented at the annual meeting of the Association for the Study of Higher Education: Miami, Fla.

Fairweather, J. S. 1996. *Faculty work and public trust: restoring the value of teaching and public service in american academic life.* Boston: Allyn & Bacon.

Feldman, D. C. 1984. The development and enforcement of group norms. *Academy of Management Review,* 9: 47–53.

Finkelstein, M. J. 1984. *The american academic profession.* Columbus: Ohio State University Press.

Finnegan, D. E. 1993. Segmentation in the academic labor market: hiring cohorts in comprehensive universities. *Journal of Higher Education,* 64: 621–56.

Fisch, L., ed. 1996. *Ethical dimensions of college and university teaching: understanding and honoring the special relationships between teachers and students.* New Directions for Teaching and Learning, no. 66. San Francisco: Jossey-Bass.

Fox, M. F. 1985. Publication, performance, and reward in science and scholarship. In J. C. Smart, ed., *Higher education: handbook of theory and research,* 1: 255–82. New York: Agathon Press.

———. 1992. Research, teaching, and publication productivity: mutuality versus competition in academia. *Sociology of Education,* 65: 292–305.

Frazier, C. E. 1976. *Theoretical approaches to deviance: an evaluation.* Columbus, Ohio: Charles E. Merrill.

Freidson, E. 1970a. *Profession of medicine.* New York: Dodd Mead.

————. 1970b. *Professional dominance.* Chicago: Aldine.

————. 1975. *Doctoring together: a study of professional social control.* New York: Elsevier.

Fulton, O., and Trow, M. 1974. Research activity in american higher education. *Sociology of Education,* 47: 29–73.

Gaff, J. G., and Lambert, L. M. 1996. Socializing future faculty to the values of undergraduate education. *Change,* 28 (July–August): 38–45.

Gibbs, J. P. 1981. *Norms, deviance and social control: conceptual matters.* New York: Elsevier.

Goode, W. J. 1957. Community within a community. *American Sociological Review,* 22: 194–200.

————. 1969. The theoretical limits of professionalization. In A. Etzioni, ed., *The semi-professions and their organization,* 266–313. New York: Free Press.

Goode, W. J., and Hatt, P. K. 1952. *Methods of social research.* New York: McGraw-Hill.

Goodwin, L. D., and Stevens, E. A. 1993. The influence of gender on university faculty members' perceptions of "good teaching." *Journal of Higher Education,* 64: 166–85.

Greenwood, E. 1957. Attributes of a profession. *Social Work,* 2: 44–55.

Gullette, M. M., ed. 1984. *The art and craft of teaching.* Cambridge, Mass.: Harvard University Press.

Hackman, J. R. 1976. Group influences on individuals. In M. D. Dunnette, ed., *Handbook of industrial and organizational psychology,* 1455–1525. Chicago: Rand McNally.

Handler, J. F. 1967. *The lawyer and his community.* Madison: University of Wisconsin Press.

Harries-Jenkins, G. 1970. Professionals in organizations. In J. A. Jackson, ed., *Professions and professionalization,* 53–107. Cambridge, Mass.: Harvard University Press.

Hook, S. 1994. The good teacher. In P. J. Markie, ed., *A professor's duties: ethical issues in college teaching,* 85–100. Lanham, Md.: Rowman & Littlefield.

Hooks, B. 1994. *Teaching to transgress: education as the practice of freedom.* New York: Routledge.

Horowitz, A. V. 1990. *The logic of social control.* New York: Plenum Press.

Jencks, C. J., and Reisman, D. 1969. *The academic revolution.* Garden City, N.Y.: Doubleday Anchor Books.

Jorgensen, A. 1995. Survey shows policies on ethical issues still lacking enforcement mechanisms. *Professional Ethics Report,* 8 (Winter): 1, 6.

Johnson, T. J. 1972. *Professions and power.* London: Macmillan.

Katz, S. N. 1995. Scholars, institutions, educational policy. Unpublished keynote address, presented at the annual meeting of the Association for the Study of Higher Education: Orlando, Fla.

Kerr, C. 1996. The ethics of knowledge. In L. Fisch, ed., *Ethical dimensions of college and university teaching.* New Directions for Teaching and Learning, no. 66. San Francisco: Jossey-Bass.

Kim, J. O., and Mueller, C. W. 1978. *Factor analysis: statistical methods and practical issues.* Beverly Hills, Calif.: Sage Publications.

Knight, J., and Auster, C. J. 1999. Faculty conduct: an empirical study of ethical activism. *Journal of Higher Education,* 70 (March-April): 188–210.

Kuhn, T. S. 1962, 1970. *The structure of scientific revolutions.* Chicago: University of Chicago Press.

LaCelle-Peterson, M. W., and Finkelstein, M. J. 1993. Institutions matter: campus teaching environments' impact on senior faculty. In M. J. Finkelstein and M. W. LaCelle-Peterson, eds., *Developing senior faculty as teachers.* New Directions for Teaching and Learning, no. 55. San Francisco: Jossey-Bass.

Larson, M. S. 1977. *The rise of professionalism.* Berkeley: University of California Press.

Lather, P. A. 1991. *Getting smart: feminist research and pedagogy within the postmodern.* New York: Routledge.

Leslie, L. L. 1972. Are response rates essential to valid surveys? *Social Science Research,* 1: 323–34.

Leslie, D. W. 1973. The status of the department chairpersonship in university organization. *AAUP Bulletin,* 59: 419–26.

Lewis, L. S. 1996. *Marginal worth: teaching and the academic labor market.* New Brunswick, N.J.: Transaction Publishers.

Lewis, M. 1997. *Poisoning the ivy: the seven deadly sins and other vices of higher education in America.* Armonk, N.Y.: M. E. Sharpe.

Liebert, R. J., and Bayer, A. E. 1975. Goals in teaching undergraduates: professional reproduction and client-centeredness. *The American Sociologist,* 10: 195–205.

Light, D. 1974. The structure of the academic profession. *Sociology of Education,* 47: 2–28.

Lodahl, J. B., and Gordon, G. G. 1972. The structure of scientific fields and the functioning of university graduate departments. *American Sociological Review,* 37: 57–72.

McGee, R. 1971. *Academic janus.* San Francisco: Jossey-Bass.

McKeachie, W. J. 1978. *Teaching tips: a guidebook for the beginning college teacher.* 7th ed. Lexington, Mass.: D. C. Heath.

———. 1986. *Teaching tips: a guidebook for the beginning college teacher.* 8th ed. Lexington, Mass.: D. C. Heath.

———. 1994. *Teaching tips: strategies, research, and theory for college and university teachers.* 9th ed. Lexington, Mass.: D. C. Heath.

Maher, F. A., and Tetreault, M. K. T. 1994. *The feminist classroom.* New York: Basic Books.

Markie, P. J. 1994. *Professor's duties: ethical issues in college teaching.* Lanham, Md.: Rowman & Littlefield.

Merton, R. K. 1942. Science and technology in a democratic order. *Journal of Legal and Political Sociology,* 1, 115–26.

———. 1968. *Social theory and social structure.* New York: Free Press.

———. 1973. *The sociology of science: theoretical and empirical investigations.* Chicago: University of Chicago Press.

―――. 1976. The sociology of social problems. In R. K. Merton and R. Nisbet, eds., *Contemporary social problems*, 3–43. New York: Harcourt Brace Jovanovich.

Merton, R. K., Reader, G. G., and Kendall, P. L. 1957. *The student-physician.* Cambridge, Mass.: Harvard University Press.

Millerson, G. 1964. *The qualifying associations.* London: Routledge.

Mitroff, I. 1974. Norms and counter-norms in a select group of Apollo moon scientists: a case study of the ambivalence of scientists. *American Sociological Review,* 39: 579–95.

Moore, W. E. 1970. *The professions: roles and rules.* New York: Russell Sage Foundation.

Mulkay, M. 1969. Some aspects of cultural growth in the natural sciences. *Social Research,* 36: 22–52.

―――. 1976. Norms and ideology in science. *Social Science Information,* 15: 637–56.

Murray, H., Gillese, E., Lennon, M., Mercer, P., and Robinson, M. 1996. Ethical principles for college and university teaching. In L. Fisch, ed., *Ethical dimensions of college and university teaching.* New Directions for Teaching and Learning, no. 66. San Francisco: Jossey-Bass.

National Academy of Sciences. 1992. *Responsible science: ensuring the integrity of the research process.* Washington, D.C.: National Academy of Sciences Press.

―――. 1995. *On being a scientist: responsible conduct in research.* 2d ed. Washington, D.C.: National Academy Press.

National Center for Education Statistics. 1997. *Instructional faculty and staff in higher education institutions: fall 1987 and fall 1992.* September. NCES 97-470. Washington, D.C.: U.S. Department of Education, Office of Educational Research and Improvement.

―――. 1998. *Digest of education statistics, 1997.* NCES 98-015. Washington, D.C.: U.S. Department of Education, Office of Educational Research and Improvement.

National Education Association. 1996. *Higher education contract analysis system: user's guide for HECAS.* Washington, D.C.: National Education Association, Higher Education Research Center.

Newble, D., and Cannon, R. 1989. *A handbook for teachers in universities and colleges: a guide to improving teaching methods.* 1st ed. New York: St. Martins Press.

―――. 1995. *A handbook for teachers in universities and colleges: a guide to improving teaching methods.* 3d ed. London: Kogan Page.

Nisbet, L. 1977. The ethics of the art of teaching. In S. Hook, P. Kurtz, and M. Todorovich, eds., *The ethics of teaching and scientific research.* 125–27. Buffalo, N.Y.: Prometheus Books.

Office of Inspector General. 1990. *Survey data on the extent of misconduct in science and engineering.* Washington, D.C.: National Science Foundation.

Parsons, T. 1939. The professions and social structure. *Social Forces,* 17: 457–67.

―――. 1951. *The social system.* New York: Free Press.

Parsons, T., and Platt, G. M. 1968. *The american academic profession: a pilot study.* Washington, D.C.: National Science Foundation (mimeographed).

―――. 1973. *The American university.* Cambridge: Harvard University Press.

Pascarella, E. T., Edison, M., Nora, A., Hagedorn, L. S., and Braxton, J. M. 1996. Effects of teacher organization/preparation and teacher skill/clarity on general cognitive skills in college. *Journal of College Student Development*, 35: 7–19.

Platt, G. M., Parsons, T., and Kirshstein, R. 1976. Faculty teaching goals, 1968–1973. *Social Problems*, 24: 298–307.

Price, A. R. 1994. Definitions and boundaries of research misconduct: perspectives from a federal government viewpoint. *Journal of Higher Education*, 65: 286–97.

Prichard, K. W., and Sawyer, R. M., eds. 1994. *Handbook of college teaching: theory and applications*. Westport, Conn.: Greenwood Press.

Reiss, A. J., Jr. 1951. Delinquency as the failure of personal and social control. *American Sociological Review*, 16 (April): 196–207.

———. 1973. Surveys of self-reported derelicts. Unpublished paper prepared for the Symposium on Studies of Public Experience, Knowledge, and Opinion of Crime and Justice. Washington, D.C..

Reynolds, C. H. 1996. Making responsible academic ethical decisions. In L. Fisch, ed., *Ethical dimensions of college and university teaching*. New Directions for Teaching and Learning, no. 66. San Francisco: Jossey-Bass.

Rhoades, G. 1998. *Managed professionals: unionized faculty and restructuring academic labor*. Albany: State University of New York Press.

Rich, J. M. 1984. *Professional ethics in education*. Springfield, Ill.: Charles C Thomas.

Robertson, E., and Grant, G. 1982. Teaching and ethics: an epilogue. *Journal of Higher Education*, 53 (May–June): 345–57.

Rokeach, M. 1973. *The nature of human values*. New York: Free Press.

Ropers-Huilman, B. 1998. *Feminist teaching in theory and practice: situating power and knowledge in poststructural classrooms*. New York: Teachers College Press.

Rossi, R. H., and Berk, R. A. 1985. Varieties of normative consensus. *American Sociological Review*, 50: 333–47.

Rothman, R. A. 1972. A dissenting view on the scientific ethos. *British Journal of Sociology*, 23: 102–8.

Rupert, P. A., and Holmes, D. L. 1997. Dual relationships in higher education: professional and institutional guidelines. *Journal of Higher Education*, 68 (November–December): 660–78.

Ruscio, K. P. 1987. Many sectors, many professions. In B. R. Clark, ed., *The academic profession*, 331–68. Los Angeles: University of California Press.

Ryan, W. 1971. *Blaming the victim*. 1st ed. New York: Pantheon.

———. 1976. *Blaming the victim*. Rev. ed. New York: Vantage Books.

Sarbin, T. R., and Allen, V. L. 1968. Role theory. In G. Lindzey and E. Aronson, eds., *The handbook of social psychology*. 2d ed. 488–567. Reading, Mass.: Addison-Wesley.

Schein, E. H. 1972. *Professional education: some new directions*. New York: McGraw Hill.

Schneider, A. 1998. Insubordination and intimidation signal the end of decorum in many classrooms. *Chronicle of Higher Education*, 44 (March 27): A12–A14.

Schurr, G. M. 1982. Toward a code of ethics for academics. *Journal of Higher Education*, 53 (May–June): 318–34.

Scriven, M. 1982. Professorial ethics. *Journal of Higher Education,* 53 (May–June): 307–17.

Shils, E. 1984. *The academic ethic.* Chicago: University of Chicago Press.

Sokolowski, R. 1991. The fiducary relationship and the nature of professions. In E. D. Pellegrino, R. M. Veatch and J. P. Langan, eds., *Ethics, trust, and the professions: philosophical and cultural aspects,* 23–43. Washington, D.C.: Georgetown University Press.

Smart, J. C. 1991. Gender equity in academic rank and salary. *Review of Higher Education,* 14: 511–26.

Smith, R. A. 1996. Reflecting on the ethics and values of our practice. In L. Fisch, ed., *Ethical dimensions of college and university teaching.* New Directions for Teaching and Learning, no. 66. San Francisco: Jossey-Bass.

Stark, J. S. 1998. Classifying professional preparation programs. *Journal of Higher Education,* 69 (July–August): 353–83.

Steneck, N. 1994. Research universities and scientific misconduct: history, policies and the future. *Journal of Higher Education,* 65: 310–30.

Storer, N. W., and Parsons, T. 1968. The disciplines as a differentiating force. In E. B. Montgomery, ed., *The foundation of access in knowledge—a symposium,* 101–21. Syracuse, N.Y.: Division of Summer Sessions, Syracuse University.

Strike, K. A. 1994. The authority of ideas and the students' right to autonomy. In P. J. Markie, ed., *A professor's duties: ethical issues in college teaching,* 101–12. Lanham, Md.: Rowman & Littlefield.

Strike, K. A., and Soltis, J. F. 1992. *The ethics of teaching.* 2d ed. New York: Teachers College Press.

Sullivan, A. V. S. 1996. Teaching norms and publication productivity. In J. M. Braxton, ed., *Faculty teaching and research: is there conflict?* New Directions for Institutional Research, no. 90. San Francisco: Jossey-Bass.

Svinicki, M. 1994. Ethics in college teaching. In W. J. McKeachie, *Teaching tips,* 269–77. 9th ed. Lexington, Mass.: D. C. Heath.

Swazey, J. P., Anderson, M. S., and Louis, K. S. 1993. Ethical problems in academic research. *American Scientist,* 81: 542–53.

Tabachnick, B. G., Keith-Speigel, P., and Pope, K. S. 1991. Ethics of teaching: beliefs and behaviors of psychologists as educators. *American Psychologist,* 46 (May): 506–15.

Tangney, J. P. 1987. Fraud will out—or will it? *New Scientist,* 115: 62–63.

Tierney, W. G., and Rhoads, R. A. 1993. *Enhancing promotion, tenure and beyond: faculty socialization as a cultural process.* ASHE-ERIC Report, No. 6. Washington, D.C.: George Washington University.

Tittle, C. R. 1980. *Sanctions and social deviance: the question of deterrence.* New York: Praeger.

Tucker, A. 1981. *Chairing the academic department.* Washington, D.C.: American Council on Education.

Tuckman, H. P., Gapinski, J. H., and Hagemann, R. P. 1977. Faculty skills and the salary structure in academe: a market perspective. *American Economic Review,* 67: 692–702.

Tuckman, H. P., and Hagemann, R. P. 1976. An analysis of the reward structure in two disciplines. *Journal of Higher Education,* 47: 447–64.

Van Maanen, J., and Schein, E. H. 1979. Toward a theory of organizational socialization. In B. M. Straw, ed., *Research in Organizational Behavior,* 1. Greenwich, Conn.: JAI Press.

Victor, B., and Cullen, J. 1988. The organizational basis of ethical work climates. *Administrative Science Quarterly,* 33: 101–25.

Vollmer, H. M., and Mills, D. L. 1996. *Professionalization.* Englewood Cliffs, N.J.: Prentice-Hall.

Wagner, P. A. 1996. *Understanding professional ethics.* Bloomington, Ind.: Phi Delta Kappa Educational Foundation.

Whicker, M. L., and Kronenfeld, J. J. 1994. *Dealing with ethical dilemmas on campus.* Thousand Oaks, Calif.: Sage Publications.

Wilensky, H. L. 1964. The professionalization of everyone? *American Journal of Sociology,* 70: 137–58.

Wilson, E. K. 1982. Power, pretense, and piggybacking: some ethical issues in teaching. *Journal of Higher Education,* 53 (May–June): 268–81.

Wilson, L. 1942. *The academic man.* New York: Oxford University Press.

———. 1979. *American academics then and now.* New York: Oxford University Press.

Zuckerman, H. E. 1977. Deviant behavior and social control in science. In E. Sagarin, ed., *Deviance and social change,* 87–138. Beverly Hills, Calif.: Sage.

———. 1988. The sociology of science. In N. J. Smelser, ed., *Handbook of Sociology,* 511–74. Newbury Park, Calif.: Sage.

INDEX

Abbott, A., 127, 164
academic departments, 115
academic disciplines: applied, 171; as community controls, 115; differences in, 166–68; and faculty characteristics, 92; four used in current research, 81; influence of, 93; knowledge base of, 163, 169; lack of attention in course planning, 81; as structural dimension, 160
Academic Ethic, The, 133
academic freedom, 150, 165, 180
Academic Man, The, 130
academic profession, differentiation in, 166
academic rank, 90; promotion in, 130
Academic Revolution, The, 131
administrative experience, defined, 89
admonitory norms: by academic discipline, 85–87; basis for, 157; behaviors of core, 75, 77; compared to inviolable norms, 41, 42; condemnation of, 169; core, 75, 77, 102–3, 159; defined, 14; and faculty characteristics, 102–3, 105, 108–13; by institutional type, 77–79; limits to, 156; nine clusters of, 42, 67–68; questions regarding, 7; sanctions for, 158; summarized, 67–68
advisement negligence, 7; and academic discipline, 86; example of, 43–45; and faculty characteristics, 103, 105, 108; defined, 43; four behaviors of, 43; by institutional type, 77; in student assessments, 152; and two-year colleges, 105
advising, 150
American Academics Then and Now, 130
American Association of Colleges for Teacher Education, 147
American Association of University Professors: on freedom and responsibility, 139; mission, 138; pertinent documents from, 138–40; Red Book, 138; on sexual harassment, 139; as source, 146–50;

Statement on Professional Ethics, 11, 130, 138
American Chemical Society, Chemist's Creed, 141
American Council of Learned Societies, 145
American Council on Education, 15
American Institute of Biological Sciences, 142
American Psychological Association, 11, 137; excerpts from code of conduct, 143–44
American Society for Microbiology, 141
American Society of Agronomy, 141
American Society of Limnology and Oceanography, 141
American Sociological Association, 13, 144–45
Anderson, M. S., 119, 121, 174
animals, treatment of, 141
Armada, G., 2
Association for the Study of Higher Education, 145
Association for Women in Science, 141n
Association of American Universities, 130
asymmetry: of expertise, 161; of power, 22
authoritarian classroom, 45–46; behaviors indicative of, 45; as core admonitory norm, 85, 87; defined, 45; example of 46–48; in student assessments, 152
authorship credit, 182
autonomy, 3, 113, 121, 125, 160–61, 165, 167–68, 171, 184

Bayer, A. E., 7, 90–92, 91n, 123, 132, 161–62, 164, 165, 167, 170, 173, 183
behavior, 180. *See also* misconduct
Bess, J. L., 165, 170
Biglan, A., 8, 16, 80, 156, 171
Bird, S., 140, 141n, 142, 144
Blackburn, R. T., 131, 171

GAYLORD FG